This brief narrative survey of political thought over the past two millennia explores key ideas that have shaped Western political traditions. Beginning with the Ancient Greeks' classical emphasis on politics as an independent sphere of activity, the book goes on to consider the medieval and early modern Christian view of politics and its central role in providing spiritual leadership. Concluding with a discussion of present-day political thought, W. M. Spellman explores the return to the ancient understanding of political life as a more autonomous sphere, and one that doesn't relate to anything beyond the physical world.

Setting the work of major and lesser-known political philosophers within its historical context, the book offers a balanced and considered overview of the topic, taking into account the religious values, inherited ideas and social settings of the writers. Assuming no prior knowledge and written in a highly accessible style, *A Short History of Western Political Thought* is ideal for those seeking to develop an understanding of this fascinating and important subject.

W. M. Spellman is Professor of History at the University of North Carolina, Asheville, USA. He is the author of *A Concise History of the World since 1945*; *European Political Thought, 1600–1700* and *John Locke*, all published by Palgrave Macmillan. He also co-authored *The West: A Narrative History* (Prentice-Hall, USA).

D0223669

A SHORT HISTORY OF WESTERN POLITICAL THOUGHT

W. M. Spellman

First published 2011 by
PALGRAVE MACMILLAN

Palgrave Macmillan in the UK is an imprint of Macmillan Publishers Limited, registered in England, company number 785998, of Houndmills, Basingstoke, Hampshire RG21 6XS.

Palgrave Macmillan in the US is a division of St Martin's Press LLC, 175 Fifth Avenue, New York, NY 10010.

Palgrave Macmillan is the global academic imprint of the above companies and has companies and representatives throughout the world.

Palgrave® and Macmillan® are registered trademarks in the United States, the United Kingdom, Europe and other countries.

ISBN 978–0–230–54558–8 hardback
ISBN 978–0–230–54559–5 paperback

This book is printed on paper suitable for recycling and made from fully managed and sustained forest sources. Logging, pulping and manufacturing processes are expected to conform to the environmental regulations of the country of origin.

A catalogue record for this book is available from the British Library.

Library of Congress Cataloging-in-Publication Data
Spellman, W. M.
    A short history of western political thought / W.M. Spellman.
        p.   cm.
    Includes index.
    ISBN 978–0–230–54559–5 (pbk.)
    1. Political science—History.   2. Political science—Philosophy—
    History.   3. Civilization, Western.   I. Title.
    JA81.S64 2011
    320.01—dc22   2011008058

10   9   8   7   6   5   4   3   2   1
20   19   18   17   16   15   14   13   12   11

Printed and bound in China

In Memory of Joseph M. Levine

Contents

Acknowledgments

Authors of short surveys always rely on the work of specialist scholars in the field. The Cambridge University Press series in the history of political thought features balanced and in-depth essays by leading historians and political theorists. Each volume in the series also contains an excellent bibliography of recent literature in the field. Once again the administration at my home institution, and in particular Provost Katherine Whatley, allowed me valuable time for working on this project. The research librarians and circulation specialists at the University of North Carolina at Asheville, including Bryan Sinclair, Helen Dezendorf, and Leith Tate, helped to locate materials and expedite the inter-library loan process. Lynne Olin and University Librarian Jim Kuhlman kindly approved my annual requests for a quiet study carrel in Ramsey Library. My colleague Bill Sabo assisted with suggestions and timely criticism at the early stages when the outline of the book was being drafted, while the two anonymous readers for the press highlighted a number of omissions and offered some important corrections. Jenni Burnell at Palgrave kept the project moving forward with gentle reminders and timely updates. The book is dedicated to the memory of one of the leading cultural and intellectual historians of our day, Joseph M. Levine, a kind and gentle man who guided generations of graduate students into the great conversation.

Introduction: Civil Society and Human Flourishing

This brief survey of Western political thought, with its subject matter originating in ancient Greece and its influence most significant in Western Europe and the Americas prior to the twentieth century, is written with the layperson and student reader in mind. The narrative is organized around views of human potential for participating in peaceful collective action. It assumes that the varieties of civil society adopted by peoples over the centuries, and the goals set for the exercise of political authority, represent an important facet of human adaptation to environment, or as the late George Sabine wrote in his 1937 classic *A History of Political Theory*, "social life and organization are primary biological survival devices."[1] Western political thought across the ages, then, represents a series of efforts to understand and solve the problems of group life and association. Often those efforts began with basic questions about the human condition. How can we as humans, given our nature and dispositions, best achieve whatever definition of the good life is accepted as proper? How can we balance the claims of the individual—much celebrated in the West since the eighteenth century—with the well-being of the entire community? To what extent is human behavior shaped by environment and culture? Are there bedrock constants, such as rationality and an innate moral sense, that distinguish humans in their efforts to live in community? Or are we motivated primarily by base passions and selfish predispositions that must be controlled or inhibited before any sort of collective social existence is possible?

Many of these questions persist into our own day, of course, but the ideas that informed creative answers—whatever the outcomes—were many and extremely varied over the past two-and-a-half millennia, and in some cases still inspire contemporary debate. The authors and issues discussed here represent examples of some key ideas in the Western tradition, beginning with the classical Greek emphasis on politics as an autonomous sphere of activity, moving to the medieval and early modern Christian view of politics as a compartment of spiritual leadership, and concluding with the modern reinterpretation of political life as an independent field without reference to any larger metaphysical agenda. Many of the authors who maintained an overcast or skeptical view of human potential emphasized the need for civil authority to play a coercive and directive role in society, while others who endorsed some form of consent and accountability shared a more sanguine reading of humankind's capacity for good and as a result tended to call for specific limits on the power of the state.

What follows, then, is an examination of some important Western thinkers and their work in historical context, providing what I hope is an accessible narrative that sets both the material and intellectual backdrop to a selective sampling of critical works. That wider backdrop includes social setting, economic patterns, religious values, and the inheritance of ideas. Since many of the key thinkers debated in this study, from Plato (c. 427–c. 348 BCE) and Thomas Aquinas (1225–1274), to John Locke (1632–1704) and Karl Marx (1818–1883), were prolific writers who addressed significant philosophical, social, and religious questions, an adequate understanding of their political thought obligates us to know something of their deeper commitments and the broader cultural and intellectual *milieu* in which they were educated. No one writes about politics (or anything else, for that matter) in a vacuum, and more often than not the prompt to authorship is a deeply held conviction, or set of convictions, about the proper ordering of society in a world perceived to have gone awry.

In their introduction to *The Cambridge History of Greek and Roman Political Thought* (2000), Christopher Rowe and Malcolm Schofield draw an important distinction between political theory and political thought. While the former is systematic and intentional, the latter is much broader, covering not only formal reflection on things political but also ideas about political action and institutions that appear in varied types of literature.[2] St Augustine (354–430), for example, was no political theorist—he was kept plenty busy on the administrative front as Bishop of Hippo in North Africa during the early fifth century—but his interest in advancing what he understood to be the right relationship between man and God, and in privileging the city of God over the city of man, had unmistakable political implications for the medieval West. Similarly, the late eighteenth-century British writer Mary Wollstonecraft (1759–1797) was concerned principally with extending educational opportunities for women in her best-known work, *A Vindication of the Rights of Woman* (1792). Wollstonecraft's work was largely dismissed during the nineteenth and early twentieth centuries by critics who disapproved of her unconventional lifestyle, but it was resurrected by modern feminists, many of whom highlighted the radical political implications of Wollstonecraft's views on Western notions of human equality. On more than a few occasions over the past two millennia, then, valuable ideas emerged from unexpected quarters to shape and inform both the location and exercise of political authority, the power to make decisions for the community as a whole. There exists no single template or platform for the genesis of political ideas that have had a lasting impact on Western culture. Religion certainly played a central role for innumerable writers; abstract principle informed by direct experience animated others; while dull suffering under the weight of oppressive material conditions, including gender, class, and racial discrimination, inspired the rest. And while most influential authors were formally educated and therefore male, there were important exceptions in every century, exceptions that deserve our attention in this short survey.

Political thought is by its very nature concerned with public matters, the inclusive property of a community. Not only do such matters typically include common defense, domestic peace, economic advancement, and the administration of justice, but they also include a more abstract sense of collective purpose and direction, a network of social meaning embedded in a particular time and place. The exact form taken by political institutions responsible for public matters and the institutionalized practices whose purpose is to direct human action are the concerns of the entire community since every member is eager to secure some approximation of a meaningful life.[3] With this in mind it is useful to recall that most of the great works of Western political thought, the ones that have outlived their original contexts, were composed during periods of deep crisis or the breakdown of established institutional forms. Whenever traditional patterns of authority and ties of loyalty came under strain due to failures of leadership, military conflict, religious division, or acute economic reversal, new visions of an ordered, civilized society were put forward in an effort to bring an end to instability and material hardship.[4]

In addition, many of the writers examined here aspired to formulate a definition of the 'life' worth living, the life of intellectual, spiritual, and emotional fulfillment. Some found ultimate meaning in the material goods of this world alone, others—especially Christian thinkers—emphasized the preparatory nature of the terrestrial passage and the type of political order best suited to spread God's kingdom on earth, while still others stressed the value of personal freedom and intellectual autonomy irrespective of economic status. Whatever the specific priorities, most were careful to address similar foundational questions in their work: what was the origin and essential purpose of political authority; where should that authority be located; how should authority be exercised; and when, if ever, was it justified to challenge established authority? Each author's responses to these questions, either explicitly or indirectly, allow us to locate their work within a larger continuum.

* * *

Since this book is targeted for the reader who is interested in the contributions of political thought, broadly defined, to the shaping of Western culture, no prior knowledge of the individuals and groups to be highlighted in the narrative is assumed. The text avoids using specialized terms without explaining them at their first occurrence and keeps scholarly notation to a minimum. The bibliography is designed to assist those who wish to explore a topic or individual in more depth and detail. The story begins with a brief assessment of early efforts at social organization before turning to the sizable Greek and Roman achievements. It was here, and especially with the Greeks, that politics was first distinguished from religion, where the uniquely Western ideals of equality, justice, personal liberty, human-made law, and responsible government were initially considered independent of formal religious prescriptions. For Plato and Aristotle (384–322 BCE), the Greek *polis* or city-state served as the focus of political thinking, and the question of living justly and happily in that community served as the ethical starting point of most early writing. But as it was Aristotle who wielded the greatest influence in later centuries, his vision of the state as a natural response to human needs will play a central role in Chapter 1.

Many surveys of political thought treat the medieval period in a cursory fashion, inadvertently endorsing the Enlightenment's disparagement of the ten centuries after the fall of Rome. Chapter 2 will attempt to address this false impression, focusing instead on continuities with the political thought of the ancient world, and on the dynamic tension between the Church and the State that began with the collapse of Roman authority in the fifth century, reaching prominence with the rise of the Carolingians in the eighth century. It will explore the competing claims, and their theological grounding, between the Church leaders (especially the Pope) and the Germanic successors to Roman authority in the West. It will address the continuing influence of Aristotelian thought, especially in the work of Aquinas, and the anticipation of resistance theory embedded in the writings of Aquinas and others like John of Salisbury (c. 1115–1176). The chapter will also trace the development in the West of the Church-inspired conciliar tradition during the central Middle Ages, the inadvertent product of papal overreach and division during the late fourteenth century. The emergence of formal consultative bodies and mixed constitutions, originating with earlier Germanic custom and reaching a high level of development in medieval England, will round out the discussion.

Chapter 3 will center on the formation of early modern national identities in the wake of the Protestant Reformation. Martin Luther's (1483–1546) challenge to Catholic universalism spurred the growth, again inadvertently, of early forms of nationalism and emboldened resistance theorists who claimed divine sanction for civil disobedience. A wide range of thinkers all found religious justification for acts of political disobedience during the sixteenth century. The integrity of the confessional state, where one faith tradition was imposed on all subjects, was severely tested during decades of religious civil war and international conflict. Calls for religious toleration during the course of the seventeenth century prepared the ground for the Enlightenment's critique of confessional politics, and for a more optimistic assessment of human potential. Parallel with the growth of contract theory and calls for toleration, however, was a resurgence of claims on behalf of divine right monarchy. The power of monarchs was enhanced in the wake of the Reformation as national churches tended to be subordinated to the temporal head of state. For their part, Europe's monarchs began to identify themselves with a larger national (as opposed to a narrowly dynastic) agenda. Political allegiance shifted away from the person of the monarch and in the direction of a broader set of cultural, geographical, and in some cases religious markers.

Although there were anticipations in the seventeenth century, the argument that the state was not responsible for upholding religious orthodoxy, and that people are by nature predisposed to work in concert to advance the collective good, received their most powerful expression in the eighteenth century. Even though most of Western Europe's foremost *philosophes* were supporters of enlightened monarchy and suspicious of popular democracy, republican political forms and natural rights language engaged a growing circle of political writers on both sides of the Atlantic. Chapter 4 will explore the nature of Enlightenment skepticism and its impact on divine right theory; the advent of social contract theory; the central (and problematic) role of natural law and natural rights theory in the political thought of leading figures and revolutionaries in Europe and North America; and the appeal of popular claims for a new science of politics. The natural and inalienable rights assertions of American and French revolutionaries; the quest for progress and preoccupation with human welfare anchored in optimistic views of human nature; the universalist assumptions behind most constitution-making of the late eighteenth century; and the struggle to extend political power to the property-owning middle class will all be explored in this chapter. Finally, the political engagement of the middle and lower classes that accompanied the American and French Revolutions, and the repudiation of natural hierarchies at the core of revolutionary thought—all of which set the stage for modern mass politics—will be examined.

Chapter 5 treats the major "isms" of the nineteenth century, including conservatism, liberalism, utilitarianism, socialism, Marxism, and nationalism. It begins with the conservatism of Edmund Burke (1729–1797) and its expression in post-Napoleonic Europe. The paternalist and interventionist strain within conservatism was challenged by liberals who, following in the tradition of Locke, were committed to limiting the scope of government intervention in the lives of private citizens. Liberal opponents of Restoration monarchies, activists in the failed 1830 and 1848 Revolutions, carried forward the American and French revolutionary ideals of responsible, constitutional government, but most preferred to restrict political participation to educated property owners.

Like the liberal movement of the first half of the century, utopian socialism was closely associated with the Romantic impulse of the age. But counterpoised to liberals who rejected any extension of the State into the economic concerns of free citizens, early socialists called for a planned, regulatory state where technocrats would manage public affairs and where economic equality was a paramount outcome of successful politics. The writings of Henri St. Simon (1760–1825), Charles Fourier (1772–1837), Robert Owen (1771–1858), and others are set against the more revolutionary, confrontational, and class-based socialism of Karl Marx and Friedrich

Engels (1820–1895). Here the chapter will address the place of progress, rationality, and confidence in human nature as embedded in liberal, utilitarian, socialist, and Marxist thought. With respect to the latter, the influence of G.W.F. Hegel (1770–1831) in shaping Marx's view of historical evolution, the tension between a dark picture of human nature inherent in class conflict across the ages and the prospect of human nature transformed after the great proletarian revolution, will be discussed. The chapter will conclude with a consideration of late nineteenth-century nationalist ideology, especially as it was formulated and employed by traditional elites to rally popular support for strong centralized states, and for imperial undertakings. The gradual extension of political rights to the working class, the achievement (near the end of the century) of universal manhood suffrage in many of the industrially advanced states of Western Europe, and the emergence of labor-oriented political parties will be analyzed within the context of the incipient welfare state and mass politics.

The rights and exemptions of the sovereign nation-state became the troubled centerpiece of twentieth-century political life, and this is the subject of Chapter 6. The fragile parliamentary democracies of the post–World War I era were eclipsed by authoritarian one-party alternatives in Germany, Italy, Spain, and the Soviet Union in the 1930s. Fascism epitomized the myopic and belligerent side of extreme nationalism, while in Stalin's Soviet Union the rhetoric of international working-class solidarity was subordinated to the power requirements of the state. Efforts to create effective transnational political institutions faltered after World War I with the League of Nations, and met with very mixed success after World War II with the establishment of the United Nations. During the Cold War decades, political thought in the West was framed by the conflict between capitalist democracy and Soviet-style communism. Marxists in the West increasingly distanced themselves from a Soviet state whose actions repeatedly betrayed its rhetorical commitment to social equality. With the collapse of the Soviet Union in 1991, some writers anticipated "the end of history," the global spread of Western-style civil liberties, constitutional politics, and market economics. But the unanticipated post–Cold War recrudescence of religious and ethnic nationalism, the emergence of racist anti-immigration politics, and the elusive threat of non-state global terrorism, all raised significant doubts about the more sanguine claims of Western-style democracies.

By the start of the new century, the forces of economic and cultural globalization, together with the challenges of environmental degradation, resource depletion, and population growth, all pointed in the direction of a need for greater international cooperation, and perhaps for a new direction in political action and debate. The unanticipated power of religious fundamentalism and ethnic nationalism posed real challenges to the viability of multiparty democracy in some states. Yet the primacy of the sovereign nation-state continued, and with the end of the Cold War, some policy makers in the world's remaining superpower embraced a universalist argument in favor of the spread of Western-style political and economic forms. This has led to resentment and backlash in some developing states, and has intensified an anti-Western strain in many Islamic countries. Once again the question of human flourishing has come to the foreground, as thoughtful women and men across multiple political divides have begun to call into question the Western-style growth imperative, the unrefined equating of material goods with a life worth living. Suddenly, and perhaps just in time, a reevaluation of the purpose of political authority has reentered the arena of popular discourse.

Chapter 1 . . . .

City-States and Republics
c. 400 BCE–c. 400 CE

Just as they inaugurated many new forms of intellectual and artistic expressions, so too Greeks gave us much of the vocabulary of modern politics, including now familiar concepts like "democracy," "aristocracy," "oligarchy," "tyranny," and "plutocracy." The very word "politics" comes to us from the unique city-state or *polis*, while the habit of thinking and writing systematically about how best to organize people in a communal setting made its first appearance with Plato, a native of Athens during the fourth century BCE. The notion of public service and civic engagement as a good, the concepts of citizenship and equality, and the linkage of justice and the decent society with reason and human law all received their initial impress on the Greek mainland.[1] Thus political thinking and formal political theorizing began rather late in the evolution of *homo sapiens*, well after a varied set of social and political models had been deployed to facilitate group living over many millennia. We know a little about these earlier efforts to coordinate human relations in larger groups, although our lack of written sources means that most of what we assert belongs to the realm of educated guesses. Still, it is useful to set the Greek achievement, which was written down, against the backdrop of prior efforts to construct communities of meaning in early civilized society, if only to highlight the truly innovative and enduring nature of Hellenic political theory and practice.

Early political communities

Humans living in community, as opposed to humans in isolation, appear to have been the essential model of social organization beginning with the emergence of *Homo sapiens* some 50–100,000 years ago. No other primates attained the tool-making, linguistic, or organizational skills of humans; thanks to the high-level analytical power of the human brain, these skills enabled early peoples to manipulate the natural environment on a scale unknown to their proto-human predecessors. Manipulation has become domination and degradation in our own day, with consequences for our children's children that have only recently come into sharper focus. But during the Paleolithic centuries, which constitute roughly 95 percent of the human past, kinship communities facilitated the gathering and distribution of food, while offering mutual aid and protection against threat, both environmental and human. A strong community orientation, as opposed to the more individualistic and acquisitive leanings of modern peoples in the West, was one of the hallmarks of kinship lifestyles.

The communitarian way of life does not mean that Paleolithic peoples were especially humane or selfless, however; such romantic notions unhappily cannot stand the test of archeological and anthropological evidence. Indeed given their relative lack of control over the forces of nature, brief lives were doubtless filled with more than a little conflict, cruelty, and heartbreak. It was, rather, a matter of self-interest being best served through cooperation and consensus. Aristotle (384–322 BCE) was right: humans are by nature social beings—they have to be in order to survive. Whether out of primal fear—a view given lasting impress by Thomas Hobbes (1588–1679) in the mid-seventeenth century—or a basic need for comity and companionship, group existence, where tool-making and food-gathering skills were shared and developed, characterized nomadic peoples on every continent long before they stopped chasing after their dinner and discovered the relative convenience of growing it.[2]

This broad sociability was first challenged with the advent of grain cultivation and pastoralism sometime around 8500–7500 BCE, as increasing numbers of humans exchanged their perambulatory, hunter-gatherer lifestyle for sedentary cultivation in populated communities adjacent to major river valleys and floodplains. The agricultural revolution, where humans became food producers instead of food gatherers, occurred first in the Middle East, along the banks of the Tigris-Euphrates and the Nile. It was here that sophisticated irrigation techniques were developed, allowing for the cultivation of crops on the same land year after year. And as irrigation technology spread east and west, the resulting increases in food production facilitated a remarkable growth in human numbers, not only in the Middle East, but in South and East Asia as well, especially along the Indus and Yangtze River valleys. The regimented labor required for successful irrigation and resulting agricultural surpluses meant the emergence of a managerial elite consisting of military and religious leaders. The former could compel massed labor resources while the latter served as liaison with the supernatural and mastered calendar systems that were essential to the rhymes of sowing and reaping. It also gave rise, for good or ill, to notions of property and accumulation, of "mine" and "thine," that were largely irrelevant in earlier nomadic communities.

It was in these inaugural agricultural zones that coordinated political authority first emerged as an essential component of common defense against surrounding human predators. The latter were keen to enjoy the benefits of the agricultural revolution without mucking about with its labor-intensive side; attack and plunder became their preferred mode of operation. And after the invention of chariot technology around 1700 BCE, nomadic raiders enjoyed a distinct military advantage over their sedentary targets. Political authority in early agricultural societies, then, had two explicit functions: Rulers were singled out to protect and preserve, and as a means to this end they had to gain control over the surpluses that were produced by the labor of simple cultivators. The coercive or tributary state, where political, military, and religious elites were freed from the demands of physical labor ostensibly to carry out the supreme tasks of common defense, the allocation of agricultural surpluses, and the arbitration of domestic disputes, now took its place on the stage of human history. Whatever measure of egalitarianism may have obtained in earlier kinship society, there was no doubt about the inequitable nature of the new model of social organization that we commonly associate with civilization. The advent of hierarchy and privilege, the birth of the coercive state, forever changed the way that humans lived—and died.

Success in agriculture allowed for the identification of political authority with a defined territory, and for the growth of urban centers characterized by a more permanent and substantial built environment. Whereas bonds of blood kinship and common origins were the main criteria of community in Paleolithic society, topography, property, and residency stood out as unifying features in the wake of the agricultural revolution. Formal institutions and mechanisms of control developed with religious, administrative, and juridical authority under the direction of some form of centralized leadership. In the lower Tigris-Euphrates valley, or what the Greeks later called "Mesopotamia" for "land between the rivers," food surpluses allowed for the growth of a wide range of specialized activities, including bronze metallurgy, plows, wheel-spun pottery, small boats, and wheeled vehicles. It also permitted the construction of public buildings, temples, tombs, and private residences of significant size.[3] The earliest aspirant kings of what were scattered cities of the Sumerian plain probably emerged out of the military, as opposed to the priestly class, but these leaders doubtless claimed to act on behalf of the gods when attempting to consolidate their power.

A not dissimilar pattern of rulership emerged soon after in Egypt, spread to South Asia's Indus River Valley about 2500 BCE, and to China's Yellow River Valley approximately 1000 years later. For the vast majority whose relentless toil made it possible for this tiny elite to focus on the nascent affairs of state, the remnants of communal life were preserved in the agricultural village, where group coordination was key to a successful growing season and where mutual aid provided the only safety net for society's weakest, most vulnerable, and unfortunate. We are left with no traces of written reflection on the evolution or operation of political authority from these long centuries, but clearly the formation of tributary states marked the beginning of sharply delineated social hierarchies and the development of religious systems and stories that served to legitimize such inequalities. As human numbers increased, relations within communities, and between settled, pastoral, and nomadic peoples, became more intentional and purposeful. Political structures arose in response to these relationships, but in a rather *ad hoc* manner, with little deliberation or forethought.

The first kings enjoyed their authority by virtue of their ability to marshal armed retainers and resources in successful combat. In Mesopotamia, inter-city rivalries and conflict led to the rise of powerful kings who could compel tribute from distant regions. Around 2300 BCE, Sargon I of Akkad imposed his will across Sumer, but he was obliged to relocate constantly from city to city in search of food and plunder for his troops. Loyalty tended to wane when the king was absent, making for a reign where perambulation was key to Sargon's empire. Only at the close of the third millennium BCE did more impersonal institutions and offices emerge that enabled Mesopotamian kings to rule through delegation across wide sweeps of territory. These embryonic bureaucracies—now mature and all too familiar to us—aligned power with official office, not with the officeholders who served at the pleasure of the king. Under Hammurabi, who ruled around 1700 BCE, the bureaucracy was strengthened through the addition of record keeping and the codification of rules that formalized important areas of human relations. Personal rulership was still important, but effective governance and predictable human relations over time and space demanded the formation of permanent institutions and bureaucratic routine.

Nowhere, it seems, was the office of the king more important than in Old Kingdom Egypt. Thanks to a favorable set of geographical conditions that protected the valley of the Nile from outside attack and an easily navigable river that facilitated the movement of men and commodities, political centralization took place as early as 3000 BCE under the conqueror Menes. The early kings or pharaohs were embraced as gods, sons of the supreme sun god Re, and Egypt's agricultural surpluses were used to support a wide array of artisans and courtiers who served the pharaoh and his court. Regular and abundant crop yields allowed for the redeployment of peasant labor on massive and spectacular building projects like the pyramids, further elevating the status of the god-king. The absolutism of the Old Kingdom era was challenged during the period 2250–2025 BCE, while under the pharaohs of the Middle Kingdom (c. 2050–1800 BCE) numerous priestly and aristocratic power bases emerged to weaken the grip on power held by the god-kings. Further revolt, political fragmentation, and even foreign invasion and occupation took place between 1800 and 1570 BCE, but when unity was restored during period of the New Kingdom, the old pattern of absolutist rule, with pharaoh as the pre-eminent god on earth, returned. The king of Egypt was the herdsman, pastor, and "feeder" of his people, insuring the fertility of the land and regulating the waters of the Nile.[4] Here more than anywhere else in the ancient world, the temporal ruler embodied the divine forces that regulated creation. Strong cultural forces programmed Egypt's masses to accept a form of rule at once deeply coercive and metaphysically reassuring. Cosmic balance and order involved everyone in his proper place, and to speak in terms of individual priorities or freedoms was simply inconceivable.

Secular foundations and the Greek city-state

Empire succeeded empire in the Middle East between 1200 and 330 BCE, with the Assyrians and subsequently the Persians temporarily uniting the entire region under tax-collecting, bureaucratic, militarized, and highly coercive governments. Only in Greece did an alternative model of political organization take root after a long "dark age" during which a sophisticated, trade-based civilization at Mycenae was capsized by Greek-speaking Dorian invaders from the north. The poet Homer (c. eighth century BCE) captured key elements of the predominant culture during these turbulent centuries, especially the belief in the capriciousness of the gods (on a super-human scale, of course), human heroism and courage (*arête*), self-assertion, physical prowess, and violence. Of central concern in Homer's *Iliad* is a conception of justice or "the right way" as determined by custom in traditional warrior-dominated society. Achilles denounces the arrogance of his commander Agamemnon when the latter seizes Achilles' war prize (a captive woman) and, as the most accomplished member of Agamemnon's army, demands to be compensated. By his arbitrary actions, Agamemnon displayed unpardonable *hubris*, the desire to affirm superiority while bringing others into shame. In the *Odyssey*, the hero Odysseus returns home after years of wandering and immediately kills the suitors who had dishonored him by wooing his wife and ignoring his son. These epic poems, and their implied moral code to honor friends and rebuke enemies, achieved their present form just as the *polis* or city-state idea, with its emphasis on justice and accountability in government, was in formation.[5]

Fleeing before the rough Dorian aggressors who occupied Greece around 1000 BCE, Greek speakers settled in a number of Aegean islands and in outposts along the coast of Asia Minor. The latter were the first to organize themselves into independent city-states or *poleis* whereby a minority of male residents mobilized for common defense, agreed a set of laws, adopted mechanisms for administration, and established procedures for choosing leaders. The leaders, in turn, held their offices on condition that they respect the gods and defend the accepted social and legal conventions. The male members of families, and not just soldiers, participated in the process, and the agreements made were expected to be permanent and not simply wartime expedients. This last feature, the permanent nature of law, was informed by a conviction that humans had the capacity to bring their communal activities into harmony with a larger order in the universe, with the underlying nature of things. Good laws and the pursuit of justice were the foundation stones of a rational society, one where arbitrary and fickle gods did not interfere. Each city-state or *polis* operated on the basis of strong citizen engagement and territorial autonomy, and each was to respect, in theory anyway, the independence of its neighbor.

The decline of kingship and the emergence of citizen administrators were forwarded by innovations in military organization and tactics. By the end of the eighth century BCE traditional cavalry formations were replaced by the hoplite phalanx, heavily armed infantrymen who assembled in close order and fought in a highly coordinated and disciplined manner. Hoplite soldiers consisted mainly of independent small farmers who were determined to protect their lands against all outside predators. Given the backbreaking and unremitting labor involved in farming (described by late eighth-century poet and small farmer Hesiod in his *Works and Days*), and the very real possibility of starvation should the harvest be expropriated, the drive to protect it at all costs is understandable. Individual courage was certainly important to the success of the hoplite phalanx on the battlefield, but group discipline and precision in formation were absolutely essential when facing an opponent's cavalry. These farmer-soldiers became ideal citizens, and their success in battle had the salutary effect of blurring some of the distinctions between aristocrats, urban craftsman, and small farmers, all of whom now fought side by side in the phalanx.

Between the eighth and sixth centuries BCE, as Greek colonies spread across the Mediterranean from the coast of Southern Spain in the West to the Black Sea in the East, trade intensified and a new commercial elite took its place alongside farmers and aristocrats. Some *poleis* succumbed to strong one-man rule (tyranny) during these centuries, where populist leaders (often aristocrats) pushed forward a series of public works projects and commercial ventures. But in general the trend in leadership by the close of the sixth century was in the direction of greater accountability and predictability under citizen control. Public discussion and debate over potential courses of action by those who had served in hoplite ranks now became normative, further strengthening the principle of consent and the idea that all had an equal stake in the success of the *polis*.[6]

What the Ionians, and subsequently their counterparts on the Greek mainland, had discovered was the possibility of politics divorced from its theocratic foundations, together with the concept of citizen engagement as the strongest guarantee of social order. Homer had expressed the idea of human excellence or *arete* in terms of individual physical prowess and achievement; now the Ionians shifted the focus onto the intellectual plane and equated the good society with the will of an informed citizenry. And with the development of the phalanx as the preferred military tactic in the seventh century BCE, comradeship, cooperation, and civic pride all coalesced around the territorial city-state. The delicate balance between freedom and order, and the solution to common problems, was to be achieved through human agency, not through gods and divine kings. Government, under this set of assumptions, was anchored in laws that had been agreed by free citizens and existed to satisfy discreet human needs. The habit of thinking and writing about these issues began in Greece, and the resulting ideas set important precedents for life in the West that remain with us even today.

How did the shift from a myth-laden and supernatural view of nature to one informed by human reason take place? The Greeks did not jettison their myriad gods and religious rituals, but in seeking an overarching principle

of order or law (*logos*) amidst the apparent chaos of physical reality, early
Ionian thinkers (sometimes termed pre-Socratic) like Thales (c. 624–548
BCE), Anaximander (c. 611–547 BCE), and Anaximenes (c. 585–525 BCE)
identified single material elements, the "stuff" of nature that allegedly
underlay all sensory phenomena. For Thales the basic element or cosmology was water, for Anaximenes it was air, while for Anaximander it was an
unidentified primary boundless mass that, in different forms, accounted for
all creation, including human beings. Collectively, the Ionians' materialist
approach to physical reality was set against a more mathematical and metaphysical view championed by a Greek speaker from Southern Italy named
Pythagoras (c. 580–507 BCE). He and his followers applied the mathematical
proportions and relations found in music to the universe at large, shifting
the emphasis away from physical substances and human sense experience
and in the direction of abstract logical relationships. Unchanging mathematical laws, under this heading, gave shape or form to corporeal bodies, the
physical world that appears to human senses. Writing from the Greek mainland, Democritus (c. 460–370 BCE) argued that tiny indestructible atoms,
imperceptible to human senses, combined in an array of forms to constitute everything in nature, while the early logician Parmenides (c. 515–450
BCE) emphasized the importance of distrusting the senses while dedicating
oneself to reason and abstract thought. For Parmenides, thought and being
were interchangeable, a formula that would have a lasting influence in the
arena of political theory. Each of these thinkers assumed an underlying
order and harmony in nature, and it was the parallel search for harmony or
justice in the social arena that would inform the great age of Greek political
theory in the fourth century BCE.[7]

Plato

The work of formalizing the distinction between the sensory world and
what some Greek thinkers took to be an absolute, permanent, and unchanging reality or metaphysic was left to Plato (c. 427–347 BCE), an Athenian
of noble birth who, living during a period of military defeat and severe
party conflict, concerned himself with the search for order and justice under
philosopher-statesmen. Athens was the largest, wealthiest, and most cul-
turally sophisticated of the Greek city-states. In the seventh century, it was
a typical *polis* dominated by aristocrats who held the best land and ruled
without a written code of law. But around 594 BCE, in the face of increasing
economic hardship and a growing disparity between the aristocratic haves
and the peasant have-nots, a majority of citizens agreed the appointment
of the poet-legislator Solon as *archon* or chief magistrate. He was accorded
extraordinary powers to cancel debts and to free those Athenians who
had been enslaved and taken abroad after their failure to meet financial
obligations to the nobility.[8]

Solon was followed in the middle of the sixth century by a military figure
named Pisistratus who, over three decades, erected a popular tyranny and

undertook a series of public works and extensive building projects, including temples, all with broad-based citizen support. The reformer Cleisthenes gained control around 506 BCE and enlarged the citizen base without regard to rank or wealth. He also created a new Council of Five Hundred for which all male citizens over 30 years of age were eligible, and declared that final authority rested with an Assembly (*Ekklesia*) composed of all citizens. With Cleisthenes, Athens emerged as the first democracy in Greece, where legislation on communal matters could be proposed and deliberated upon by many minds, irrespective of wealth or lineage, and without fear of intimidation. Also with Cleisthenes we begin to see the emergence of that core belief of Greek political culture, the assumption that in the final analysis government rests on conviction or consent rather than force.

Occupying an area of approximately 1000 square miles and with a citizen base of between 30 and 40,000 out of a total population of perhaps 200,000 in Plato's day, Athens served as the premier intellectual center for Greek speakers from across the eastern Mediterranean. Economically and demographically it overshadowed all of its neighbors. There were over 700 Greek *poleis* scattered across the eastern Mediterranean during Plato's lifetime, with most of them operating as small and intimate communities of 500–2000 citizens. Athens, then, was very much the exception in Greek politics, having by far the largest population of free males who participated in the political process and who assumed civil offices on a rotating basis.[9]

During the Age of Pericles, who led Athens from 461 until his death in 429, the Assembly held approximately ten meetings per year and additional extraordinary sessions as called by the Council. All male citizens were eligible to participate in setting policy in domestic and foreign affairs, military action, and public finance. Thanks to a salary supplement for public service—including jury duty—even the landless citizen who lacked leisure time could afford to take on the responsibility of office holding. Political offices and committees were filled by lot on a term-limited basis, thus assuring that a large number of citizens secured some practical experience in government.[10] Perhaps a third of the total population was in this way, and through participation in the Assembly, engaged in the political life of the city-state. Excluded, of course, were the wives and other female relatives of free males, together with non-Athenian Greeks (metics) and the large population of slaves (a universal institution throughout the ancient world). But in general Athenian democracy presupposed that common men were capable of acting wisely in a political capacity and that specialization and training were not essential to the operation of the city-state. Plato would come to disagree with both assumptions.

Ironically, Athenian democracy or direct rule by citizens flourished over a period of two centuries when the *polis* was involved in a series of debilitating military conflicts. The city and its allies rebuffed powerful Persian invaders in 490 and again in 480, but fought a long and unsuccessful war against a coalition led by Sparta from 431 to 404, and struggled, again without success, against Philip of Macedon in 388. It was near the end of the campaign against Sparta that Pericles encapsulated the spirit of Athenian democracy when he commemorated those soldiers who had fallen in battle. They had fought to preserve a state in which "the administration is in the hands of the many and not the few." Only Athenians "regard a man who takes no interest in public affairs, not as a harmless, but as a useless character; and if few of us are originators, we are all sound judges of policy." For Pericles and his fellow citizens, Athens was "the school of Hellas," but in the aftermath of the disastrous Peloponnesian War (the city was starved into capitulation in 404 BCE), democratic governance temporarily gave way to an oligarch clique under the so-called "Thirty Tyrants," some of whom were related to the young philosopher.[11]

Plato was a first-hand observer of these reversals, and for a brief time he aspired to have a career in public life. He became instead the first Western political theorist by devoting himself explicitly and systematically to addressing issues of governance anchored in a formal assessment of human nature and human potential. It was not a particularly upbeat evaluation. Like his teacher and mentor Socrates (who was executed in 399 BCE by a scapegoating democratic government that convicted him of corrupting youth and subverting state religion with his inveterate questioning), Plato was disillusioned by the incapacity of most politicians for ethical theorizing, and by the intensity and pettiness of factional rivalries. Too often it appeared that self-serving leaders, appointed by a democratic but unreflective Assembly, were consumed by immediate and practical gain. They had neither the time nor inclination to investigate the nature of justice and truth, right and wrong, nor the will to advance the common enterprise of civic life. According to Plato, these individuals, having neglected to examine the state of their own immortal souls before assuming public leadership positions, were incapable of attaining to the level of knowledge necessary to secure the good of all citizens.[12]

Convinced that few people were fit for public office, and of the need to build a rational foundation for human conduct and social organization, Plato abandoned his earlier desire to enter politics and instead focused his energies on the theoretical construction of an ideal state. Founding a school called the Academy in 388 BCE, he continued to lecture and to write about needed reforms in a series of dialogues that employed the dialectical, or question and answer format employed by his beloved mentor Socrates. The impact of the judicial murder of Socrates on Plato was profound. Several of the early dialogues are connected to this watershed event. The *Apology* treats Socrates' defense at his trial, in the *Crito* he outlines his reasons for not attempting to escape after his sentencing, and in the *Phaedo* the condemned man argues in favor of the immortality of the soul.[13] The dialogue format continues in the three works that are essential to Plato's political philosophy. The *Republic* was written in the author's early manhood and probably soon after the founding of the Academy; the *Statesman* was most likely composed mid-career; and the *Laws* was completed toward the end of his life, and almost certainly after his disastrous experience as an advisor to the young king of Syracuse in the 360s.

The wide-ranging *Republic* features Socrates as the main protagonist, and not surprisingly we find him dedicated to the pursuit of ethical knowledge and justice, or how best to live in community. This ambitious agenda was of a piece with Plato's idealist metaphysics, the belief that the world of matter and sense experience was no more than a pale shadow of the real world of unchanging eternal truths. Like his master Socrates, Plato believed that the only way to know the higher reality of truths, which he called Forms, was through highly disciplined rational investigation. In the seventh book of *The Republic* he introduced the now-famous allegory of the cave to illustrate the difficulty involved in humankind's quest to understand the Forms. In the "cavernous chamber" ordinary mortals are chained in a fixed position where they are able to see only the wall of the cave in front of them, which reveals but shadows of the real world at the cave's entrance. The shadows represent the perspective available through sense experience, and only when one of the prisoners is permitted to ascend to the light of day at the mouth of the cave does he realize that the shadow world is in fact far removed from reality.

It would be a shocking experience to be thus abruptly disabused of widely accepted views of reality, and the released prisoner, who is the philosopher, "would need, then, to grow accustomed before he could see things in the upper world." Even harder would it be for the prisoner, returning to his fellows in the cave, to explain to them the error of their ways. They are, after all, relatively comfortable in their shadow world. "And if it were possible to lay hands on and kill the man who tried to release them and lead them up, would they not kill him?"[14] Plato's philosophers, who understood the illusory nature of the world of sense and its fleeting attractions, were not destined to make much headway with the vast majority of citizens who did not possess a strong capacity for reason. Nevertheless, the philosophic search for knowledge of the Forms is antecedent to the realization of the good life on earth, prerequisite to the establishment of justice.

Plato recognized that every association of men in social groups was animated by a desire to satisfy specific needs. No person is truly self-sufficient but depends upon others for survival and human flourishing. The state, he claimed, is designed to assure "the harmonious interchange of services."[15] In observing that humans possessed differing natural talents, he insisted that each should focus on tasks that were appropriate to their skill set, developing those skills to the highest possible level. The versatility and absence of specialization that is celebrated in Periclean Athens is sharply disparaged in the *Republic*. Working from this elitist premise, Plato wrote that just as there was a division of labor in functions related to material production, so too there should be a parallel division with respect to the locus of political power. In particular, Plato held that society is divided into two essential classes, the producers who commit themselves to a variety of forms of economic activity, including agriculture, trade, and manufacture;

and the guardians who carry out military and executive functions depending on their aptitude. The military guardians exhibit extraordinary courage under pressure, while those charged with executive functions are distinguished by their intellectual abilities and selfless devotion to the betterment of the community.

In the utopian world of the *Republic*, prospective rulers undergo extensive training from childhood, living in garrisons where they are freed from the distractions of property, marriage, and family life. An aristocracy of intellect is created, with rulers highly skilled in the art (*techne*) of governance living an austere existence that mirrored life in Sparta, Athens' great rival. In a state built on natural principles, the philosopher-statesmen would be prepared to exercise political power wisely, for they alone would be capable of recollecting the knowledge that all men unconsciously possess, including the Form of Justice. As experts in the science of governance they are able to inspire and direct others to strive toward the absolute standards of Beauty, Goodness, Equality, and Justice, the unalterable foundation stones of the life worth living in community.

Clearly there was no mistaking the fact that peasant producers and artisans, whose lives are guided by appetite, have no right to question such political authority. Their duty is to obey, and to supply the community with the material products that are essential to the flourishing society. What freedom is allowed individual citizens relates to their realization of a particular calling in the service of others, about meeting collective, not individual needs. The philosopher-statesmen, freed from the distractions of getting and exchanging, focus instead on leading the lower orders to work in community to satisfy the highest human needs. In order to advance this noble cause, the ruler is free to adapt existing laws to fit particular circumstances, and is not personally subject to man-made law. In the end, justice is achieved when each of the three orders in society—artisans and laborers, military men, and rulers—carries out complementary and harmonious functions: supplying physical needs, affording protection, and providing skilled statesmanship.

Plato's later works on politics, the *Statesman* and the *Laws*, do not approach either the literary or speculative quality of the *Republic*, but their considerable influence upon subsequent theorists is undeniable. Whereas the philosopher-king of the *Republic* was very much a figure above the law in the sense that he was empowered by virtue of his specialized training to know the Good, in the *Laws* the author recognizes the difficulty of identifying such selfless statesmen and concedes that in a second-best state the rule of law must prevail over all citizens. Nevertheless, Plato throughout his adult years remained committed to a form of what we might term "political authoritarianism" in his insistence that politics and rulership were specialized fields of human inquiry, much like medicine or mathematics, and that only a handful of persons are capable of making definitive statements respecting objective values and the nature of the good life. The majority can neither know nor consistently pursue the good life, thus it is the function of the paternalistic—and ultimately coercive—philosopher-king, the expert in these all-important matters, to have the final word.

Aristotle

Although not an Athenian by birth, Aristotle joined Plato's Academy as a student from Stagira in Macedon around the year 367 and stayed on as a fellow teacher until the master's death in 347. He then left Athens and after brief stays in Asia Minor and on the eastern Aegean island of Lesbos, accepted an appointment as tutor to the young prince Alexander of Macedon in 343. In 335, he returned to Athens where he opened his own school, the Lyceum. Aristotle's written works prior to the establishment of the Lyceum—four-fifths of his total output—have not survived, but the extant materials doubtless draw upon earlier efforts. His interests were wide-ranging and included natural history, ethics, rhetoric, the physical sciences, and comparative politics. Athens was by now firmly under the control of Aristotle's former student, who was about to embark upon the extraordinary military campaigns that would take him as far south as Egypt and as far east as the Indus River Valley. But when Alexander the Great died suddenly at the height of his power in 323 BCE, anti-Macedonian sentiment in Athens affected all non-resident aliens from the north. Charged by his enemies with impiety, Aristotle hastened to avoid the fate of Socrates and departed Athens, dying in Chalcis on the island of Euboea the following year.[16]

Despite his Macedonian roots, Aristotle was not in favor of the imperial project undertaken by his former student. Like his mentor Plato, Aristotle pursued his theoretical work assuming that the *polis* or self-governing political community was normative, and that the trend toward great territorial states was an aberration. And again like Plato, he believed that the city-state encompassed more than forms of deliberation, administration, and the official exercise of power; it included an entire pattern of living, including intellectual production, cultural output, and religious values. Both men were convinced that individuals found the highest level of human flourishing (*eudaimonia*) as active, rational participants of the *polis*, not as rights-bearing individuals who asserted personal freedoms against the state, nor as subjects of large and powerful empires. Indeed for Aristotle, human beings living outside of the city-state were potentially the worst type of wild beasts, always guided by selfish instinct. Ironically, the very citizenship that Aristotle held to be essential to the flourishing life of the city-state was denied to him as an outsider living in Athens.[17]

In the *Politics*, his major work on government and constitutions, he continued the Platonic project by claiming that the state was similar in many ways to the family unit. Just as the family was the first form of association instituted to meet our survival needs, and as the village represents the interests of multiple households, so the *polis* cultivates human potential at the highest level. Distinguished from the animals by the ability to exercise reason, the very spark of the divine within them, Aristotle believed that humankind's purpose or teleology consisted of intellectual activity in community with others.[18] To be fully human one must exercise the power of speech to debate the collective choices that every community must make. But he also recognized that most persons were driven oftentimes by ambition and greed, resentment of others' prosperity, and fear.[19] Key to ameliorating these tendencies was education in general, and knowledge of justice in particular. As social animals, humans look to the state, and in particular the *polis*, as the natural instrument for promoting the worthwhile life and common welfare—the greater good of human beings. Where he parted ways with his teacher, Aristotle did so in an effort to achieve the same end: the formation of the good society under the leadership of rational political actors.

The parting began with the abstract theory of Forms. For Plato the Forms of beauty, justice, and the good did not exist in the particular instances that were accessible through sense experience, but instead in an abstract realm of ideas. Aristotle rejected the doctrine of Forms as no better than idle metaphor, and he argued that any attempt to arrive at universals must be anchored in concrete examples that embody them. As the son of a Macedonian court physician, Aristotle insisted that observable facts mattered, and that only from a study of the particular could one graduate toward objective and universal truths. His inductive approach to knowledge informed the research agenda at the Lyceum, where students gathered detailed information on the history and administrative structures of 158 Greek city states. The ideal *polis*, Aristotle reasoned, was best approached by studying the strengths and weaknesses of existing city-states, by observing and classifying institutions and behaviors. Empirical and historical investigation, not abstract speculation, became essential prerequisites to the improvement of life in community.

Although the study of Athens is the only extant example, Aristotle's inductive approach overturned Plato's commitment to the philosopher-king who alone is fitted to rule because he allegedly knows the Forms as they exist beyond the realm of sensory experience. The top-down, highly elitist structure of political authority, where one class of rulers, the philosopher-kings, monopolize access to higher learning and determine the state's well-being for everyone, was called into question by Aristotle precisely because it lacked any empirical basis. Plato assumed that altruism would prevail in an ideal communal society, and that Guardians would divest themselves of all personal interests. The communalism of the *Republic* assumes that human nature will be changed, and altruism abound, once institutions are reformed.

Aristotle took a more skeptical approach, preferring to evaluate humans as they are and to look for ways to improve communal sentiment. In Book II of the *Politics* he took issue with Plato's abolition of the traditional family and private possessions, and the close regimentation of daily life that emerges from the definition of the Good in the *Republic*. He was more supportive of Plato's approach to the political community in the *Laws*, however, where greater emphasis is placed on efforts to improve existing constitutional structures through reasoned dialogue and the supremacy of agreed legal conventions. He also believed, like Plato and many others, that slavery was natural, and that the institution was part of the hierarchy of relationships that were essential to the proper functioning of society. Just as children are subject to parents, wives to husbands, and citizens who are deficient in practical reason to those with superior intellects, so too slaves are in subjection to their masters for their own well-being. They are the essential food producers in Aristotle's ideal *polis*, but as a permanent underclass can never enjoy the fruits of citizenship irrespective of their loyalty and dedication.[20]

Since both the family and the neighborhood were natural forms of association emerging out of human needs, Aristotle viewed the *polis* as a capstone association dedicated to human well-being. Books III through VI of the *Politics* examine a range of political systems because Aristotle was convinced that no one model was suited to every society. In those rare instances where one man was more virtuous than all others, monarchy would be appropriate. But monarchy, under a corrupt leader, would quickly degenerate into tyranny. Similarly, a small group of virtuous leaders might form a strong aristocracy. Wealthy and educated, they would bring their collective wisdom to bear on public issues. But there would always be a danger that group ambition would transform the aristocratic leadership team into an oligarchic clique.

In those places where the great majority of non-wealthy freeborn citizens consistently followed high moral standards and governed in the common interest, a "polity" was formed, but selfish ambition at this level resulted in what Aristotle termed "democracy." He was willing to concede that ordinary citizens collectively may exhibit a degree of wisdom comparable to the just king or aristocratic few, but where the high standards were absent— and Aristotle was not particularly hopeful on this account, there was a danger that democracy would quickly degenerate into rule by the indigent to the distinct disadvantage of the wealthy minority. In the end he did not endorse any one model, counseling instead the need for elites and common folk to compromise in the interest of securing justice for every citizen. Most states contained mixed populations, and Aristotle believed that a properly constructed mixed constitution, with a large middle class, had the best chance of fostering consensus and moderate rule amongst all ranks of citizens. Recognizing the claims of the many in a lasting political system, Aristotle pressed for the need to educate every citizen in state-supported and controlled institutions.[21]

If habits of character strengthened the moral virtues and constituted the ethical side of politics, and if constitution-making involved the application of those virtues to the specific structure of political life, then for Aristotle the neglect of education was the greatest threat to the constitution. No citizen should suppose that he belongs to himself, "for they all belong to the state,

and are each of them a part of the state, and the care of each part is inseparable from the care of the whole."[22] Educators might differ over the content
and contours of a curriculum, but since virtue is neither innate nor a divine
gift, taking pains to form a life of well-doing must be the primary task of
state-controlled education. At the close of the *Nicomachean Ethics*, a work
that in many respects is the companion to the *Politics*, Aristotle observed
that "it is difficult to get from youth a right training for excellence if one has
not been brought up under right laws; for to live temperately and hardily
is not pleasant to most people, especially when they are young." This is
why their education, what Aristotle referred to as "nurture and occupation" should be fixed by law. Habit and practice were essential to right
living; without them the coercive arm of the law was necessary, "for most
people obey necessity rather than argument, and punishments rather than
what is noble."[23] This generic observation, cutting across rich and poor,
oligarchs and democrats, further strengthened the defense of mixed constitutions where abuse of power is controlled by the fact that no one class
(or individual) can act without the approval of the others.

The social contract state, where government serves to defend the rights
of citizens against one another, and against the state, was anathema to
both Plato and Aristotle. Theirs was vision of the state as the agent of the
good life, where the definition of what constitutes such a life is informed
by rightly constituted laws, an educated citizenry, and community-minded
legislators. A successful state is one with a distinct ethical purpose in which
opportunities for leisure are reserved for self-improvement and not for
indulgence or inactivity. Formal education was not to be the handmaid of
occupational training but instead training for a life of inquiry and intellectual growth. Knowing how to rule and, in turn, how to be ruled, involved a
picture of public authority that assumed an objective and discoverable good
that all reasonable persons could discover and embrace for themselves. For
Aristotle in particular, the "final and perfect association" of the *polis* was
the indispensable instrument in advancing humankind's natural end, as he
stated at the outset of the *Politics* that man "when perfected, is the best of
animals, but, when separated from law and justice, he is the worst of all . . . .
That is why, if he has not excellence, he is the most unholy and the most
savage of animals, and the most full of lust and gluttony."[24] The civilizing
capacity of the state, and the ability of legislators to make men function in a
common and reciprocal fashion, were the defining features of Athenian politics as understood by Plato and Aristotle. Both men embraced the principle
of consent, but only in the context of an educated citizenry.

From city-state to Roman Empire

In the wake of the collapse of the small, self-contained and demographically homogeneous Greek *polis*, new challenges arose for political thinkers
in what was increasingly an age of huge states with diverse populations.
Macedon, Egypt, Syria: Each repudiated the intimacies of the Greek polity

in favor of unabashed empire. In these states, where the *polis* gave way before the *cosmopolis*, few were afforded the opportunity for direct participation in matters of governance. Alexander's Macedonian Empire, no matter how short-lived, fundamentally altered—some would say destroyed—the notions of civic duty, participation, and political accountability that were at the heart of the Greek experiment. The very word "political" traced its etymology to "things concerning the *polis*," making it difficult to redefine political space in an environment where decision-making was removed from the lives of most subjects.[25] The trend toward giantism would reach its full measure under Roman auspices, especially after the obliteration of Carthage in 146 BCE and the establishment of the empire soon thereafter. Stretching across enormous distances and embracing peoples of widely dissimilar cultures and traditions during the first two centuries of the Common Era, the imperial idea shifted attention away from local actors and metropolitan concerns, highlighting instead the propriety of allegiance under a single, distant, unchallenged, and godlike ruler.

Rome, of course, had itself begun as a small city-state on the banks of the Tiber River in 509 BCE and attempted to retain the administrative architecture of a small community even as its territories expanded throughout the Italian peninsula. As the historian J.M. Roberts has observed, the Romans "always showed a fondness for old traditions and liked to keep alive old ways of doing things."[26] They felt proud of their mixture of three types of government: monarchy in the form of annually elected consuls; aristocracy as represented by the Senate; and democracy in its citizens and tribunes. The gods looked favorably upon this arrangement whereby one part of the state cancelled out the vices of another, but the balance was hard to maintain in practice.

In fact the Republic was dominated early on by a powerful Senate, and as territorial expansion proceeded apace, immense wealth was concentrated in the hands of the landed elite.[27] The independent small farmer, long the economic backbone of Roman society, lost his position in the face of slave labor on massive estates. A democratic surge in the second half of the second century BCE resulted in a series of civil wars and the eventual establishment of a tyranny under military strong men. The instability was only eliminated with the accession of Augustus (63 BCE–14 CE), adopted son of Julius Caesar, in 30 BCE, and the formation of a world empire.

As the effort to maintain city-state governmental structures became increasingly untenable and alternative models were adopted to deal with new spatial realities, Roman political thinkers responded in a highly practical manner. Leading jurists or legal scholars, for example, incorporated elements of the legal codes of the various subject peoples into Roman law, creating over time a *jus gentium* or law of nations or peoples that would later apply to inhabitants across the empire. The formation of this body of legal precedent testified to the need for common regulations to govern relations between faraway strangers, and Roman magistrates became key figures in implementing these laws in the provinces. Under Augustus the provinces were organized for the first time with some regard to the welfare of the inhabitants, further legitimizing the adoption of comprehensive law codes.

And while it may be fair to say that there were few exceptional or systematic thinkers during the long centuries of the Roman Republic and Empire, there were numerous important contributors in jurisprudence, ethics, and administration. Most of these men, recognizing the cultural and intellectual sophistication of their neighbors to the East, developed a strong admiration for classical Greece, mastered the Greek language, and set out to learn from those they had conquered. During the centuries of expansion under the republic, thousands of educated Greeks—some slave and some free—came under Roman control, beginning an informal process of Hellenization that had a deep and lasting impact on Roman, and later Western, thought. Greek science, medicine, art, and philosophy all made inroads into Roman culture. But perhaps the most important result of the consolidation of Roman power was the creation of a common intellectual heritage and a cosmopolitan set of values embraced across much of the Mediterranean world and beyond. Rome set the foundations of Western civilization, and while today we rarely look back on the achievements of the empire as eclipsing anything in the modern West, for a millennium after its decline and fall the peoples of Europe measured their own political and cultural life against the long shadow of the West's first super-state.

Cynics, Epicureans, and Stoics

What did membership in a political community entail after the eclipse of the city-state, as the ties that bound men together in the *polis* slowly dissolved? If docile obedience was the prescription for all but a few of the subjects of the new imperial authorities, how were thoughtful individuals to view their relationship to distant state structures? By the late fourth century BCE, a new move toward disengagement from public life was led by thinkers known as Cynics. Diogenes of Sinope (c. 400–325 BCE) was the earliest recognizable figure in this grouping or school, earning for himself the appellation "dog" for his vocal attacks on all forms of convention and for his shameless behavior in public.[28] Diogenes insisted that a simple life and the satisfaction of basic physical desires, not the Socratic pursuit of abstract knowledge, was the most elevated of callings. A highly individualized form of freedom was to be achieved outside of society, in what the Greeks called autarky or self-sufficiency. So-called eternal truths, and the laws and institutions that buttressed them, were no more than social conventions to be ignored in the interest of seeking a personally defined life of virtue. There was a marked anti-intellectual streak in Cynicism, at least to the extent that it considered human misfortune the product of a distorted natural order— the imperial order. The distortion was brought about by civilization itself, a hotchpotch of institutions and rules that were at odds with nature.

The general retreat from the public sphere championed by the Cynic school was affirmed by the followers of Epicurus of Athens

(c. 341–269 BCE). Unfairly identified as a self-indulgent hedonist by later generations, Epicurus doubted that humans could obtain real knowledge of the world of atoms around them and instead counseled the pursuit of insights that would advance both individual happiness and mutual friendships. His followers defended themselves as principled proponents of physical and emotional well-being and a quiet life within political communities they could no longer influence. The pursuit of fame, power, and wealth, they believed, was insatiable and always ended in frustration and misery. The desire-less state or *ataraxia*, together with the cultivation of friendships that might re-create some of the best aspects of the polis, was to be preferred to the usual scramble for worldly success or political power. So too the fear of angry, interventionist gods did nothing but sap humankind's strength to live healthy, balanced lives. Epicurus believed in the existence of the gods, but he insisted that they cared nothing for human affairs.[29]

The leading Roman Epicurean was Lucretius (c. 96–c. 55 BCE), an atheist who pursued the goal of philosophical tranquility in his work *On the Nature of Things*. In a world of near constant political and military strife, the highest good, not to mention freedom from anxiety, could be realized only by living a simple "unnoticed" life, one that excluded political activity. Epicureans paired a minimum commitment to the state in the interest of maintaining peace and civil order with a heightened sense of individual autonomy and self-interest. It was a worldview in stark contrast to the Socratic emphasis on the civilizing function of political activity.[30] The biographer Plutarch of Chaeronea (c. 46–c. 122 CE) charged the Epicurean with parasitism, seeking the advantages of life in a polity without making any contribution to its well-being. It was a criticism that did not take into account the mood of ambivalence fostered by the imperial paradigm, where meaningful civic action now was limited to distant capitals and where rules seemed arbitrary.[31]

The radical disengagement of the Epicurean school was countered by perhaps the most productive intellectual response to the challenges associated with the growth of empire: Stoicism. The Stoic outlook, product of one of the great Athenian schools founded by Zeno of Citium in Cyprus (335–263 BCE) at the end of the fourth century BCE, became immensely popular amongst educated Roman aristocrats of the second century of the Common Era. Convinced that there was an underlying rational order or divine *logos* in the universe, Stoic thinkers emphasized devotion to duty, common citizenship, and the pursuit of justice under universal law. Every person had an element of the divine spark within them, and at the time of death—which was not to be feared—that spark returned to the eternal spirit.

It was in many respects a perspective ideally suited to a civilization that was expanding rapidly under the *pax Romana* or Roman Peace. Rejecting the old distinction between Greek and barbarian (not unlike Pauline Christianity, that other great belief system of the early empire), Stoics embraced a form of ethical universalism that was anchored in practical common sense. And with this insistence that all men were alike irrespective of birth, social status, or possessions (again the parallels with Christianity are clear), the Stoics provided an important fillip to the deeply influential belief in a common humanity that easily transcended artificial borders and geographic distance. Some of them also contributed a revolutionary rejection of slavery in a world where unfree labor supported the entire economic order. During the first century BCE, approximately one-third of Italy's total population were slaves who were thought to be property that produced and served at the pleasure of the master. To question such a system and to suggest that slaves were human was, to say the least, deeply subversive.[32]

The Roman statesman, lawyer, and orator Cicero (106–43 BCE) was one of the strongest advocates for the rational, universalist values embedded in the Stoic outlook. Coming from undistinguished ancestry, Cicero rose to become one of the leaders of the Senate and to serve as consul in the year 63 BCE, the most important executive office in the republic. The internal upheaval and civil wars that troubled the republic he ascribed to the failure of men to live by constitutionally agreed principles. In his *Republic* and *Laws*, together with a work *On Duties* addressed to his son, and in over 900 letters, Cicero affirmed the Stoic doctrine of natural laws and the obligation of men to live in subjection to reason the noblest faculty of the soul.

During the early empire, the voice of Epictetus (c. 55–c. 135) carried forward the Stoic message. Born into slavery but winning his freedom on the strength of his teachings, his *Discourses* and *Handbook* (composed by his student Flavian Arrian) counseled patience and resoluteness in the face of overwhelming misfortune, acceptance of one's place and duty in the world, and indifference toward material accumulation. Banished along with other philosophers by the Emperor Dometian (r. 81–96) around the year 89, Epictetus settled in Nicopolis in northwestern Greece and established a school that was popular with Roman citizens. Whereas happiness in Aristotelian terms required a modicum of freedom and physical well-being, Epictetus claimed that one could find meaning and purpose even in the worst of circumstances. It was, after all, mistaken beliefs about what is good in life, and our investment of time and talent in pursuing transient prizes, that formed the core of human ill. Many events and circumstances are not in our power to control; what is in our power is the ability to adapt to all that we face and to maintain a virtuous disposition.

The most recognizable of the Roman Stoics was the Emperor Marcus Aurelius (r. 161–180), whose posthumously published *Meditations* truly encapsulated the devotion to duty, irrespective of adverse circumstances, that best defined Stoicism. Although the emperor was almost constantly at war throughout his reign, during the last 12 years of his life he managed to compose his famous notebook of reflections and practical ethics which he called "To Himself." The unimportance of a single human life, and the transitory nature of human accomplishment within the context of infinite time, are recurring themes of the work. "In a brief while now you will be ashes or bare bones; a name, or perhaps not even a name—though even a name is no more than empty sound and reiteration. All that men set their hearts on in this life is vanity, corruption, and trash; men are like scuffling puppies, or quarrelsome children who are all smiles one moment and in tears the next."

Having lost all but one of his five children (his monstrous successor Commodus being the only survivor), the emperor knew more than a little about the fragility of the human passage. Even the social distinctions that humans placed great store in were meaningless, for in death "Alexander of Macedon's end differed no whit from his stable-boy's. Either both were received into the same generative principle of the universe, or both alike were dispersed into atoms."[33] The emperor admonished himself to accept his fate as part of an unknown divine plan and to always act with reason and restraint, to fulfill one's duty and to remain unperturbed in the face of another's evil behavior. The many burdens associated with personal rule over Western Europe, North Africa, Asia Minor, Armenia, and Syria were to be assumed with equanimity. So too was the plague that afflicted most of the empire during these decades, the intrusions of Germanic barbarians, and the floods that destroyed the grain stores in Rome.

Recessional and the city of God

While Stoicism may have provided intellectual consolation to Roman aris-tocrats who lived under an increasingly bureaucratized and militarized empire, the poor, humble, and outcast were beginning to turn to another source of comfort in the new millennium. For the first two centuries of its existence Christianity was but one of a number of small "mystery reli-gions" that afforded compelling narratives about the nature and purpose of human existence. Officially suspect because of their privileging of the osten-sible "king of kings" over the Roman state, Christians suffered intermittent persecution at the hands of provincial authorities. Even St Paul's admoni-tion to followers in Rome that "there is not authority except from God, and those that exist have been instituted by God" did not free the Christian community from suspicion.[34] It seemed only appropriate that a civiliza-tion specializing in the practical—building towns and cities, pioneering transportation infrastructures like paved roads and sophisticated bridges, and keeping things clean with breakthroughs in plumbing and sanitation—would look unfavorably on a ragged lot that preached the imminent end of the world. A starker contrast with the action-oriented citizens of Rome would be hard to imagine.

But ironically it was the *pax Romana* that expedited the movement of people and ideas, including Christianity, across the empire, and by the start of the fourth century under the Emperor Constantine, persecution of the nascent Christian community was ended. Church leaders had softened their rhetoric about the proximity of the end time, and Roman authorities were astute enough to recognize the potential upside of a strategic alliance with an organization that commanded the allegiance of approximately 5 percent of Rome's subjects. The empire benefited greatly from its increas-ingly close relationship with religious leaders who counseled obedience to the Roman state as the indispensable protector of the Christian evangelical project. It was not surprising, then, when the Emperor Theodosius made Christianity the official religion of the Roman Empire in 378.[35]

Before this pivotal alliance was realized, however, the Christian view of humankind's place in God's creation had been solidified by the tribulations of the empire. Augustus and his successors maintained the old forms and trappings of the republic, especially the Senate, and were elected consuls on an annual basis, but the realities of political power had changed fundamentally. As *princeps civitatus* or first citizens, the emperors exercised control over the armed forces and the paid bureaucracy. They became *de facto* monarchs, but their tenure was contingent upon the maintenance of good relations with the Roman army. In the century after the death of Augustus in 14, Rome would be governed by a total of 12 emperors, and despite periods of cruelty early on occasioned by conflict over the succession, in general a period of peace obtained that continued until the death of Marcus Aurelius in 180.

Things took a decidedly violent turn under Marcus's son Commodus, who shared none of his father's virtues and whose assassination signaled the start of a period of instability and decline that inadvertently strengthened the otherworldly outlook of Christianity. During the disastrous third century, German tribes who increasingly adopted Roman military techniques began to penetrate into the empire along the Rhine-Danube frontier. It was in the midst of this crisis that the Emperor Decius attempted to eradicate Christianity because of its ostensible disloyalty and apocalyptic rhetoric. The autocratic Emperor Diocletian (r. 285–305) also launched a concerted attack on the Christian Church while strengthening military defenses against the Germanic barbarians. But Rome's largely agrarian economy was incapable of shouldering the tax burden required by the expanding military and bureaucracy. When the emperor resorted to confiscating the property of his affluent subjects, aristocrats fled the cities and retreated to their rural estates, further undermining the urban cosmopolitan culture of the empire.

Constantine's (r. 312–337) dramatic reversal of policy brought the Church into the fight for the survival of the empire. The 313 Edict of Milan legalized Christianity and put an end to all official persecution, and by the end of the century all other faith positions were proscribed. Church authorities adopted Roman administrative and legal structures, organized missionary activities out of Roman towns and cities, and erected a governing hierarchy that resulted in claims by the Bishop of Rome to spiritual hegemony over all other churches. The early Church of saints and martyrs became a bulwark of establishment respectability and the recipient of imperial largesse on an unprecedented scale. It now enjoyed the luxury of quarreling with itself, and doctrinal disputes became commonplace. As the locus of imperial power and stability drifted eastward to the richer and more densely populated portion of the empire, the Roman Church assumed *de facto* authority over the affairs of Roman territories in Western Europe. Christian bishops began to exercise the functions previously held by civil magistrates, and

people looked to the Church for both physical security and emotional comfort in a disorderly world. This was especially true for slaves and members
of the lower classes, who found the Christian promise of salvation, together
with its insistence upon equality of membership in the community of faith,
a bracing cure to their difficult daily existence. Germanic attacks intensified during the fourth and fifth centuries, until the substance of Roman civil
authority was completely undermined.[36]

The neo-Platonic and Augustinian antidote

It was within this unhappy context that Augustine (354–430), Bishop of
Hippo in North Africa, reflected upon the fortunes of empire and counseled
a radically separate path for Christian soldiers. Augustine had himself traveled a long and laborious road to Christianity, detailed in what is arguably
the most powerful spiritual autobiography of the late classical world, the
Confessions. A highly educated pagan who was born and lived most of his
life in North Africa, he became a Christian only in midlife. He claimed to
have lived a youth of unbridled dissolution before his conversion, and his
estimate of human nature seems to have been informed by his own experiences. Ordained a priest in 391 and quickly ascending the ecclesiastical
ladder to become Bishop of Hippo in 396, Augustine was a prolific author
who ranged widely in works that defined him as perhaps the most influential of all Christian philosophers. And at the core of his intellectual makeup
was a strong familiarity with and admiration for the idealist philosophy
of Plotinus (204–270), a Egyptian-born thinker who lived through some of
the worst reverses in the history of the Roman Empire but whose work
makes no mention of these ruinous events. Reaffirming the Platonic message, Plotinus wrote about the real world of ideas and dismissed the illusory
world of appearances. According to Bertrand Russell, the metaphysics of
Plotinus, translated for a Christian audience by Augustine, offered "tran-
scendental hopes that consoled men when everything terrestrial inspired
despair."[37]

Augustine concentrated his greatest energies on how to make sense of a
world that was filled with an inordinate share of cruelty and danger (when
he died his own city was under assault by the Vandals). After Visigoths
sacked the city of Rome in 410, pagan critics of Christianity blamed the
catastrophe on those who had long refused to worship traditional Roman
deities. Augustine responded with his most important work, the *City of God*.
In this path-breaking Christian analysis of the history of the Roman Empire
and a great deal more, Augustine commanded his fellow believers to continue supporting the Roman state, but he insisted that the worldly city of the
senses was destined for destruction and that only the righteous would live
forever in the heavenly "city of God." Those who do not belong to the heavenly city "shall inherit eternal misery, which is also called the second death,
because the soul shall then be separated from God its life ...." Accord-
ingly, the earthly city could never be the central concern of true Christians;

empires and cities would rise and fall, but so long as an individual's principal interest was the forgiveness of sin through the unmerited saving act of Christ, the worldly obligations of subjects could be met.[38]

Augustine's neo-Platonic distinction between the eternal city and the corruptible life of the flesh, together with his insistence that reason without faith resulted in the futile pursuit of wisdom, would shape the outlook of the Church throughout the Middle Ages and beyond. The classical centering of humans to shape their own destiny, the bedrock of ancient city-states and republics, was replaced with a quest to fulfill God's will on earth in preparation for the real life after death. By the close of the fifth century the admonition seemed to make sense, at least in the Western Roman Empire, where barbarian tribesmen had made a shambles of a once proud civilization. The Vandals took their turn at sacking Rome in 455, and when the loathsome Huns were turned back from the West in 451, the "Roman" army that repelled them was actually a congeries of Visigoths, Franks, Celts, and Burgundians in the employ of a Visigothic king. The miserable fiction was brought to a close in 476 when the last Western Roman emperor, a 15-year-old boy named Romulus, was ousted and killed by the German warlord Odovacer.

The tribulations of leadership in the late imperial West seemed to confirm the Augustinian view of human nature. It was a view that owed much to St Paul, whose sense of the omnipresence of sin dominated his thinking. Disobedience and a natural penchant for thought and action in opposition to God's will would result in damnation for the majority, and no level of human effort could overcome the crippling effects of the first sin of Adam and Eve. Unlike the Platonic claim that there was no essential defect at the center of personality, that reason most clearly resembles the divine in humans, and that the fully rational person could act in a virtuous manner, the Augustinian dissent highlighted incapacity and depravity. When an obscure British monk named Pelagius (c. 354–c. 420) arrived in Rome and took issue with the doctrine of predestination and inherited corruption, Augustinianism had already won the day. The Emperor Honorius (r. 393–423) condemned Pelagius' opinions, and Pope Zosimus (r. 417–418), who had initially defended Pelagius' orthodoxy, soon reversed his position. Humans were empowered to know something of the heavenly city, but were obliged to concede that the majority would be forever excluded from its borders, and that God's method of election would remain a great mystery.[39]

Augustine extrapolated from the fallen nature of individual humans to the impossibility of social life without the coercive arm of the state. Rome may have had its full share of nasty reprobates who wore the imperial purple, but in a world where even the saved are sinners, Augustine was prepared to allow that the wicked ruler was most likely an instrument of God's anger. The hope, of course, was that the Christian prince would fulfill his obligations to rule justly as a matter Christian practice. But when monsters wield power and take aim at God's law, passive resistance is the strongest permissible recourse. The faithful must avoid complicity in the ruler's perversions, but so too they must accept punishment and even death in a spirit of humility. Righteous tyrannicide found no place in the Augustinian moral universe, even though the State—unlike the Church— was of no value when it came to issues of eternal moment. Its portfolio involved outward compliance, not inward conviction. The latter was the business of the visible Church. Necessary due to humankind's sinful nature, but birthed in blood and illegitimate by any standard of Christian brother- hood, the state was no better than a provisional entity led by sinners who kept a fragile check on even deeper depravity, "evil against the greater evil of social chaos."[40]

The sin of Adam made the coercive arm of the state an essential bulwark of order in an otherwise anarchic world; it was certainly not an agency in the advancement of human happiness on earth—nor should it be. Life was meant to be grim and problematical; what small pleasures might come by and by were wholly fortuitous and undeserved. In answer to the question why one should obey the state, Augustine answered that obedience makes possible a focus on the really important business of life, the abandonment of distractions within the world, and compliance with the will of God. Here was a perspective very much removed from the common assumptions of the classical Greek mind, a perspective that would come to dominate the political consciousness of Western Europe for the next millennium.

The advent of natural law theory

The Greek *polis* had both encouraged and celebrated particularism. Essen- tial rights and duties were affiliated with the well-being of the city-state and the successful interactions of a comparatively small community of men in the public square. The age of empire required a much more expansive defi- nition of "community," together with guidelines for people united under an imperial banner and across vast geographical areas. A deepening conscious- ness of a common human nature was one of the most important long-term by-products of the Macedonian Empire under the leadership of Alexander the Great. Three centuries later the apostle Paul captured the essence of this consciousness, and skillfully grafted it onto the nascent Christian agenda when he declared that "as the body is one and hath many members, and all the members of that one body, being many, are one body, so also is Christ."[41] But what were the rules governing relations between persons irrespective of locale and leadership? Could a law for the whole of the civilized world be discovered and agreed after the failure of the city-state? More immedi- ately, could the concentration of coercive power in the hands of emperors be checked by a higher law that was both innate and affirmed by reason? Would the individual retain any moral standing, any indisputable rights against arbitrary power, and if so, how was a framework for universal justice to be agreed and implemented?

The Roman state provided some preliminary answers to these questions. By the late imperial period a large body of civil law had emerged from a variety of sources, rules that survived from the period of the republic, including the decisions of provincial judges, the interpretations of specialist scholars, and imperial decrees. Never static, the law expanded and evolved over the centuries, and a comprehensive summing up and codification was not attempted in any systematic way until the reign of the eastern Emperor Justinian (r. 527–565) in the early sixth century. But as citizenship was extended to foreigners in the wake of Rome's dramatic expansion, the idea of universal standards governing people irrespective of their locale began to take hold within the legal community. Classical Greek culture provided the foundation for thinking about human relations in terms of overarching law. If the phenomena of physical nature adhered to general principles, it seemed logical to assume that analogous principles obtained in the social sphere. Epicureans lodged a powerful dissent to this position on the grounds that the underlying essence of things could not be perceived, but in general the direction in Greek thought moved toward ubiquitous, if dimly perceived, laws governing all of creation.

When Roman lawyers and judges addressed cases involving citizens and non-citizens of the empire, they found it helpful to seek a common ground of agreement, and from there a vision of what ought to be, with respect to the experiences and practices of litigants on both sides of a case. They did this by comparing and analyzing existing laws in a variety of local settings and across differing political units, always with an eye toward identifying shared elements. It was in these circumstances that lawyers began to establish what came to be called the *jus gentium* or law of peoples, as distinguished from the *jus civile* or Roman law. Stoic philosophy, with its commitment to a broad cosmopolitanism, was enormously helpful in this effort. Affirming an underlying unity and rationality in all things, Stoicism smoothed the way to an understanding of law that was no longer particular to time and place, to one people exclusively, or to one geographic location in isolation. Beneath the apparent variety and clutter of sensory experience, Stoicism maintained, lay a world of uniformity, commonality, and deep order—a "natural law" that could be discovered and agreed by all reasonable persons. In the words of Cicero, whose views carried enormous influence both on his contemporaries and on his admirers throughout the Christian Middle Ages: "True law is right reason, consonant with nature, spread through all people. It is constant and eternal; it summons to duty by its orders, it deters from crime by its prohibitions." Under this reading, Natural law was innate, engraved on the hearts of humans and known through the cultivation of the rational intellect. It governed both moral behavior and the order of physical creation.[42]

The work of Roman jurists who repeated and elaborated upon Ciceronian general principles became part of the *Corpus iuris civilis* that was published under the Emperor Justinian in 533. Roman precedents informed the legal structures of both the Orthodox Church in the East and the Roman Catholic Church in the West, not to mention many of the successor states to Rome in the medieval West. The concept of a natural law of human relations, and the corollary understanding of justice as a knowable divine ordinance brought down to earth, would have an enormous influence on both medieval Christian and modern secular political thought.

But natural law theory in its early Christian context also had to account for the Augustinian picture of fallen human nature. Cicero had argued that only the fully rational person would act on the natural instinct to sociability and consensus building. Such a person knew his duty and would act in harmony with eternal law. With God as its author, those individuals who disobey the innate natural law are in effect denying their own human nature. And this was precisely Augustine's point. Human nature was flawed in a fundamental sense, its restoration no longer an act of volition but rather a magnanimous gift for which the recipients were completely undeserving. Cicero acknowledged that some have weaker minds and that most would not be able, unassisted, to see and obey the requirements of the natural law. But weakness for Cicero did not signal evil predisposition; for Augustine the matter was entirely otherwise, and the function of the State—and the Church—was to act in response to this unhappy reality. The medieval centuries, anchored in a pessimistic view of human nature and committed to the necessity of coercion in civil matters, were now underway.

Chapter 2.

Heavenly Mandates, 400–1500

The millennium between the fall of the Western Roman Empire and the start of the Renaissance, while recognized by scholars as a period of profound change and intellectual dynamism, is still disparaged in popular discourse as a gigantic detour in the march of human progress. The loaded term "Dark Ages" calls attention to all that was wrongheaded about the successor societies to Rome. A world of ignorance, chronic warfare, grinding poverty, poor hygiene, bad manners, and dogged superstition all presided over by self-serving clerics and illiterate warrior kings—these were the essential material and intellectual conditions in the lands of the former Roman Empire. According to this reading of the past, medieval people knew little about and cared less for the achievements of the ancient world. Once the Germanic barbarians were brought into the Christian fold, the pre-eminent concern of Europe's landholding elite was the advancement of the Christian commonwealth, the organization of confessional kingdoms in line with transcendent guideposts. It was only in the late fifteenth century, thankfully but inexplicably, that the darkness began to give way before a new dawn of culture and enlightenment, a new dedication to the affairs of this world known as the Renaissance.

It is an appealing analysis on the surface, especially for those who feel compelled to justify their own cultural priorities by highlighting the alleged inadequacies of others long deceased, but in the end it is nothing more than a caricature of the medieval millennium, what one recent scholar called "an adventure playground for prejudice."[1] Western European society after the collapse of Roman authority was fundamentally altered, and the forms of political thought and organization that emerged—so unfamiliar to modern notions of government and statehood—have no doubt contributed to the popular disparagement of things medieval. Our penchant, for the most part, is to applaud history's great centralizers, and in the Middle Ages the list is short. The modern growth imperative, together with the drive to concentrate power, simply did not inform the thinking of most medieval leaders.

Indeed during the formative centuries of Germanic rule, it is the failure to re-establish the unity realized under Roman auspices that stands out to us. The political culture centered on the personal bonds of illiterate warrior elites, around oaths of fealty, contractual dependence, service, dispersed authority, and mutuality within local lordships and principalities.

This seemingly anarchic state of affairs did not trouble common people at the time, most of whom accepted without much reflection the normalcy of small units of government and communal perspectives. As long as the real needs of the population were met, as long as a modicum of physical security was achieved, medieval people did not spend their days lamenting the demise of the Roman *imperium*. The manorial lord with his local courts, the diocesan command of the bishop and his priests, the village council, and the custom of the ages all these were the serviceable reference points for most subjects, both free and unfree, when it came to law and order, food and shelter, and—most importantly—eternal salvation.[2]

There was one consolation for advocates of the growth imperative during the Middle Ages, although even this was, at the end of the day, a rather mixed blessing. The institutional home of nascent Christianity, the Roman Catholic Church and its leader, the Bishop of Rome or the Pope, aspired throughout most of the medieval millennium to make good the claim to hold the mantle of Roman authority in the West. Moreover, this same Bishop of Rome, as Vicar of Christ and successor to St Peter, was tireless in claiming universal sovereignty throughout Christendom by virtue of his supreme pastoral role. Authority over, and care for, the eternal souls of men and women, not their fragile bodies or transitory possessions, was the extraordinary charge of the Pope and his clerical subordinates.[3]

It followed, then, that kingship was simply an office under the Church, and the person of the monarch (or emperor) a subsidiary representative of the Pope whose duty was to enforce God's law in the temporal sphere. Failure to complete the charge carried with it the likelihood of rebuke and the outside possibility of a sacking—at least in theory, anyway. The latter action was attempted on occasion, with uneven results for the papacy's overall prestige, but the assertion when combined with the sanction of excommunication, at least allowed the popes to define "temporal rulership" as a religious charge. Western Europe during the Middle Ages was a unified quasi-state in the sense that religious heterodoxy was disallowed everywhere. Almost everyone agreed that dissent was to be crushed, the "other" reproached and, if need be, eliminated.

But the Middle Ages also bequeathed early forms of consultative government that were deeply embedded in the culture of Germanic society. Feudal land systems, rising to prominence in the tenth century, emphasized reciprocal obligations amongst the military elite, and the propriety of customary land tenure for the unfree serf. During the central Middle Ages (c. 1000–1300), free cities and commercial urban communities in northern Italy and the Low Countries set precedents for autonomy and guild-dominated governance. The outlines of modern representative systems, state sovereignty, property rights, the centrality of law, and the separation of church and state all can be traced back to the central and later Middle Ages (c. 1200–1450). There were only a handful of medieval writers prepared to argue in favor of the unlimited exercise of power by either kings or prelates. Christian teaching about the intrinsic sameness of immortal souls and of God's purposes for humankind helped to insure that the dignity of the individual would not be forgotten, just as precepts concerning the essential equality of humans before the King of kings would shape political structures anchored in a deeper moral code. Indeed the very existence of two distinct centers of power, lay and religious, insured that the drift toward absolutism emblematic of other major centers of civilization around the world would not be replicated in Western Europe. The dynamic tension between Church and State, the competing claims of prince and bishop, would inadvertently set the stage for the growth of constitutional theory in the early modern age. Responsible government and the principle of consent, the rule of codified law, the rejection of claims to omnipotence—these conceptual products alone should make us wary of careless ascriptions like "The Dark Ages."

Germanic kingship and Christianity

The Germanic successor states to Rome were both modest in size and fragile in terms of political stability. The pagan invaders and migrants who hailed from central and Southeastern Europe settled amongst a provincial population that was largely Christian and for whom Latin remained the language of the elite. Local bishops, often recruited from the landed aristocracy, assumed some of the political authority abdicated by Rome, while Benedictine monastic establishments controlled estates that were worked by rent-paying peasants and slaves.[4] Latin learning was kept alive in these monasteries, but little else of the Roman heritage remained. Urban centers atrophied and commercial activities that once intersected the entire Mediterranean basin were now reduced to local trade and barter. Subsistence agriculture and self-contained economic units under the control of ambitious churchmen and former imperial officials became the norm.

During the course of the fifth century there emerged a series of regional kingdoms—Visigothic in Spain, Frankish in Gaul, Ostrogoth and later Lombard in Italy, and a number of smaller Anglo-Saxon territories in Britain—but none were especially successful. Some of the barbarian states attempted to maintain fragments of the old imperial administration. Former Roman counselors and fiscal experts, for example, served the Visigoths and Ostrogoths. But bureaucratic efficiency and formal institutions of governance were never top priorities for the bellicose invaders. Instead, leadership tended to revolve around military prowess and the ability of war leaders to maintain the allegiance of their supporters. It was personal charisma and success on the battlefield that anchored the authority of the tribal leader or king. The *comitatus* or war band took pride of place within the social fabric of Germanic society as warriors organized themselves through an unwritten code of honor and courage in the service of their leader.[5] Another central feature of this pugnacious culture was the bond of kinship. Defending one's own against real or perceived affronts and the frequency and attending chaos of blood feuds necessitated the evolution of an informal system of man-money (*wergeld*) whereby the perpetrator of a crime might buy off the victim's kinship group.[6] Notions of law centered on custom, precedent, community consensus, and appeals to divine judgment, not the rational abstractions of Roman jurisprudence.

Historians once claimed that Germanic kingship strictly followed the elective principle, but recent scholars have questioned the validity of this generalization, pointing to the paucity of source material at its core. It seems far more likely that the authoritarian tendencies within Roman and Christian thought informed the construction of Germanic monarchy. In fact, many of the early rulers enjoyed the sanction of the Roman emperors whose territorial base of power was now in the Eastern capital of Constantinople. Such was the case with the Ostrogothic king, Theodoric, who ruled in Italy from 493 to 526 and won the support of the old landholding class of aristocrats. A similar relationship emerged in the former Roman province of Gaul, where the barbarian Clovis was awarded an honorary consulate and ruled from 482 to 511 in nominal subordination to the eastern Roman emperor. Although a thoroughly repellent ruler who had most of his potential rivals murdered, Clovis won high praise from church leaders, including Bishop Gregory of Tours, for his adoption of Trinitarian Christianity in the face of a growing heresy known as Arianism that denied Christ's divine nature. Not for the last time in the Middle Ages would the Church lend its support to a reprobate monarch so long as he was on the side of theological orthodoxy.[7]

With Roman law largely lost to the West and the works of Aristotle unavailable until the twelfth century, the main source of political ideas, aside from theological treatises and sermons, was the Bible.[8] And an important element in Christian thought that buttressed the power of barbarian kings who embraced the Catholic faith was the belief that God was the sole source of royal authority. In Romans 13: 1, for example, St Paul enjoined everyone to respect higher authorities, "for there exists no authority except from God, and those who exist have been appointed by God." Churchman, of course, understood that kings who held their office by the grace of God remained under the watchful eye of Christ's ordained ministers. The purpose of earthly power, not its origin, was for the church key to limiting the excesses of temporal rulers. Monarchs were constantly reminded that their commission to govern was a Christian service for the advancement of God's kingdom, not their own. And in the event that the message was not received, bishops, abbots, and popes began increasingly to assume the trappings of temporal rulers. Churchman regularly emphasized the kingship of Christ and the royal status of the Virgin Mary. And the papal seat in the city of Rome took on the appearance of a royal court, with court officials, militias, and banners all designed to impress the occasional imperial visitor.[9]

But to illiterate and battle-hardened warriors, the heady doctrine of rule by heavenly appointment suggested something quite different. Subjects owed complete obedience to their earthly superiors, and the least resistance to established authority was a sin. Leading magnates may have had a role in the selection, acclamation, and legitimization of the king, but once in office all subjects were duty-bound to follow royal injunctions. Every sub-sequent formulation of the royal office would include strong elements of theocratic divine right, with the exact nature of the relationship between the monarchy and the Church a matter for some debate and dispute. Germanic kings heartily welcomed the endorsement of the Church, but their actions often belied the stewardship principles that lay at the core of Christian kingship. When they did exceed the bounds of customary law, the ques-tion of appropriate allowable recourse, either by church authorities or by the people at large, loomed very large indeed.[10] Not until the twelfth cen-tury would a Christian writer (John of Salisbury) concede the possibility of tyrannicide, and then only under extreme circumstances.

The Byzantine exception

There was no room for such ambiguity in the Eastern Roman Empire. In fact, the contested nature of monarchical authority in Western Europe is best illustrated by juxtaposing it with developments in the Greek-speaking lands of the Eastern Mediterranean. Constantine's decision in 323 to estab-lish a new imperial capital at the intersection of the Black Sea and the Mediterranean made sense on a number of levels. Easily the most popu-lous, literate, urbanized, and affluent portion of the empire, the lands of Asia Minor and the Middle East also enjoyed strategic advantages that were to prove invaluable in an age of aggressive Germanic, Asiatic, and Muslim migrations. Imperial taxes supported a well-trained army that was capa-ble of protecting what later historians would label the "Byzantine" Empire after the old Greek town on the same location, and for the next thousand years Byzantium would stand in a strong defensive posture as the legitimate successor to the defunct Western Empire.[11]

With a long history informed by Greco-Roman culture and Christianity, the political system that emerged in Byzantium was characterized by dis-tinctly autocratic elements, giving the emperor (*Basileus*) extraordinary power over military, civilian, and church affairs. The empire was nothing less than a fully developed theocracy, where the emperor was accepted as God's vice-regent on earth and where the armed forces fought in defense of a religious ideal whose embodiment was the reigning sovereign. The earliest apologist for this model of governance was Eusebius of Caesarea (263–339), a contemporary of Constantine who was influenced by neo-Platonic ideas. For Eusebius, the earthly kingdom, when properly ordered, was a microcosm of God's heavenly abode.[12] When disputes arose in the theological sphere, the emperor did not hesitate to intervene by calling general church councils and influencing their deliberations. The patriarch of the Byzantine orthodox church, himself the distinct subordinate of the emperor, refused to recognize the claims to primacy of the Bishop of Rome, and while Byzantine scholars eventually lost familiarity with the Latin lan-guage and Byzantine armies lost their foothold in the West, the notion that Constantinople was anything other than a continuation of the Roman imperial project was rejected out of hand.

During the mid-sixth century, the Emperor Justinian (r. 527–565) directed scholars to bring together the myriad imperial laws, edicts, and precedents from earlier reigns into a comprehensive survey of Roman jurisprudence. This enormous undertaking resulted in a body of civil law known as the *Corpus iuris civilis*. The final work heavily reflected the more authoritarian tone of the later Roman Empire, and when it was reintroduced into Western Europe during the course of the twelfth century it served as a counterweight to Germanic customary law. All temporal authority is of divine origin, and all imperial laws are sacred and everlasting: This was the overarching message of the *Corpus iuris*, and church authorities were ill-prepared to contest the formulation. As the living source of law, the emperor was bound neither by its jurisdiction, nor by the clerical establishment. Here was a position that later would buttress the claims of Europe's monarchs to hold absolute power by divine mandate. But it would take centuries before the practice found widespread support in the West.

Papal inheritance

According to early church tradition, St Peter, who was the chief of Christ's apostles, had designated a successor Bishop of Rome as head of the emerging Catholic community. The key text for the original commission was found in the Gospel of St Matthew (16: 18–19) where Christ refers to Peter as the rock upon which he will build the church, assigning him "the keys of the kingdom of Heaven" and telling Peter "whatever you bind on earth shall be considered bound in heaven; whatever you loose on earth shall be considered loosed in heaven." After Roman authorities proscribed paganism in the late fourth century, papal theory envisioned a Christianized super state where temporal leaders willingly accepted the spiritual guidance of priests and bishops, all under the direction of a saintly bishop of Rome. The tomb of St Peter in Rome, and the popular belief that the martyred saint commissioned each living pontiff, strengthened the claims of the Holy See to primacy in all worldly and otherworldly affairs.[13]

A church synod held in the city of Sardica in 343 was the first to attribute primacy of jurisdiction in religious matters to the Bishop of Rome. And Pope Leo I (r. 440–461), who bravely stood down the fearsome Attila the Hun while the western Emperor Valentinian III fled from Rome in 451, ably demonstrated the capacity of the Church to assume the temporal functions that were being abdicated by the State. As the Germanic kingdoms took shape, the popes consistently advanced a reading of Church–State relations that defined each new temporal ruler as a son (*filius*) of the universal church. Religious and moral matters, which frequently had direct political implications, were to be the exclusive province of church law and governance. The precedent had been set as early as 390, when Ambrose, Bishop of Milan (c. 340–397), successfully censured the Emperor

Theodosius I (r. 379–395) after a massacre of civilians in the rebellious city of Thessalonica. The emperor was obliged to undergo public penance for his sinful actions before being allowed back into the communion of the church.[14]

One century later, in a letter of 494 addressed to the eastern Emperor Anastasius I (r. 491–518), Pope Gelasius (r. 492–96) stated that in treating the respective powers of the Church and State, "the responsibility of the priests is more weighty in so far as they will answer for the kings of men themselves at the divine judgment."[15] With such language a parallel monarchy was in the making, one where the Pope was responsible for matters pastoral, and by extension for the eternal well-being of all Christians under his charge. A separate church government and legal system evolved alongside this nascent monarchy, until by the reign of Pope Gregory the Great (r. 590–604) the jurisdictional reach of the episcopal see of Rome extended as far north as the British Isles. Concerned over the survival of the Church in an area of Europe where temporal rule seemed so ineffective, Gregory went so far as to affirm that the ultimate sanction of excommunication, a move that would leave the accused without hope of personal salvation, could be employed against secular rulers as well as clergy.

An ephemeral Carolingian Empire

Control over land and those who labored upon it was the foremost measure of power and authority in the post-Roman West. Even church authority, while ostensibly spiritual in nature, was strengthened by the fact that so many members of the episcopate were from the old Roman landowning aristocracy. These men enjoyed jurisdiction over their flocks through their church office and lordship (*dominium*) over tenants, serfs, and slaves by right of land ownership.[16] For Germanic kings, the recruitment and retention of ambitious fighting men depended on the alienation of land. The insecurity that marked life after the collapse of Roman authority meant that men of violence were eager to commend themselves to those who were more dominant. A reciprocal relationship developed whereby legitimate political authority slowly emerged out of network of relationships centered on land, its acquisition through conquest, and its alienation by compact.

The most successful of the new type of warrior-king was Charlemagne (r. 768–814), head of the Carolinigian family of rulers, who displaced the successors of Clovis in Gaul during the early eighth century. Clovis had established the Merovingian dynasty by virtue of success on the battlefield, but those who followed him on the throne carelessly alienated crown estates, ultimately weakening their own position in relation to their nearest potential rivals. In addition, the Merovingian kings tended to allocate portions of their lands to each of their male heirs, further eroding the royal patrimony and prompting ruinous civil conflicts among equally undeserving children. By the time that Muslim forces moved into Gaul in the 730s, it was a Carolingian warrior, Charles Martel (c. 688–741), not the Merovingian king, who commanded the fighting assets required to defeat the invaders at the Battle of Tours (732).

The balance of power shifted quickly under the leadership of the next Carolingian leader, Pepin the Short (r. 741–768). Allying himself with a reform movement in the Church led by the English Benedictine monk St Boniface (c. 672–754), Pepin sought papal backing for his plan to usurp the crown from the do-nothing Merovingians. Searching for a strong military partner in its own struggle against Lombard aggression, and in its dispute with the Byzantine church over the propriety of religious icons or images, the papacy decided to cast its lot with the upstart Carolingians. In 751, Pepin's palace *coup d'etat* against King Childeric was recognized by Pope Zachary (r. 741–752), and Boniface, acting as papal representative, formally anointed the new monarch in the Frankish city of Soissons.

Three years later Pope Stephen II (r. 752–757) journeyed across the Alps to the new Carolingian kingdom and anointed the king and his queen, together with their sons, and gave Pepin the title "patrician of the Romans." Anointing transformed the royal office into something distinctly other than an autonomous secular responsibility. At this time and for the next few centuries anointing with holy oil was viewed by the Church as a sacrament. The royal recipient was now afforded special grace to carry out a unique ministry within the Church, defending and advancing its earthly interests.[17] Pepin was not remiss; he dispatched his forces to Italy in 754 and again in 756, routed the troublesome Lombards, and graciously "donated" a large portion of central Italy to the papacy. A fateful alliance had been formed, one where the precise nature of the relationship between spiritual and temporal power remained altogether ambiguous.[18]

Pepin's son Charlemagne greatly enhanced the strategic alliance with the Church of Rome during a reign lasting over 45 years. He funded the building of churches and supported liturgical reform, encouraged monastic scholars and their schools, and protected missionaries as they carried out their work of proselytizing among pagan tribes. Charlemagne spent most of his reign engaged in expansive military operations that were designed with the dual purpose of land aggrandizement and Christian crusade. In a letter composed by Alcuin of York to Pope Leo III, Charlemagne stated that "Our job is the defense of the church and the fortification of the faith; yours to aid our warfare by prayer."[19] As a successful warrior-king in the tradition of Germanic leadership, Charlemagne absorbed the Lombard kingdom into his domains, led an offensive push against Muslim armies in northern Spain, routed a powerful Avar state in Southeastern Europe, and fought multiple battles against the pagan Saxons on the Northeastern frontier.[20] On the domestic front, he and his closest advisors issued capitularies or laws covering topics as wide-ranging as the construction of fortifications, coinage regulations, and the treatment of rebels against the Crown.

At the height of Charlemagne's military power, with all of Western Christendom, excluding the British Isles, securely under his control, the king was eager for Constantinople to recognize him as an equal, and to restore the lapsed title of Western emperor. A series of diplomatic overtures were made and marital alliances proposed, but there was little enthusiasm on the Byzantine side. Finally, in the year 800, Pope Leo III took matters into his own hands. Charlemagne was in Rome to arbitrate a protracted dispute between the Pope and the city's quarrelsome aristocracy. During a Christmas service at St Peter's Basilica, Leo took the opportunity to crown the king "Emperor of the Romans." A new western protector of Christendom in the person of an illiterate German warrior-king had been chosen to resurrect the Roman *imperium*.[21]

In truth, the reconstituted Western Roman Empire was but a pale imitation of its original, with the ship of state dependent largely upon the personal influence of Charlemagne. Administrative units led by regional officials—counts, dukes, and margraves—took oaths of loyalty to Charlemagne and served as the eyes and ears of the government, but constant vigilance and royal oversight were essential to public order. Indeed the nobles who served Charlemagne were also his electors; they had elevated him to the office of king and they jealously guarded their right to elect each successive ruler. There was no room for Eastern-style absolutism in such an environment. For his part, the emperor commissioned the building of an imperial capital in the city of Aachen, well North of the old Roman administrative center at Trier, in an effort to centralize control after the fashion in the East. An impressive stone church in the Byzantine style served as the architectural centerpiece of the new Rome. Byzantine ambassadors visited Aachen late in Charlemagne's reign to acknowledge his title, but the capital never blossomed into a major commercial or political center that could equal cities in the Eastern Roman Empire.

The larger significance of the coronation ceremony of 800 was the message that the papacy hoped to deliver both to the Byzantine emperor, the Church's former protector, and to the newly minted German emperor and his successors. In what purported to be a third-century letter from Constantine to Pope Silvester I known as the "Donation of Constantine," the first Christian emperor transferred the imperial insignia and imperial power over the Western portions of the empire to the Pope.[22] The forged document, probably written in the middle of the eighth century, conveniently made its public debut just before Charlemagne's Christmas day coronation. The statement of papal temporal supremacy embedded in the Donation was clear to all but the most obtuse. The new emperor, although illiterate, was certainly not in this last camp. He maintained a very different view of the ritual. And just to insure that the Pope understood the imperial reading of Church–State relations, in 813 Charlemagne took it upon himself to conduct the coronation of his own son, Louis the Pious, as the emperor apparent. The historian R.W. Southern was right: The idea of a Western empire was a mistake from the start "primarily because in creating an emperor the pope created not a deputy, but a rival or even a master."[23]

Feudal recoil

When Charlemagne died at the age of 71 in 814, his sole surviving heir was unable to win from his regional aristocrats the high level of personal allegiance that was essential to the functioning of a Germanic warrior state. Just as the imperial capital at Aachen failed to develop into a major urban showpiece, so too the Carolingian imperial project never gained sufficient traction to overawe the wider aristocratic penchant for factionalism. Charlemagne held his vassals in check through the strategic distribution of conquered territories. Plunder and tribute, not the peaceful pursuits of commerce and internal development, were the transient economic drivers of the Carolingian state.[24] Once the expansionist phase of the reign came to an end at the start of the ninth century, a mood of restlessness appeared within the ranks of the landed elite. While a conscientious leader, Louis the Pious (r. 814–843) was not the man to restore the mantle of martial leadership, and during the final years of his reign his sons rebelled against him, and then against each other, plunging the Carolingian Empire into civil war. Three truncated successor states, all bulwarks of provincialism, eventually emerged from the wreckage.

The break-up of the ephemeral Carolingian Empire was hastened by the last wave of invasions that would afflict Western Europe during the Middle Ages. Vikings from the North, Magyars from the East, and reenergized Muslims forces from the South all carried out devastating attacks against the borders of the former empire. All but the last eventually settled down, intermarried, and adopted Christianity, but for upward of two centuries the surprise attacks, pillaging, murder, and mayhem continued across the continent.[25] For common people, what little protection there was typically came through the offices of the local lord or bishop, who in the latter instance became a *de facto* temporal ruler in an otherwise lawless environment. With armed and mounted vassals of a great lord owing allegiance to no higher authority, political life reverted back to a simple network of personal relationships. From the ninth century until the middle of the eleventh, contract and consent between the independent nobility and their vassals in a set of relationships known as "feudalism" eroded the coercive claims of theocratic monarchy. Personal service and mutual advantage, all in an environment where public authority was exercised by private individuals and where everyone was looking for protection from someone stronger, set the foundations of consensual government. When Hincmar, Archbishop of Rheims, and a leading elaborator of mid-ninth century West Frankish coronation rites, wrote that the realm could only be ruled rightly through the counsel of leading men, both lay and clerical, he was expressing the consensus view during a period of deep political crisis.[26]

The significance of the contractual component of feudalism cannot be overemphasized. The vassal was expected to do homage and swear an oath of fealty to his lord. It was, ostensibly, a life-long commitment to be faithful but it did in practice have limitations. The lord was obligated to provide

the vassal with a benefice—the use of land, including its serfs and its pro-
duce. And the lord was charged with organizing his individual vassals
into an effective fighting force that could meet all external threats. As dis-
agreements arose within this structure, an informal system of feudal courts
evolved to hear claims and adjudicate matters through the use of peers or
social equals. In some cases, the feudal ladder reached all the way up from
the poorest knight to the king as the major landowner. Whether or not such a
king could enforce the feudal obligations of his leading vassals was another
matter entirely, since in effect he was no more than first among equals.

Popes and emperors

In the German-speaking lands of East Francia, strong monarchy rebounded
after the Saxon King Otto I (r. 936–973) crushed a powerful Magyar army at
the Battle of Lechfeld in 955. The victory signaled the end of the nomadic
incursions from the East and provided a foundation for the emergence
of a strong state in central Europe.[27] Following earlier Carolingian precedent, the Saxon magnates had elected Otto to the throne, but in 962 Pope
John XII (r. 955–964) offered further legitimacy by crowning him Roman
Emperor. This time the title would stick, as Otto's successors would retain
the imperial designation until Napoleon Bonaparte abolished it in the
early nineteenth century. The geographical sweep of the empire was much
smaller than its Carolingian predecessor—only the German-speaking lands
were included—but its relationship with the Church was more productive
in terms of strengthening royal authority.

   German bishops and abbots, not restive (an occasionally disloyal)
regional magnates, emerged as the key administrators in what would later
become known as the "Holy Roman Empire." The emperor was active in
establishing new bishoprics and selected candidates for all episcopal offices
when vacancies occurred. Bishops were entrusted with large estates and
oversaw secular as well as ecclesiastical matters in their dioceses. They functioned as agents of the Crown and even provided soldiers to the royal army
when called upon.[28] When Pope John later turned against the ambitious
Otto, the emperor arranged for a synod to depose the pontiff. It was a critical precedent, fueling the belief among future Holy Roman emperors that
high churchmen served at the pleasure of the sacred monarch. Such was
the relationship in the East, where, as we have seen, the Byzantine emperor
selected and then directed the patriarch of Constantinople. It was only natural to expect the Western Roman emperors to demand the same relationship
with the Western church.

   The Ottonian move to solidify its claim to royal theocracy came at a pro-
pitious moment. The papal office during the early eleventh century had
degenerated into a tarnished prize that was contested by equally objec-
tionable aristocratic factions in the city of Rome. The political situation
throughout Italy was dire: Muslims controlled Sicily and much of the South;
the Byzantines held on to a few administrative outposts in the Northeast;

and a series of small independent kingdoms managed to survive in the Northwest. In Rome the pope claimed territorial authority over a wide stretch of lands in the central part of the peninsula, and it was this juris-diction that proved so attractive to rival noble factions. The result was the elevation to the Holy See of a number of very undeserving successors to St Peter. The Pope who Otto removed from office in 963, for example, stood accused of a long list of crimes ranging from incest to murder.[29] The ideal of apostolic succession, where popes represented Christ and held the keys to eternal salvation, had become a distant memory.

Internal church reform

For those in the Church who were deeply troubled by this untoward state of affairs, and there were many conscientious priests, monks and bishops appalled by the situation in Rome, the only possible course of action was to insist upon a wholesale reform and re-affirmation of the autonomy—and supremacy—of the Church. They were joined by a handful of powerful but pious laymen who were similarly concerned with the state of Western Christendom. One of these was the Emperor Henry III (r. 1039–1056), who in 1046 marched his troops into Rome and ended a sordid three-way dis-pute over the papal throne by installing his own German-born reform pope, Leo IX (r. 1049–1054). The new pontiff cracked down on simony, removed corrupt bishops, and began traveling around Europe to raise stan-dards, weed out clerical malefactors, and enforce church rules known as "canon law." In a move to bring greater centralization to the reform effort, Leo IX restructured the previously ceremonial office of cardinal and made the incumbents his key advisors. Since he could not visit every diocese, the Pope was assisted in on-site inspections by a group of loyal papal legates. In a dramatic show of papal power, one of them, Cardinal Humbert (c. 1015–c. 1061), delivered a papal bull of excommunication to the patriarch of Constantinople, rupturing bilateral relations and, tragically, inaugurating a schism that continues to this day.[30]

Henry III was no saint; he supported the reform effort for his own dynastic purposes. The emperor wished to appoint responsible bishops and abbots, entrust them with royal fiefs, and secure their loyalty in the ongoing struggle against the provincial aristocracy. Henry believed that this was the only means by which he could unite Germany under his leader-ship. But during the second half of the eleventh century, the papacy turned against its imperial ally in the reform movement, hoping to restore its right to select bishops and to invest them with the ring and staff, traditional symbols of episcopal office. Acting in an environment where larger areas of Europe, including the kingdoms of Hungary, Bohemia, Poland, and the British Isles, were embracing Roman Christianity, the reformers believed that the Church's independence was essential to future growth. Insisting that lay investiture of bishops was without basis in canon law, the religious leaders who called for greater autonomy were convinced that layman had no right to interfere in the administration of the Church, especially at the senior levels.

The stakes could not have been higher. Since the Church owned upward of one-third of the property in Europe, the emperor was destined to forfeit considerable political influence in his own lands should the reformers win the day.[31] In an opening salvo, a council at Rome issued a decree in 1059 stating that papal elections were to be the sole responsibility of the cardinals of the church. Henceforth, the emperor's role was to be one of affirmation, not selection. The most idealistic and uncompromising of the reformers, a monk by the name of Hildebrand, was elected to the papacy in 1073 as Pope Gregory VII. His 12-year reign would be marked by a dramatic clash with an emperor who understood fully the political implications of the new thinking in Rome.

Henry IV (r. 1056–1106) had already quarreled with Pope Gregory's predecessor over the right to select the Bishop of Milan, the most important administrative and religious office in Northern Italy, and over the Church's excommunication of some of Henry's ministers of state. Gregory pushed the issue of supremacy in a church synod held at Rome, going so far as to assert in 1075 that the Pope was empowered to depose emperors and absolve subjects from their allegiance. As successor to St Peter the Pope asserted that he was answerable to no earthly authority and that only he could revise his own judgments.[32]

Gregory was reclaiming for the papacy the supreme direction of a unified religio-political Christian society. The Pope and his advisors believed that imperial divine right proceeded not from God directly but instead through his intermediary on earth, the Bishop of Rome. And as the temporal monarch was answerable to his spiritual counterpart, so too the monarch's subordinates, his vassals, lay counselors, and ecclesiastical appointees were similarly bound to obey the directives of the Pope whenever dissension existed between *regnum* and *sacerdotium*. Under this formulation, lay vassals with a grudge against their temporal lord might be sympathetic to the papal claim, while bishops who were jealous of their regional and national autonomy might be expected to stand against the centralization campaign.[33] The emperor quickly rejected all of these provocative assertions and assembled his own synod of German bishops who promptly declared the Pope to be a usurper. Unwilling to make any concession, Gregory imposed his most severe sanction, excommunicating Henry and declaring forfeit his imperial office. Dissident German princes, long restive under the emperor's centralizing regime, sided with the papacy in an effort to undermine Henry's power. Losing key support within his own realm, the emperor made a tactical decision to beg the Pope's forgiveness in the short term and await an opportunity to strike back over the larger principle of sacred monarchy and the traditional practice of royal oversight of the Church.[34]

He did not have to wait long. After prevailing over his princely enemies North of the Alps in a 3-year civil war, the emperor returned to Italy at the head of a powerful army and forced the Pope to seek the support of his Norman allies from Sicily. Gregory died in exile in 1085, believing that he had failed to secure the revolution in Church–State relations that was his goal. But while the battle had been lost, the larger issue had not been resolved. The dispute between pope and emperor occasioned a series of theoretical pamphlets exploring the respective claims of each side. An anonymous English author at the turn of the twelfth century defended the royalist position, insisting that by divine authority "kings are ordained in the church of God and are consecrated at the alter with sacred unction and benediction, that they may have the power of ruling the people of the Lord, the Christian people, which is the holy church of God." But the German Augustinian canon Manegold of Lautenbach (c. 1030–1103), a supporter of the papal position, claimed that the Roman Church "is distinguished with such great authority" that "anyone who has not remained in communion with it is a stranger and a sinner and an enemy of God, and whatever is done against its discipline can in no wise be held lawful." The Frenchman Hugh of Fleury (d. c. 1118) offered a middle ground, allowing a king, "inspired by the Holy Spirit" to elevate a churchman to the office of bishop so long as the archbishop "commit to him the care of souls."[35]

By the early twelfth century the forces of moderation seemed to secure the upper hand. In England the upstart Norman kings, sensing the value of strong church support for their dynasty, were content to allow bishops to undergo canonical election and receive their symbolic ring and staff from an archbishop. The newly elected bishop would then be presented—in a separate ceremony—with his royal estates and take an oath of homage to the king as a feudal vassal.[36] A similar consensus was agreed between the kings of France and the papacy. And in the Holy Roman Empire, agreement was finally reached in 1120 with the Concordat of Worms, where Henry V (r. 1106–1125) and Pope Calixtus (r. 1119–1124) adopted a formula whereby the bishop was elected by fellow churchmen but received the symbols of administrative and territorial authority from the emperor.[37] The compromise allowed the papacy to prevail in its view that spiritual authority originated within the Church. In practical terms this meant that the powers of the bishops—the right to ordain priests and appoint them to their offices, supervise dioceses, adjudicate violations of canon law, and enforce clerical discipline, all lay within the exclusive purview of the hierarchical Church. Monarchs, on the other hand, preserved their role in the nomination of candidates to high ecclesiastical office who would simultaneously serve the state in a landowning, administrative, and advisory capacity. The dynamic tension between Church and State thus continued long after the original Investiture Controversy, leaving two centers of jurisdiction in Western Europe firmly entrenched, each equally determined to deny the other the coveted title of "universal sovereign." And the struggle ensured that broader claims to coercive authority without some level of consent would not go unchallenged.

Kingdoms and politics in the central Middle Ages

In tracing the heated clash between Europe's spiritual and temporal rulers over the respective powers belonging to each, it is easy to lose sight of the fact that both sides accepted the reality of one, not two distinct societies that strove for alignment with divine law. Church and State, formally speaking, remained one project inasmuch as everyone was a member of the Christian community. Temporal leadership was Christian leadership, just as spiritual authority was exercised within the context of a Christian Kingdom or Empire. Controversies that arose were always jurisdictional in nature, not foundational in the sense that one party wished to free itself from the requirements of confessional orthodoxy. Kings and emperors readily allowed that their decisions were in the service of divine truth, while their claim that royal authority came directly from God was parallel to the papal case for spiritual jurisdiction.[38] Into this extended debate over the location and exercise of political authority entered new voices by the start of the twelfth century, the voices of urban dwellers and university scholars.

Metropolitan rebirth

The social and economic landscape of Western Europe changed markedly during this period. Better agricultural techniques and new technologies like the tandem harness, water mills, and heavier plows resulted in additional arable land being brought under cultivation. The result was an increase in food supplies and a more varied diet for rich and poor alike, which helped set the stage for a doubling of Europe's population from approximately 40 to 80 million between the years 1000 and 1300. All across Europe, new urban elites or burghers, pressed hard for greater autonomy in carrying out their business affairs, and this in turn accelerated demands for greater personal freedoms and an end to the servile labor obligations long associated with feudalism. Powerful merchant and craft guilds took shape with members acting collectively to protect and advance their common economic interests against the exactions of the landed aristocracy. By the twelfth century, the latter were issuing charters to the urban centers located on their lands, allowing town leaders to establish their own courts and municipal governments with tax-collecting powers.[39]

Urban life fostered educational reform. The intellectual rebirth of the twelfth and thirteenth centuries was centered on the new universities, former church and cathedral schools established and staffed by the new mendicant religious orders of Franciscans and Dominicans. These *studium generale* or institutions of higher learning attracted students eager to explore philosophy, theology, medicine, and civil or canon law in a comprehensive and systematic manner under the direction of specialist scholars. Bologna in Italy, Paris in France, and Oxford in England each attracted some of the keenest intellects of the period and fostered widespread discussion on the ends of human life and the obligations of the subject to prince and pastor. Gradually the *studium* or scholarly career took its place alongside the *imperium* or political administration, and *sacerdotium* or the priestly function, as a recognized and admired feature of urban civilization.

The twelfth-century churchman, statesman, and scholar John of Salisbury illustrated the combination of all three professional interests. In his *Polycraticus* or *Statesman's Book* (1159), a wide-ranging treatise dedicated to his friend Thomas Becket and concerned largely with the search for the common good in a society of multiple competing interests, John of Salisbury employed an expansive familiarity with classical literature, biblical study, and logic to defend the divine nature of kingship while also highlighting the natural limits on royal power. In what many scholars recognize as the first complete political treatise of the Middle Ages, the author, who had clashed repeatedly with King Henry II of England (r. 1154–1189), employed the analogy of the human body to outline the appropriate functions and offices of the state. With the clergy representing the soul while the magistrate was analogous to the head, John argued that the former must always serve in a directive capacity to the latter. Judges and magistrates are charged with carrying out the duties of the eyes, ears, and tongue, while the job of the military corresponds to the work of the hands. Finally the feet, always resting upon the earth, stand for the laboring peasantry, without whose contributions the state would surely perish. "Remove the help of feet from the strongest body and it will not proceed by its own strength," he wrote, "but will either basely, uselessly and laboriously crawl with its hands, or will be moved by the aid of brute beasts."[40]

John of Salisbury's endorsement of limited, responsible monarchy reflected a growing sense of the importance of law in addressing the question of the purpose and extent of political authority. "There is wholly or mainly this difference between the tyrant and the prince," he wrote in the *Policraticus*, "that the latter is obedient to law, and rules his people by a will that places itself at their service, and administers rewards and burdens within the republic under the guidance of law in a way favourable to the vindication of his eminent post." Human law was a distillation of divine law, "a sort of discovery and gift from God, the teaching of the wise, the corrective to excesses of willfulness, the harmony of the city, the banishment of all crime."[41] Making and recording law for future reference and the establishment of precedent would become an essential function for a society that was coming to rely more and more on the written record.

With improved rates of literacy thanks to the growth of church-affiliated schools and universities, oral tradition atrophied—especially in urban areas—and the sanction of custom was increasingly linked to written records. Everything from epic poems to judicial decisions was now committed to writing. Deeds, property transfers, surveys, tax rolls, judicial transcripts, business contracts—all became symbols of a more efficient and professional administrative structure that characterized royal government across Western Europe. As records were stored at government offices for future reference by bureaucrats who could read, write, and make calculations, the equation of knowledge with power became transparent to ambitious students who were eager to advance their careers in business or government service.

A large part of the content informing the acceleration of learning in the twelfth century was the rediscovered Roman law, some elements of which had been preserved in Italy and Southern France during the early Middle Ages. The sixth-century *Corpus Juris Civilis* of the Emperor Justinian became a featured study at Bologna, and Roman legal studies subsequently informed the curriculum at Paris and Oxford. Once these scholars initiated the work of organizing and clarifying classical jurisprudence, efforts to systematize and codify regional legal traditions began in earnest. In the mid-thirteenth century, for example, the English jurist Henry Bracton authored an important treatise on English common law, while French, Spanish, and German scholars undertook similar compilations for their own regions.[42] The academic commentaries and textbooks based on Roman law sought to organize subjects by rational categories. More importantly, these texts assumed the legitimacy of the state as an authority separate from the private ownership of land and feudal prerogative. Slowly and imperceptibly, monarchs were empowered to make new law on behalf of their subjects instead of simply enforcing age-old custom. Lawmaking as a creative act, as a deliberative response to felt societal need, became an acceptable function of the state.

A parallel development in the Church centered on canon law, rules, and precedents drawn from a wide range of religious sources, including the Bible, papal pronouncements, and the decisions of general councils. Canon lawyers worked assiduously to organize a vast array of material in a manner that would highlight the prerogatives of the Church in general and the pontiff in particular. In 1140, the Bolognese canon lawyer Gratian completed an important synthesis known as *The Concordance of Discordant Canons* that offered readers an orderly, topically organized set of legal principles.[43] Subsequent compilations in the thirteenth century gave the Church a body of detailed law that was the ecclesiastical equivalent of the Roman law in the secular sphere.

The return of "the philosopher"

Starting as early as the eighth century, Muslims scholars undertook to translate a large body of Greek scientific and philosophical works into Arabic. At the core of their efforts were the encyclopedic writings of Aristotle. Prior to the twelfth century, European Christians were all but ignorant of Aristotle's works on metaphysics, cosmology, ethics, and politics. At first the job involved retranslation from the Arabic texts, but by the start of the thirteenth century new translations directly from the Greek into Latin were being made available.[44] Despite the reservations of early church fathers like Tertullian, who had asked the rhetorical question: "What has Athens to do with Jerusalem?", the work enjoyed the patronage of Christian church leaders and enabled educated Europeans to once again consider the full range of Aristotle's scientific and philosophical thought.

More than the particular subject areas, it was the underlying theme in each of Aristotle's works that was of greatest value to the scholastics, especially his claim that reason was the indispensable tool in the advancement of knowledge. The world as viewed from an Aristotelian perspective was no longer a stage upon which miracles were performed, and where an interventionist God regularly used supernatural means to punish sinners and reward saints, but an orderly place whose underlying principles might be grasped by humans. Peter Abelard (1079–1142) was one of the earliest medieval scholars to view creation as open to human investigation through the employment of reason, a perspective that was soon endorsed by many other leading theologians. The challenge facing these university types was to integrate a philosophically oriented pagan perspective into a faith-anchored worldview, to assimilate pagan reason and employ it as a servant and complement to Christian revelation.

It was a challenge that was engaged brilliantly by the thirteenth-century Italian Dominican Thomas Aquinas, who authored no comprehensive political treatise but instead wove his analysis of politics into a vast tapestry of philosophical and theological writings. With the appearance in the mid-thirteenth century of Aristotle's *Nichomachean Ethics* and *Politics*, Aquinas began to reevaluate the Augustinian position on sinful human nature and the purpose of the state. Concurring with Aristotle that humans were social and political by nature, he accepted the state not as a necessary evil due to sinfulness, but as a natural institution, a positive value, and a vehicle for realizing the life of faith informed by reason, justice, and law.[45] Since people inevitably have conflicting interests, the state's role was to serve as the embodiment of the common good, making cooperation and social life possible under the care of the responsible monarch.

For Aquinas, as for Aristotle, a hierarchical ordering of relations was essential to the smooth functioning of the state just as it was in the world of nature, where from the tiniest of elements and creatures there rises in a great chain of being a vast panoply of sentient beings.[46] But every person, irrespective of their particular station in life, is in the end equal to their social and political superiors by virtue of their rational and soul-bearing nature. All have the same purpose, the same teleology, although each carries out different earthly functions for the common good. Given this deeper human equality, rulership became for Aquinas an office or trust, and the ruler, like all others on the great chain of being, must contribute to the advancement of a natural order that leads, ultimately, to God.

For Aquinas, the natural order of creation was informed throughout by law. He set human law firmly within a fourfold hierarchy of rules that emanated from God. The Eternal Law was synonymous with the will of God, the orderly plan by which everything is regulated but which is outside the direct grasp of humans. Natural Law was the divine spirit informing all creation, each according to its nature. In living things it includes the natural desire for self-preservation, to live a life in community, and in alignment with one's natural endowments. In humans the Natural Law is a window into the Eternal Law, fostering an inclination to actions and ends that are fitting for rational agents. Divine Law was revealed truth, a gift of grace and not the discovery of reason. Finally, the Human Law applies solely to the most gifted of God's creatures and at its best strongly affirms the principles of the three higher forms. Human Law, a statute-based corollary of God's eternal precepts, always puts the general good or community before the interests of the individual. Reason and justice must inform the decisions of every secular magistrate. According to Aquinas "in order for the things commanded to have the character of law, will must be regulated by reason. And thus we should understand that the will of the prince has the force of law, otherwise the will of the prince would be iniquity rather than law."[47] The enterprise of scholasticism culminates in the work of Aquinas, setting the task of coercive governance firmly within the context of rational conduct in pursuit of communal well-being.

Diversity of thought in the later Middle Ages

By the start of the fourteenth century, the Church–State question had lost its status as a Europe-wide issue and had devolved into a matter of provincial relations between the papacy and specific monarchies. The whole idea of united Christendom and the international hegemony of the Church under the direction of the successors to St Peter began to lose credibility as autonomous kingdoms successfully pressed their claims and waged war against their Christian neighbors. Instead of debate over the respective purviews of spiritual and temporal power, the focus of attention shifted to the relationship between the prince and the corporate body over which he ruled. This shift from Church–State to ruler–subject relations represented a momentous change in political sensibility, signaling the birth of the sovereign state and the eclipse of universal Christendom.[48]

When Pope Boniface VIII (r. 1294–1303) demanded in the papal bull *Clericis Laicos* (1296) that the kings of France and England cease taxing the clergy of their respective realms in order to pay for their internecine wars, the French King Philip IV (r. 1285–1314) responded by cutting off all church revenues to Rome. Mutual recriminations followed, and with the promulgation of the bull *Unam Sanctum* in 1302—probably the most sweeping of medieval papal documents—the theory of papal empire reached its definitive conclusion as Boniface declared "that it is altogether necessary to salvation for every creature to be subject to the Roman Pontiff."[49] But with an assembly of the Three Estates of the realm denouncing Boniface, and French troops even taking the aged Pope prisoner for a brief period, Boniface's gambit represented the last serious effort to assert medieval papalism as a political theory. The next pontiff, the Frenchman Clement V (r. 1305–1314), hastily conceded the issue of taxation and in 1309 moved the papal court from Rome to the city of Avignon, just beyond the jurisdiction of the French Crown, where it remained for the better part of the fourteenth century.[50]

Additional disasters, some natural and others self-inflicted, befell the official Church during what one historian called "the calamitous fourteenth century." Europe's economic expansion and technological innovation slowed after 1300, while population pressures undercut the standard of living for peasants who were obliged to subdivide plots repeatedly and begin cultivation on less fertile land. As families struggled with higher grain prices and poor harvests due to unfavorable weather, catastrophic bubonic plague arrived from the East in 1347 and spread rapidly across the continent. Over the next 3 years, an estimated one-third of Europe's population perished, with mortality rates in congested cities and towns much higher still. There were, of course, no medical explanations, much less treatments, for an affliction that spread rapidly, took no account of social standing, and, according to some eyewitnesses, shattered all existing norms of parental, spousal, and familial obligation.[51]

As if natural disaster were not enough of a blow to the official Church authority, in 1377–1378 infighting amongst French and Roman cardinals led to a division in the Church and the election of two rival popes, one in Rome and a second in Avignon. The rupture known as the Great Schism continued for the next 37 years, with rival pontiffs hurling excommunications at one another with debilitating regularity, while support for contending claimants split along national lines. The leadership crisis intensified between 1409 and 1417 as the efforts of successive church councils to find a solution only led to the emergence of a three-way papal schism. And while the Church finally was reunited under the leadership of Pope Martin V (r. 1417–1431), irreparable damage had been done to the international standing of the Holy See, with popes of the early Renaissance conceding greater control over national churches to secular rulers.[52]

The secular turn in government

Even before the disaster of the Great Schism seriously eroded the argument for papal hegemony, the Italian poet Dante Alighieri (1265–1321) called for the restoration of imperial power and the establishment of world monarchy as the only sure path to lasting peace and the realization of a rational life. Exiled from his home city of Florence by partisans of the papal party, Dante's *De Monarchia* (c. 1314–1318) attributed the incessant quarrels of the Italian cities to the malevolent influence of the Church, and he adduced from Scripture arguments to demonstrate that temporal power is contrary to the nature of the Church's other-worldly mission.[53] But it was another Italian writer, a physician by training, who was able to look forward and anticipate the birth of the autonomous sovereign state. In 1324, Marsilius of Padua (c. 1275–c. 1343) offered an unequivocal endorsement of the supremacy of the secular polity with his *Defensor Pacis* or *Defender of Peace*, a work that was condemned as heretical by Pope John XXII (r. 1316–1334) in 1327.

A student of Aristotle who viewed his work as a supplement to the *Politics* in its treatment of the causes of civil unrest, Marsilius began the *Defensor Pacis* with a detailed consideration of the nature, function, and organization of the state. Like Dante he was appalled by the political turbulence and chaos of his day. As a natural outgrowth of household government, he argued that the state's principal function is to assure that everyone can live well and in peace. In a truly stable political order, the ruler enforces laws that are the product of an agreed legislative process, not divine mandates. And while Christians are to remain united in faith, their first loyalty must be to the temporal ruler, who is the sole guarantor of peace and civil order. Marsilius was emphatic in his declaration that the Church should have no civil jurisdiction, and in his claim that clergymen must recognize their subject status within the borders of the kingdom. Indeed the human legislator, if he were to ensure the well-being of the unified community, must have control over all clerical appointments. The exclusive role of the priesthood, according to Marsilius "is to teach and educate men in those things which, according to the evangelical law, it is necessary to believe, do, and omit to attain eternal salvation and avoid misery."[54] Looking to the civil strife in Italy that was fed by papal meddling, he reminded his readers that Christ and his apostles excluded themselves from worldly rule, eschewed coercive power, and preferred a life of evangelical poverty to the perquisites of temporal authority.

Embedded in Discourse I of the *Defensor Pacis* is the naturalistic assumption that the unitary authority of government rests on the support—the consent—of the whole corporation of citizens. Represented by legislators who in turn elected the executive or ruler, the powers wielded by the ruler are in the end by delegation from the community.[55] According to Marsilius, human law is the product of legislative action, not of a piece with divine or eternal law as Aquinas insisted. The legislator "or first and proper efficient cause of the law, is the people or whole body of citizens, or the weightier part thereof, through its election or will expressed by words in the general assembly of the citizens, commanding or determining that something be done or omitted with regard to human civil acts, under a temporal pain or punishment."[56] The state, therefore, is a self-contained, omnipotent corporation whose members owe their obedience to law, not to pontiffs, not to kings, and not to persons. The executive, be that a monarch or an assembly, is charged with forwarding the mandate of the corporation as distilled through the legislature. Spiritual imperatives are recognized as important to human well-being, but they are not the purview of the state. Here was nothing less than a sweeping reinterpretation of the function of temporal authority, an anticipation of limited, responsible government that characterizes many modern states.[57] It was also an affirmation of a more confident view of human nature and human potential than anything offered by the Church and its representatives since the time of St Augustine.

Consolidated monarchies and the principle of consent

By the close of the fifteenth century, the consolidated monarchies that were emerging in England, France, and Spain could readily embrace the argument contained in *Defensor Pacis*. Across Western Europe the territorial state began to take its place as the object of prime allegiance for subjects of the Crown. In England, the French-speaking Norman kings who ruled after 1066 built an impressive administrative and legal structure whose power radiated out from the capital in London to embrace the entire island kingdom and eastern portions of Ireland. The Crown enjoyed wide latitude in the selection and appointment of clerics to major church offices, and the rapid growth of the country's commercial economy during the central Middle Ages brought new sources of revenue to the court. The Norman kings shrewdly adopted the Anglo-Saxon royal practice of consulting with key nobles and prelates when important decisions were to be made. The old Anglo-Saxon council or *witenagemot* evolved into the Norman *curia Regis* or king's court, with a shifting body of advisors traveling with the monarch and helping to frame royal policy. When an unpopular King John (r. 1199–1216) attempted unilaterally to impose excessive taxes to fight an unsuccessful war in France, his leading magnates rebelled and forced him to issue a "Great Charter" or *Magna Carta* in 1214. The document stripped the monarch of the power to raise non-customary taxes without the consent of the leading men of the kingdom. By insisting the Crown respect custom and tradition, the barons were setting the stage—inadvertently perhaps—for the subsequent development of limited monarchy and the rule of law.

By the middle of the thirteenth century, members of the country gentry and wealthy urban burghers were being invited to join with the great nobles in attending consultative councils. The inclusion of social inferiors into what had been a select advisory body limited to the feudal elite reflected the changing economic power structure in the country. When kings needed extraordinary revenues to conduct the affairs of state, the consent of the landed gentry and the urban commercial elite was deemed imperative since a significant portion of the national wealth was now being generated by these segments of society. King Edward I (r. 1272–1307) called frequent great councils or parliaments, and included knights of the shires and affluent townsmen in these gatherings. By the middle of the fourteenth century, these knights and burghers began the practice of meeting separately from the members of the high nobility, inaugurating the historic division into the House of Commons and the House of Lords. The Crown remained the driving force behind the evolution of parliament, and the institution remained very much a creature of the Crown, called and dismissed at the monarch's discretion, well into the early nineteenth century. Still, although it was viewed by England's monarchs as another tool of royal policy and not as any kind of fundamental right to representation, the periodic meeting of parliament buttressed the medieval concept of limited, responsible government, where the principle of consent was inherent in the overall architecture.[58]

The Capetian kings of France traversed a more arduous path to political centralization, taking upward of two centuries to make good their claim to authority over insubordinate barons and widely dispersed feudal principalities. The business of consolidation began in earnest under King Philip Augustus (r. 1180–1223) and his successors. Salaried officials took the place of local aristocrats as the major judicial and military figures in the provincial counties and duchies, and Paris was transformed into a permanent capital for the entire realm. By the end of Philip IV's reign (1285–1314), the monarchy had clearly established its pre-eminence over the Church and the nobility of France. Under Philip IV, the central government successfully imposed taxes on the Church, plundered the wealth of the crusading order known as the Knights Templars, and after seizing the property of the vulnerable Jewish community, expelled them from the country. Yet even the autocratic Philip, who was constantly in need of revenues, occasionally was obliged to call upon the support of his leading subjects in carrying out his centralizing agenda. In 1302, the first meeting of the Estates General took place at the request of the monarch, and while it never became a central component of French royal government after the model of the English parliament, the meeting of the clergy, nobility, and leading townspeople in one assembly did provide opportunities to plant the seeds of a distinct national consciousness.[59]

Machiavelli and the politics of command

Perhaps no single political thinker in the Western tradition has been the subject of as much opprobrium as Niccolo Machiavelli (1469–1527). The streak of bad press began, not surprisingly, with the leaders of the Catholic Church, who angrily associated Machiavelli's best known book, *The Prince* (1513), with the malevolent mission of Satan. This native son of Florence composed the work, along with his less read but still influential *Discourses on the First Ten Books of Titus Livius*, during a long period of personal political exile that began with the downfall of the Florentine Republic in 1514. Not just Florence, but early sixteenth-century Italy as a whole was wracked by political division, city-state rivalries, foreign occupation, princely ineptitude, and, most eviscerating of all, church interference in the affairs of state. Machiavelli's anti-clericalism, born of a deep sense of shame over Italy's misfortunes, assured that his trenchant and uncompromising analysis of political affairs, and his bold prescription for renewal, would rarely receive a dispassionate hearing. No one was surprised when, in 1559, his writings were placed on the Catholic Church's Index of forbidden books.[60]

At one level Machiavelli, former statesman and diplomat, was simply interested in rescuing Italy from the grip of foreign domination. In the *Discourses* he looked back to the period of the Roman Republic as an age in which citizens acted heroically and decisively in defense of their freedoms and territorial integrity. Most of Machiavelli's contemporaries would have agreed with him that internal unity was the essential prerequisite to international respect. At a deeper level, however, what was so disturbing—and revolutionary—about Machiavelli's political thought was its complete independence from the intellectual conventions of late Medieval Europe. In that tradition the good ruler was always held up as the embodiment of human virtues, the exponent of natural law, and the mirror of divine justice and mercy. Politics itself, according to the historian Sheldon Wolin, was viewed "as a microcosm displaying the same structural principles of order prevalent in creation as a whole . . . ."[61]

Machiavelli daringly advanced a separation of politics and ethics that remains controversial even today, arguing that actions are never right or wrong in any fixed of defined sense, but instead must be judged within the context of their final outcomes. For the reforming ruler "it is a sound maxim that reprehensible actions may be justified by their effects, and when the effect is good . . . it always justifies the action."[62] There was no Platonic form of the good, no natural law, no universal morality, Christian or otherwise, at work in the world, only the situational morality of the end in view. And in politics the appropriate end is always the unity and security of the state. That crucial goal will never be realized by focusing on how saints and philosophers of the past have insisted people should act, but rather through the exercise of *virtu* or what Machiavelli understood as courage, craft, steadfastness, and valor.[63] Christian morality, with its emphasis on self-denial, lowliness, turning the other cheek, and contempt for this world, was for Machiavelli the antithesis of *virtu* and therefore lethal to civic order.

The Prince was designed as a handbook of practical advice for the monarch or autocrat, the man who would restore the greatness of the state in the face of the lethargy and/or degeneracy of the citizenry. Machiavelli was not enamored of hereditary rulers and loathed the fractious nobility who had made such a mess of life in Italy, but he did support reforming monarchy.[64] The *Discourses*, on the other hand, while composed at the same time as *The Prince*, highlights the advantages of republican government in a society characterized by courage and a strong practice of civic virtue. Although Machiavelli favored the latter form, he acknowledged the need for autocracy whenever law and public spirit were in decay.[65] What is consistent in both works is the privileging of hardnosed command and the conviction that private and public morality must not be conflated, "For when the safety of one's country wholly depends on the decision to be taken, no attention should be paid to either justice or injustice, to kindness or cruelty, or to its being praiseworthy or ignominious."[66] Successful rulers must sin with impunity for the greater good of the state, and politics must cease to be cast as a by-product of theology.

Machiavelli believed that in order to achieve political stability, people should be treated in a manner consistent with how they behave in fact. Although a harsh critic of church leadership and practice, he embraced Catholicism's deeply Augustinian picture of human nature. It was an unhappy fact, observable in every society in every age, that men "are ungrateful, fickle, liars and deceivers, they shun danger and are greedy for profit; while you treat them well, they are yours."[67] But they are also quick to turn against their fellows in time of danger. Human appetites are insatiable and "the human mind is perpetually discontented, and of its possessions is apt to grow weary." As a result, we forever "find fault with the present, praise the past, and long for the future."[68] In light of this troubling anthropology, the effective ruler was advised to cultivate the love and regard of his subjects, and to rule with justice and restraint, but he also must recognize that it is better to be feared rather than loved by one's subjects.[69] Violence and force, he claimed, are not infrequently the appropriate remedies to civil decay.

This new-style ruler, ambitious, ruthless, efficient, defiant of convention, and scornful of those who would conflate reasons of state with personal codes of morality anticipated the profile of Europe's sixteenth-century monarchs, Catholic and Protestant alike. They believed, following Machiavelli's advice, that in a world of competing states, each populated by avaricious and self-serving subjects "a man who wants to act virtuously in every way necessarily comes to grief among so many who are not virtuous." In order to survive and do the good work of building the state and enhancing the security of all, "he must learn how not to be virtuous, and to make use of this or not according to need."[70] The Aristotelian and Thomistic unity of politics with ethics, morality, and religion was now a legitimate focus of question and debate. A world of moral stillness, bereft of a divine monarch who created meaning, was slowly emerging on the stage of European political thought. Egotism and appetite, both constants of human nature that were lamented and deplored by St Augustine, were now to be employed in the service of national greatness without regard for theological absolutes. With Machiavelli the "new man" of the Renaissance, confident and ambitious, this-worldly and concerned with personal greatness, takes his place on the contested stage of the secular state. It is a state that is to be treated as a human artifact, a work of art, and no longer as the directing force behind a great drama, either chivalrous or divine, that is enacted under a larger canopy of meaning.

Chapter 3 . . . .

The Emergence of the Sovereign State, 1500–1700

Although it is both arbitrary and misleading to date the end of the Middle Ages, it is difficult to avoid the conclusion that some fundamental demographic, economic, military, and cultural changes were underway in Western Europe by the mid-point of the fifteenth century. And all of these changes paralleled the growth of state power, the formation of truly sovereign territorial states under the control of ambitious and aggressive monarchs. In 1400, the leading feature of European political life remained its restricted nature. Monarchs talked much about imposing their royal prerogative over local law and custom, and on extraordinary occasions they were successful. But real power lay mostly with the hundreds of nobles, princes, and city and town councils or corporations that acted in a largely independent manner. By the start of the eighteenth century all of this had changed. Monarchs now directed cohesive states staffed by thousands of professional administrators. They also commanded large, well-equipped armies, headed national churches, and collected taxes on a regular, country-wide basis. Distant government and the idea of the secular state as the object of highest allegiance had taken their place on the European stage, and political thought reflected and endorsed the change.[1]

Material life and the humanist contribution

As the indiscriminate ravages of the Black Death lessened in intensity by 1400, Europe's population rebounded over the following century to a pre-plague level of about 70 million. This surge in population led to greater competition for land and jobs, forcing many landless peasants, some recently freed from serfdom, into urban areas in search of employment. And it was in the cities, first in Northern Italy and subsequently across much of Western Europe, that commercial, cultural, and political ferment defined daily life. It was here that medieval protective feudalism and its communal values gave way to competitive capitalism and its individualistic ethic. New wealth created by long-distance trade allowed merchants to become patrons of the arts and education while supporting ambitious rulers who could provide the level of domestic security essential to the growth of a capitalist economy. For autonomous cities and royal governments alike, the advent of gunpowder and the destructive potential of artillery led to the imposition of higher taxes, increased spending on the latest weapons of war, and the recruitment and training of heavily armed and non-noble military forces. Warfare on the continent became more commonplace, more expensive, and more apt to disrupt the lives of civilian non-combatants.[2]

Superior military technology accounted for much of the success enjoyed by European adventurers who took the first steps in what would become a centuries-long process of overseas exploration, exploitation, and colonization. The "discovery" of the Americas exposed Europeans to a wide range of non-Christian belief systems and social practices. A renewed interest in the intellectual and artistic cultural output of pre-Christian Greece and Rome called into question the hegemony of the Christian worldview. And a radically altered picture of physical nature, more mechanistic and impersonal than anything described in the Bible, emerged out of the work of leading astronomers and natural philosophers. Dramatic advances in the natural sciences prompted some to hope that an analogous science of politics might be possible. Finally, in the early sixteenth century, Christian Europe split into a number of distinct religious communities, with national churches and increased royal control over those churches shattering the medieval conception of one Christian commonwealth under papal guidance.

Ironically, the great changes and innovations that signaled an end to medieval Europe were inspired by an admiration for and emulation of the distant past. And nowhere was this retrospective temperament more pronounced than in the movement known as the Renaissance. This diffuse intellectual and cultural movement was anything but the coherent phenomenon that modern historians began to write about in the nineteenth century. To be sure, by the close of the fourteenth century there were a handful of Europeans who looked to Greek and Roman antiquity for models of artistic and philosophical excellence. But the wider rejection of the Middle Ages that is so often associated with the spirit of the Renaissance did not surface in a truly identifiable form until the mid-1400s.

Characterized by an emphasis on secular concerns and power, and by a celebration of human creativity and individuality, Renaissance artists, scientists, and thinkers sought to recapture the spirit of human-centeredness that lay at the core of antiquity. Beginning in Italy and spreading northward as the cities of Western Europe revived, the Renaissance was always associated with urban culture. Educated Europe's fascination with, and emulation of, ancient Greece and Rome was predicated on the conviction that the values of antiquity, especially its educational priorities and its ethical principles, offered eternal standards that had been inexcusably cast aside by self-interested priests and princes during the medieval centuries. For the humanists who called for a restoration of classical standards in literature, the arts, rhetoric, and even political life, Europe's new dawn was to be modeled after pagan, not Christian, precedents; after rational, not faith-based guideposts.

An essential part of the humanist temperament, the quest to restore ancient harmonies, was a commitment to the active life of service (*vita activa*) as opposed to the medieval privileging of the contemplative, other-worldly existence. Even Renaissance artists and their wealthy patrons tended to subsume private commissions under a didactic and world-affirming heading, with paintings and statues emphasizing secular themes and the value of human achievement. With the advent of the printing press in the late fifteenth century, humanist ideals were communicated more easily—and often in the vernacular—to a wider audience, both within universities and at court where administrators were as likely to be appointed on the basis of their educational attainments as they were for their military accomplishments.[3]

Each of these transformations contributed in unique ways to the growth of centralized state power and a corresponding decline in both the provincial authority of the landed aristocracy and the transnational claims of the clergy. The widespread diffusion of political power that was characteristic of medieval society was based on the personal relations between ruler and ruled, whereas the new notion of centralized sovereignty stressed national consciousness and an understanding of the state as a legal entity within pre-scribed territorial boundaries.[4] In political thought, reasons of state and the will of the Crown began to engage the attention of writers, whose range of output after 1500, both in terms of the diversity of national sources and the social position of important authors, dwarfs anything available from the Middle Ages. For most of these authors, human ends continued to be defined mainly in religious terms, but the mundane requirements of the nation were accorded a new position of prominence. Machiavelli's dismissal of the moral and religious foundations of the state may have shocked most of his contemporaries, but the trend toward the secularization of political power gathered force even as kings and queens affirmed their fiduciary role in defending the interests of their national churches.

Religious reform and confessional politics

The Reformation occupies an ambiguous place in the intellectual history of early modern Europe, in part in forwarding the emergence of the now familiar territorial state and the sanctity of individual conscience, but also in holding fast to the medieval world of theocratic government and confessional loyalty tests. Despite the myriad doctrinal differences within sixteenth-century Protestantism, all but the most radical of sects shared a strong belief in the necessity of a church-directed civilization, where moral principles and inclusive codes of conduct were determined by the Church on the basis of revelation and enforced by the State using the instruments of persuasion and coercion. In the words of one scholar, the Reformation "arrested an incipient secularism and made religion and even confessionalism dominant concerns even in politics for another 150 years."[5] As in medieval Catholicism, the Protestant care of souls necessitated the power to discipline and regulate the worldly affairs of sinful humans.

The two leading figures of the early Reformation, Martin Luther (1483–1546) and John Calvin (1509–1564) were deeply conservative Christians whose preferred path to spiritual renewal followed Pauline and Augustinian lines. Neither man was interested in more inclusive models of secular governance, especially in light of their pessimistic view of human nature, and neither stood as proponents of social change and the political empowerment of the emerging commercial class. Instead, they were fully committed to a restoration of primitive Christianity, and they renounced all forms of accommodation with the world.[6] But their willingness to confront the absolute authority of the Pope and the legitimacy of the Church's hierarchical structure, coupled with their insistence upon the equality of Christians in the most important business of life (one's relationship with God), served as a powerful, if unintended, corrosive of established order in every compartment of life. In the words of Franklin Le Van Baumer:

> The reformers contributed to individualism, although none of them were individualists in the modern sense; to nationalism, although they hoped to restore Christian unity; to democracy, although hardly any of them were democrats; to the "capitalistic spirit," although they were extremely suspicious of capitalists; indeed, to the secularization of society, although their aim was exactly the reverse.[7]

The church and its allies

Prior to the Reformation, the Catholic Church could arguably lay claim to being the one genuinely international power on the continent. With its own trained personnel, diplomatic corps, legal system, power of taxation, and communications network in the form of thousands of pulpits across Europe, the Rome-based quasi-state commanded the allegiance of tens of thousands of ordained clergy who enjoyed multiple exemptions from temporal jurisdictions.[8] And so long as the Church maintained its position as a state within a state, no European monarch could claim exclusive authority within his or her dominions. The Lutheran revolt that began in 1517 changed the equation entirely. Within one generation not only Northern Germany, but all of Scandinavia, England, Scotland, the Netherlands, and Switzerland had broken with Rome and taken control over church property, personnel, and religious teachings. Even in Catholic countries like France and Spain, aggrandizing monarchs prevailed in the centuries-old contest for power over clerical appointments and taxation, allowing for much greater royal autonomy in pursuit of routine national interests.

As we saw in the last chapter, lay criticism of the Church was not a new phenomenon. Avaricious clergy and politicized popes had been the targets of reform-minded Christians at least since the time of John Wycliffe (c. 1324–1384) and Jan Hus (c. 1369–1415). In the early sixteenth century,

Renaissance humanists like the Dutch scholar Desiderius Erasmus (1466–1536) and the English statesman Thomas More (1478–1535) continued the critique of church practices and counseled a life of simple piety and benevolence after the example of Christ. But the Renaissance papacy doggedly resisted each and every call for reform, preferring to silence those who questioned established orthodoxies by enlisting the support of secular monarchs who sought a greater role in the appointment of senior church officials. In 1516, King Francis I (r. 1515–1547) won extensive power over the Church in France through the Concordat of Bologna, but it was Spain's monarchs who emerged as the central bulwarks of papal authority and the doctrinal standard-bearers in what became a continent-wide fight against heresy.

It is important to remind ourselves that there was nothing inevitable about the growth of national states and consolidated monarchies in the sixteenth century. In fact, the concept of universal sovereignty that was appropriated by the Church during the Middle Ages was almost achieved by Catholic Spain during the course of the sixteenth century. The accrual of power began with the Emperor Charles V (r. 1516–1556), whose remarkable inheritance at the age of 19 included all of Spain and its Italian dependencies, the American colonies that had been acquired since 1492, and the lands of the expansive Holy Roman Empire together with the imperial title. With such an impressive portfolio of territories, and the gold and silver of the American colonies to underwrite a large and well-trained military force, Charles was in a position to entertain the notion, forwarded by his chancellor Mercurio Gattinara (1465–1530), of a world monarchy after the model proposed by Dante. A decisive victory over rival French forces in Italy in 1525, and the capture of the emperor's opponent Francis I seemed to confirm the viability of such an objective.[9]

Charles heartily embraced the medieval idea of one pope as the spiritual head of Christendom and one emperor as its temporal leader. For nearly 40 years he battled to achieve his goal against the French, against German Protestant princes, and against the Turks who attacked his empire from the east, but in the end his far-flung territories, each held by separate right and lacking any common central institutions, never cohered as an imperial unit.[10] When the emperor retired to a monastery in 1556, his son Philip II of Spain (r. 1556–1598) redoubled efforts to forge a Catholic super-state, and while he too fell short of his ambitions, the outcome lay very much in the balance as late as the 1590s.

Luther's unintended legacy

When the Augustinian monk Martin Luther, after a long spiritual journey marked by considerable personal anguish, began to discount the efficacy of liturgical rituals and good works in the search for salvation, few in the Church took notice. But when his quest for union with God led him to attack the Church's revenue-enhancing practice of selling indulgences (papal letters that promised sinners reduced time in purgatory) as theologically suspect, the newly elected Holy Roman emperor took action against him. Excommunicated by the Pope in 1520, Luther was summoned the following year to a meeting of the imperial Diet in the city of Worms. There he boldly defended himself in the presence of Charles V, and with the support of Frederick "the Wise" of Saxony (r. 1486–1525), one of the seven princes who elected the Holy Roman emperor, was protected from imperial retribution and provided safe haven in a fortress at Wartburg. Widespread lay sympathy for this frontal attack on Rome, the product of long-standing resentment of ecclesiastical taxes, clerical malfeasance, and imperial encroachments on local autonomy, provided Luther a further measure of popular support.[11]

Luther's arguments, although directed exclusively against papal claims, had crucial long-term implications for Western political thought. His criticism of Rome was predicated on the belief that a true church was a fellowship bound by faith, not a coercive institution with sovereignty over lands and rulers and wielding its own code of discipline and enforcement mechanisms.[12] For centuries the Catholic sacrament of Holy Orders elevated the priest above ordinary men, exempting him from civil jurisdiction and charging him with the power to absolve men and women of their sins. Luther shattered this distinction between clergy and laity. In 1520, he wrote "An Appeal to the Ruling Class" in which he repudiated clerical exemptions from the jurisdiction of secular rulers. Describing how "our baptism consecrates us all without exception and makes us all priests," Luther maintained that when a bishop consecrates "he simply acts on behalf of the entire congregation, all of whom have the same authority."[13] The Church is not the Pope, neither is it the clerical hierarchy; it is, rather, the whole community of Christians. Laymen who exercise civil authority are similarly priests and bishops and wield their authority "as an office of the Christian community and for the benefit of that community."[14]

These audacious statements, although limited to Church government and leadership, implied a form of equality in life's most important journey that Luther found to be consistent with early Christian practice. The death of ecclesiastical fiat and the repudiation of canon law as forms of spiritual direction were not without their long-term significance in fostering novel ideas of personal autonomy. By inviting his contemporaries to question the infallibility of one institution, the path lay open to question others; if the burden of salvation—the most important business in life—now rested on Everyman as priest, why should the individual be denied a voice in civil affairs, the realm of the fleeting and probationary earthly pilgrimage?

Luther's appeal resonated with middle-class urban dwellers offended by the wealth and worldliness of so many members of the higher clergy. His translation of the Bible into German and resolve that every individual was capable of reading and understanding scripture for themselves put an end to the clerical monopoly over God's word. Insisting that believers were obligated to establish their own personal relationship with God based on ready access to printed copies of vernacular scripture, he provided an unintended fillip both to emerging notions of human equality and to a

form of individualism that would later come to shape Western consciousness in the eighteenth century. The message of reform also made practical
sense to members of the German nobility. Like Luther's protector the Elector of Saxony, these nobles saw an opportunity to enhance their regional
independence while confiscating church lands and eliminating burdensome
church taxes. The peasantry, on the other hand, saw Luther as a champion
of the poor in the struggle against both lay and clerical oppression, misin-
terpreting his call for Christian freedom as an endorsement of direct action
and radical social change. When a widespread peasant rebellion erupted in
1524–1525, Luther swiftly condemned the insurgents and called upon the
princes of the Holy Roman Empire to be both judge and executioner in the
interests of social order.[15] Vastly outnumbered, poorly led, and inadequately
armed, upwards of 100,000 peasants died in the ensuing conflagration.

The fact that Luther sided with Germany's Protestant rulers is not surprising given his need for their material support and protection in the
greater fight against papists on the right and emerging radical sectarians
on the left. But in defining the Church as a community of the faithful lacking disciplinary and coercive power rather than a hierarchical government
backed by canon law, Luther magnified the role of the godly prince in
the work of sustaining the Christian polity. In fact, he put an end to the
medieval doctrine of the two swords, charging the prince with the impos-
sible task of defining and upholding the true faith.[16] Eight years after the
great reformer's death, in 1555, the Emperor Charles V, having failed to
end through military force the religious schism inaugurated by Luther,
signed the Peace of Augsburg with his rebellious Protestant subjects. By its
terms the princes of the Holy Roman Empire were given legal sanction to
choose between Catholicism and Lutheranism as the faith of their respective
states.[17] And once the choice had been made, every subject was expected
to follow the lead of the prince. The Lutheran Reformation brought politics and religion together again, but this time making the Church a virtual
department of state while anchoring the obligation to obey the prince in the
providential will of God.[18]

Given his deeply pessimistic view of human nature, Luther was wary
of politics and political figures, and in *Temporal Authority: To what extent it
should be obeyed* (1523) he reflected on the scarcity of wise princes. Despite
the myriad failings of temporal rulers, however, he concluded that the
state must hold a monopoly over the use of coercive force, and in a world
of inveterate sinners the prince alone must be responsible for maintaining peace and true religion. A gathered community of believers bound
together by love and faith was not enough to insure the temporal well-
being of every member. Order had to be enforced, and therefore Christians
were obliged to accept divinely appointed rulers even if they acted in a
tyrannical or immoral fashion. Some tyrants, after all, might even be instruments of divine wrath, and while Luther conceded that subjects must refuse
to do what is evil, they also must be prepared to suffer the immediate
consequences of their disobedience at the hands of the state.

Luther's assertion that active resistance to the magistrate was sinful and therefore forbidden (a position at odds with his own resistance to Emperor Charles V) helped to "legitimate the emerging absolutist monarchies of northern Europe" and became one of the more contested issues faced by political thinkers during the following 200 years.[19] Luther's shadow was long and, ironically, ecumenical. Toward the close of the seventeenth century, for example, one of the leading Catholic apologists for absolute monarchy, Bishop Jean Bossuet of France (1627–1704), deployed arguments that were closely allied with Lutheran precedent. In his *Politics Taken from the Works of Holy Writ* (1679), Bossuet argued that political principles must be derived from the Bible, that royal authority extends to all compartments of life, secular and sacred, and that the obedience of subjects must be entire and admit no possibility of resistance.[20]

The absolutist impulse

For nearly a century between 1559 and 1648, the key principle of the Protestant Reformation—the freedom of the individual to be guided by conscience in matters of religion—was rejected by every European head of state and by most religious leaders on both sides of the confessional divide. Ever since the Roman Emperor Constantine threw his support behind the Catholic Church in the fourth century, it was widely assumed that an identity of belief between rulers and subjects was both synonymous with political loyalty and essential to the peaceful ordering of society.[21] The notion that a state's sovereignty was in any measure compatible with religious pluralism (a commonplace in modern democracies) was rejected out of hand, and coercion of religious minorities became standard practice across the continent. Internal wars of religion, together with international conflicts involving most of Europe's major powers, were a debilitating and chronic feature of life until the end of the seventeenth century. The most costly of the religious wars occurred in the lands of the Holy Roman Empire. Between 1618 and 1648, Protestant princes and their Swedish and French allies engaged the armies of the Catholic emperor in a series of battles that featured some of the worst atrocities ever witnessed on European soil. Opposing armies laid waste to everything in sight, making no exception for civilian life or property. Only war weariness and the repeated failure of duress led some political writers and a handful of rulers to imagine the possibility of national cohesion amidst the splintering of Christian communities.

Jean Bodin and royal sovereignty

France was one of the first countries to be afflicted by a combination of weak leadership and internecine religious conflict, and the resulting disorder served as a backdrop to one of the earliest calls for nonsectarian monarchical authority. Protestantism was outlawed in France after 1534,

but legal directives were powerless to arrest the spread of dissenting principles. The ranks of the French Protestant minority, or Huguenots, grew to
almost 7 percent of the population by mid-century and included members
of the nobility, the urban bourgeoisie, and the rural peasantry. King Henry II
(r. 1547–1559) steadfastly rejected every appeal for greater religious freedom, but his accidental death as the result of wounds inflicted in a joust left
the country under the ineffective regency of his Italian widow Catherine de
Medici (1519–1589). Fighting between two great noble families, the Catholic
Guises and the Protestant Bourbons, erupted in 1562 and immediately took
on religious overtones. Excesses marked the conflict on both sides, with the
worst atrocities taking place in August 1572 when Catholics, with the consent of the young King Charles IX (r. 1560–1574) set upon the Huguenot
population of Paris. The massacre continued for 6 days, reaching into the
countryside and resulting in the deaths of thousands of men, women, and
children.[22]

It was in the midst of these civil wars that the French jurist Jean Bodin
(c. 1529–1596) published his *Six Books of the Commonwealth* (1576). Over the
next two decades, ten French editions of the book, together with three Latin
ones, would appear in print. It was translated into English in 1606 and was
cited by a range of writers in the decades before the outbreak of the English
civil wars.[23] Although a Roman Catholic, Bodin was associated with a group
of thinkers known as *politiques* that advocated toleration for Protestants on
the grounds that religious persecution was both ineffective and divisive.
The central function of political authority was to defend the state against
potential aggressors while ensuring justice and domestic tranquility, not
to advance a particular religious orthodoxy or transcendent vision of the
good. Progressive and community-oriented goals, he believed, could best
be achieved in France through a toleration enforced by a supreme authority.
Competing centers of power in the form of church establishments, customary rights, and time-honored provincial privileges must be subordinated to
the demands of the sovereign in the interests of domestic order.

In light of the dire circumstances in which he wrote, Bodin prioritized
structures that he believed were conducive to long-term domestic harmony
and social interaction. How could people live together in an orderly fashion
so that they might undertake the work of utilizing nature for productive
purposes? Bodin's conception of sovereign secular power, unchallenged by
any other temporal or spiritual authority, put an end to the plural alle-
giances of the medieval world. The untrammeled power of the sovereign, be
it in the form of an assembly, a small group, or (Bodin's strong preference)
a monarch, must have full law-making power and the right to appoint all
inferior officials and magistrates. Anything less was a recipe for chaos. Identifying a parallel to absolute political sovereignty in the "natural" order of
the family, a hierarchical and patriarchal model that traced its roots back to
biblical precedent, Bodin allowed for passive disobedience, but following
Luther's position, defiance of the sovereign always carried with it penalties
that must be endured in silence.

France's politico-religious conflict continued until the Protestant Henry of Navarre assumed the throne in 1589. Although the new monarch converted to Catholicism in deference to the sentiments of the majority of his subjects (and would be assassinated in 1610 by a fanatical Catholic), the king issued the precedent-setting Edict of Nantes in 1598, affording religious toleration for Protestants in France in an effort to staunch the confessional bloodletting. Although it was repealed in the late seventeenth century, the Edict of Nantes exemplified the principles of the *politiques* and built upon the theory of state power outlined by Bodin. In its tacit recognition of the possibility of civil peace under strong executive leadership in the midst of confessional diversity, the *Six Books of the Commonwealth* offered a way out of the debilitating cycle of religious civil war.

The Tudor Reformation and royal power

That the Reformation in England was triggered not by the spiritual anguish of the faithful but instead by the dynastic requirements of the supreme egoist Henry VIII (r. 1509–1547) indicates the extent to which Protestantism was vulnerable to cooption by the state. In 1529, when Henry inaugurated the break with Rome over his perceived need to off-load his Spanish wife in favor of a more youthful and fecund Anne Boleyn, the king showed little interest in or sympathy for Protestant theology. His would be an administrative Reformation, a jurisdictional change, not a doctrinal housecleaning. During the 1530s, Henry would assume the supreme headship of the Catholic Church in England, end all appeals and payments to Rome, and expropriate and then sell-off the Church's extensive monastic properties. Whereas Lutheranism had redefined the Church as a community of the faithful lacking all coercive powers, Henry boldly appropriated the jurisdictional powers of the Church, maintaining all of its legal rights under royal control. Comparable steps were taken later by the monarchs of Denmark and Sweden.[24]

In England, repression and coercion were applied irrespective of the victim's social standing; all officers of the Crown were obliged to accept the king's supremacy and those who demurred, like the humanist Thomas More, were tried and executed as traitors. The leading architect of the Henrican Reformation was Thomas Cromwell (1485–1540), principal secretary to the king and consummate technocrat who, like his mercurial master, was largely indifferent to the spiritual dimensions of the Protestant Reformation. Cromwell was interested in forging the unitary state, where the monarch became the sole object of every subject's allegiance, and he employed a sophisticated propaganda apparatus to move public opinion into the king's camp.[25]

But there were others in England who wished to move beyond the liberation of the Church from Rome to a program of serious doctrinal reform. Thanks to extensive commercial and intellectual links with the continent, Lutheran ideas began to make significant inroads in England as early as the

1520s. The groundwork that had been prepared by the Lollards outlawed followers of Wycliffe who kept alive the anti-clerical heresy despite vigorous state persecution. Others, like the Cambridge scholar William Tyndale (c. 1494–1536), had spent time with Luther in Wittenberg in the early 1520s and subsequently published *The Obedience of a Christian Man* (1528), the first exposition of Lutheran political ideas in English. Perhaps more importantly, Tyndale secured the financial support of some dissenting English merchants in London and produced an English-language translation of the New Testament in 1526 that was heavily influenced by Lutheranism.[26]

Henry VIII was able to suppress the reform movement, but his son and heir Edward VI, who reigned as a child-king from 1547 to 1553, allowed the Lutheran ideas of his tutor Sir John Cheke (1514–1557) to influence official policy. When Edward died, his Catholic half-sister Mary made the restoration of papal authority the chief policy objective of her government. The queen made martyrs of a number of high-profile Protestants who refused to conform while forcing others into extended exile on the continent. Mary's marriage to Philip II of Spain, champion of the Catholic cause across Europe, served to strengthen the association of Protestantism with English nationalism. When the queen died, childless, in 1558, her younger sister Elizabeth assumed the throne, bringing with her religious sensibilities that were firmly in the tradition of her father Henry VIII.

James I and divine right theory

During a reign lasting more than four decades, Elizabeth I skillfully protected royal prerogative and headship of the state church while acknowledging the role of parliament in its advisory and legislative capacity. She also refrained from persecuting those whose religious sensibilities lay outside of the official Church, preferring not to "make windows into men's souls" so long as religion was not used a pretext for disloyalty. The threat from Catholic Spain, which reached its climax in 1588 when King Philip II launched an ill-fated naval expedition to topple the heretic queen, served to rally the kingdom around Elizabeth as the embodiment of English national identity. The last of the Tudor monarchs held strong views of the royal prerogative that often frustrated her loyal subjects, but she was disinclined to force the issue with unequivocal statements on monarchical power.[27]

Her successor, James I (r. 1603–1625), was less circumspect when it came to public reflections on the nature of the kingly office. A seasoned executive who had already served as king of Scotland for more than two decades when he inherited the English throne, James authored two works that enlisted history and scripture in defense of hereditary right and royal absolutism. *The Trew Law of Free Monarchy* (1598) and *Basilikon Doron* (1599) both argued that religiously inspired civil conflict could be prevented only under the auspices of strong monarchy. Because monarchs "sit upon God his throne in the earth, and have the count of their administration to give unto him," man-made laws do not constrain the ruler whose first concern

must be the good of the commonwealth. The wise king will rule in accordance with established law, "yet he is not bound thereto but of his good
will, and for example giving to his subjects."[28] James combined a Bodinian
emphasis on the duty of the divine right monarch to uphold the established
law with opposition to the view that subjects possess a right of resistance to
the prince, even if he were to act in a tyrannical manner and command in
opposition to divine law.[29] His son Charles I, who reigned from 1625 until
1649, shared this strong view of royal prerogative and his intransigence
in the face of growing parliamentary opposition to his policies led to the
outbreak of civil war in 1642.

Thomas Hobbes and secular absolutism

Critics of absolutism associated it with tyranny, despotism, fanaticism, privilege, and prejudice. But defenders were quick to point to the chaos that so
often accompanied the breakdown of strong government and to the realities of competitive international politics in making the case for rule by
one. In dangerous times, where the oppressions of over-mighty subjects, the
threats of religious fanatics, and the constant dangers from rival states jeop-
ardized the well-being of the whole, undivided authority with a monopoly
over the use of physical coercion seemed both practical and progressive.
And no one more effectively made the case for pragmatic absolutism than
the Englishman Thomas Hobbes (1588–1679). Writing in the midst of the
fratricidal civil wars that resulted in the execution of King Charles I and the
temporary triumph of Puritans who condemned the half-way reformation
of Henry VIII's Church of England, Hobbes was determined to end both the
notion that political power can be divided or shared between people and
king, and, more importantly, the association of political power with the will
of the divine. In its place he would, like Machiavelli, disengage the function of the magistrate from transcendent purposes while simultaneously
extending the power of the ruler with the consent of the people.[30]

Hobbes began his efforts with the publication of *The Elements of Law* in
1640. The Puritan members of parliament, all staunch opponents of King
Charles I, found nothing to admire in the work, and fearing for his life
Hobbes fled to France. He spent the next 11 years in exile, watching his
country descend into civil conflict and composing two additional works
of political theory: *De Cive* (1642) and *Leviathan* (1651). In the latter work
Hobbes boldly combined consensual agreements respecting the origins of
sovereign power with traditional absolutist arguments on the scope of that
power. It was a position guaranteed to offend both divine right royalists
and Puritan leaders in parliament. Viewing human behavior in a hypothetical state of nature, Hobbes described a pre-political condition dominated by
envy, selfish passion, and the potential for hostile action. Pride and passion
invariably moved people to define "good" and "evil" on the basis of their
own perceived needs, thus in the pre-civil state "notions of right and wrong,
justice and injustice have there no place." Absent an agreed civil authority,

"there is no law, no injustice" and force and fraud become "the two cardinal virtues." The terrible conclusion is that life for everyone in the state of nature is "solitary, poor, nasty, brutish, and short."[31]

Despite this pessimistic assessment, Hobbes believed that people in the state of nature had the ability, as a function of rational self-preservation, to combine forces, enter into contract, and create a common power whose exclusive purpose was to insure the physical security of all. They do not enter into a contract with the sovereign but with themselves, creating a mortal god against which there is no right of resistance.[32] For Hobbes civil society was not the natural predisposition of man, as Aristotle had assumed, but a necessity built and maintained by humans (not God) on the foundation of hard experience. Similarly, positive law is not derived from a higher, eternal law; it takes its origin from convention grounded in circumstance. In agreeing to give up the right of nature to do whatever they deem necessary for their own preservation, subjects willingly charge one man or group of men to maintain order, "stable and trustable social relations."[33] They obey for the sake of protection, and in pursuance of that goal the sovereign must be allowed autocratic discretion, making law and doing in effect "whatsoever he shall think necessary to be done, both beforehand, for the preserving of peace and security ... and when peace and security are lost, for the recovery of the same."[34] The power of the state is justified solely on a utilitarian standard—the security of individual human beings, ignoring as irrelevant any consideration of custom, tradition, or supernatural sanction. Under Hobbes's iconoclastic formulation, law, morality, even religious truth, exist simply as the will of an absolute sovereign who is fulfilling the conditions under which it has been created. Even the most tyrannical government, he held, was better than no government at all.

Seventeenth-century trends

The practice of absolutism appeared to gain significant ground during the course of the seventeenth century. Noble privileges, local and national legislative assemblies, clerical exemptions from civil jurisdiction, and judicial power in the hands of local elites all retreated before the expanding prerogatives of the Crown. In France, the royal advisory body known as the Estates General ceased to meet after 1615, undermining the notion that taxation required the consent of the taxed. King Louis XIII (r. 1610–1643) successfully subdued the Huguenot minority with the help of his principal minister, Cardinal Richelieu, whose *Political Testament* (1624) set the ambitious goal of making the king supreme in France and France supreme in Europe.[35] During the long reign of his successor Louis XIV (r. 1643–1715), the centralizing project continued apace. Even the Catholic Church acquiesced when, in 1682, a formal declaration by the clergy of France asserted the independence of the king from papal control. Similar trends were noticeable elsewhere. In 1660, the Danish Estates met for the last time, while in Spain the once powerful Cortes of Castile did not convene after 1667.

Absolutism was introduced in Sweden in the 1680s, and in Prussia the Elector freely taxed his subjects without their consent and employed a highly trained army to enforce his will. Further to the East in Tsarist Russia, the autocratic Peter the Great (r. 1682–1725), a monarch who much admired Western ideas and practices, set the standard for rule unhindered by the countervailing interests of the landed elite.

Whether absolutism was framed as divine right authority derived immediately from God, or more controversially as an irreversible grant made by the people, the underlying assumption that the ruler was the unconstrained maker and interpreter of law was based on a negative conviction. Absent strong and unitary leadership, to return to the words of Bishop Bossuet, "all is confusion and the state returns to anarchy."[36] In other words, absolutism was deduced from deeply held views of human nature, views that were equally informed by Christian theology and the empirical data of contemporary domestic and international conflict. For absolutists, mixed or limited government was tantamount to divided sovereignty, and given the constants of sinful human nature since the Fall, was a recipe for disaster and an affront to God's will. Monarchs, of course, were not exempted from the consequences of Adam's transgression, for they too were sinners and equally prone to misuse their power. But for the proponents of absolutism, punishment in the case of royal malefactors was to be delayed until he or she encountered the awful majesty of God. Here was the concluding movement to the Lutheran political odyssey, one man's understanding of the biblical directives regarding how people ought to live with one another.

Resistance theory and constitutionalism

For many other Protestants, however, and not a few Catholics, this reading of scripture was seriously flawed. Theirs' was a more activist, indeed contractual, reading of their relationship with God and with those whom they acknowledged as their temporal rulers. It had been Luther's pious, if in retrospect *naïve*, contention that free access to scripture would result in a fuller and more widely agreed understanding of God's purposes for humankind. Unhappily the Protestant encouragement of free inquiry led almost immediately to multiple interpretations of primitive Christianity that precluded the emergence of anything approaching a unified theological position. Luther and the Swiss reformer Ulrich Zwingli (1484–1531), for example, met in Marburg, Germany in 1529, but instead of an alliance against a common Catholic opponent, the two men fell into disagreement over the nature of Christ's presence in the Eucharist and left the summit harboring reciprocal ill feelings. Within 2 years Zwingli was dead, killed in battle against the armies of the Catholic cantons of Switzerland, and more radical Swiss Protestants, impatient with the slow pace of reform and committed to alternate interpretations of early Christian living, proceeded to create their own biblical havens.

The Swiss radicals were led by Conrad Grebel (1498–1526), whose efforts to restore the Kingdom of God in its biblical purity attracted both peasant and urban lower-class support, a deeply troubling combination in the eyes of traditional landed elites. Insisting that adult members must be re-baptized into the voluntary community of believers and that Church membership was not synonymous with membership of the State, the radicals—labeled "Anabaptists" by their opponents—demanded a complete separation of the Church and the State and refused to take oaths, pay taxes, or bear arms on its behalf. The movement spread rapidly into other states on the continent, prompting Lutheran and Catholic authorities to crack down hard on those who claimed religious sanction for political disobedience.[37]

Events in the German city of Munster in Westphalia afford but one of many examples of the extreme measures taken against the Anabaptists. The city became an Anabaptist theocracy for 1 year (1534–1535), with its residents adopting the practice of adult re-baptism and emphasizing the inner light of conscience as the guide to religious truth, burning all books other than the Bible, refusing the take oaths, and practicing polygamy. In preparation for the second coming of Christ, the leadership forced Catholic and Lutheran residents of the city to convert or emigrate. Those who took the second option had their property confiscated. Well-armed Protestant and Catholic armies crushed the movement, and its rank and file—men, women and children—were brutally tortured and slaughtered as an example to other would-be radicals. Recognizing the anti-hierarchical and separatist implications of the "inner light," Anabaptism was declared a capital offense throughout the Holy Roman Empire.

Calvinism and the godly magistrate

Whereas Lutheranism was deferential to the secular state, relying upon the prince to lead the movement for Church reform and to define the proper nature of that reform, the interplay between Protestant theology and political authority was more problematical for the French-born lawyer and religious reformer John Calvin (1509–1564). After fleeing persecution in his native country, Calvin eventually settled in Geneva, where after 1540 he played a leading role in the creation of a strictly regimented theocracy where a tightly knit oligarchy regulated personal conduct and punished violations of God's law. Calvin embraced a rigidly Augustinian view of sinful human nature, which he took to be "blind, darkened in understanding, and full of corruption and perversity of heart."[38] In addition, he was convinced that every person, irrespective of good works, had been predestined either to salvation or eternal damnation. The only sign of salvation (there were no guarantees) was a person's unfailing adherence to divine ordinance and its robust imposition on others.

By the 1550s, Geneva had became a destination city for the Elect of God. Protestant exiles from England, Scotland, the Netherlands, France, and the Holy Roman Empire gathered there and eagerly absorbed the teachings of

Calvin, set out most persuasively in his *Institutes of the Christian Religion* (1536). The book became, after the Bible, the leading source of Protestant theology in Europe during the second half of the sixteenth century. As political circumstances allowed, Calvin's followers returned home carrying a message that redefined the relationship between people and magistrates in the godly state. For while Calvin endorsed Luther's argument that people must obey even the unjust magistrate, leaving punishment to God, some of his disciples adopted a more militant stance borne of the fact that they lived under governments that were opposed to their theological perspective.

In the final chapter of the *Institutes*, Calvin stated unequivocally that Christ's spiritual kingdom and civil jurisdiction are both ordained by God but separated by function. It was the Church and not the State that defined pure doctrine; the leaders of the Church, the Elect of God, were alone to set the standards of morality and right conduct based on their reading of scripture. The function of the State, on the other hand, was to enforce these prescriptions while preserving common peace and security. As George Sabine observed, Calvin's theory of the Church "was more in the spirit of extreme medieval ecclesiasticism than that held by nationalist Catholics."[39] In light of this lofty conception of church power, it is not surprising that Calvinists who formed a minority in states that were actively hostile to the Genevan formula should begin to rethink the doctrine of passive obedience. France, Scotland, and the Spanish-controlled Netherlands were such states, ruled by Catholic monarchs who set the terms of orthodoxy and took heavy-handed actions to enforce it. In each country, rebellion against existing secular authority in the name of true religion became the preferred course of action by men who were confident that obedience to God sanctioned their disobedience to man.

In the Spanish-controlled Netherlands, open hostility between Protestants and Spanish authorities stretched, intermittently, from 1568 until 1648. Philip II of Spain was determined to crush the Calvinist minority and sent an enormous occupying army into the country, but the Dutch, with the full support of their Calvinist ministers, fought back and won *de facto* independence in 1609 and official separation in 1648. In Scotland, Calvinist forces under the determined leadership of John Knox (1510–1572) upended the French-backed Catholic government and undertook a complete overhaul of Church and State. Knox was one of the more famous figures living in Geneva during the 1550s, where he was deeply influenced by Calvin and served as pastor to an English exile community. Back in Scotland, he effectively organized nobles and commoners against the Monarchy, and when the Catholic Mary Stuart assumed the throne in 1561, Knox called for armed resistance against the "idolatrous" queen.[40] It did not take long for the queen, a master of poor judgment and indiscretion, to alienate most of her leading subjects before she was expelled from the kingdom in 1567.

The leading apologist for the new government was George Buchanan (1506–1582), a humanist who had spent most of his career on the continent, and who was now employed to justify the removal of a hereditary monarch by her subjects. In a series of influential works, including an unflattering biography of the deposed queen, a history of Scotland that emphasized precedents for the removal of rulers, and most importantly, in a dialogue titled *De jure regni apud Scotos* (1579), Buchanan encapsulated a quickly maturing position on the right to resistance. Scrutinizing both biblical and Roman law injunctions to obedience, he claimed that none of these directives was meant to apply to tyrants, who must be removed by legal action, military force, or as a last resort, by assassination.[41]

Such severe views appealed to many Puritan dissenters. One of Knox's co-pastors in Geneva was the Oxford-educated Christopher Goodman (1520–1603), who had fled England upon the accession of the Catholic Mary I. In a tract of 1558 justifying rebellion against the queen, Goodman referred the reader to the 19th verse of the 4th chapter of Acts, where Peter and John answered the rulers of Jerusalem with the words: "Whether it be right in the sight of God to obey you rather than God judge you." Goodman's reading was unequivocal, insisting "that to obey man in anything contrary to God, or his precepts though he be in highest authority . . . is no obedience at all, but disobedience." In language so strident that even the Protestant Queen Elizabeth was unwilling to allow Goodwin to return home until 1570, the dissenter wrote that unless subjects resisted the godless ruler, "you which are subjects with them shall be condemned except you maintain and defend the same laws against them . . . for this God hath required of you."[42] And Goodwin was no lone voice. Fellow exile John Ponet (1514–1556), bishop of Winchester under the Protestant Edward VI, concluded in *A Short Treatise of Politic Power* (1556) that a ruler who violated his or her sacred trust should be treated like a common criminal. Obedience to one's sovereign was important within its proper bounds, "for too much maketh the governors to forget their vocation and to usurp upon their subjects."[43]

In the wake of the 1572 St Bartholomew's Day Massacre, France's Huguenot minority abandoned what had been their steady allegiance to the monarchy. In a major work of historical jurisprudence, the Huguenot Francis Hotman (1524–1590) set out to describe the constitution of pre-Roman Gaul. His *Franco-gallia* (1573) asserted that absolutism was a recent innovation, usurping the ancient Frankish constitution where kings "did not have boundless, absolute and unchecked power but were bound by settled law, so that they were no less under the people's power and authority than the people were under theirs."[44] In addition, Hotman's researches convinced him that a public meeting of the entire realm had been in place since the earliest days of the kingdom. This precursor to the Three Estates originally held the power to create and depose kings and to exercise authority over areas normally reserved for the executive, including the power to make war and peace, regulate religion, and appoint regional governors.

While never calling for overt resistance to the Crown, Hotman's contemporaries were emboldened by his antiquarian research. Theodore Beza (1519–1605), successor to John Calvin in Geneva after the latter's death in 1564, communicated with Hotman while he was composing his own work on the problem of legitimate resistance, the *Right of Magistrates* (1574). Although he never acknowledged the right of individuals to challenge a sovereign who had degenerated into a tyrant, he did allow for lesser magistrates "who have public or state responsibilities either in the administration of justice or in war" to resist any "flagrant oppression of the realm" by virtue of their sworn duty to uphold established law, both human and divine. The book appeared in ten French editions in the decade after its publication, while Latin translations—often bound with copies of Machiavelli's *The Prince* and another anonymous work, *Vindiciae contra tyrannos*—appeared in print regularly through the middle of the seventeenth century.[45] Beza's willingness to go beyond the cautious principles of his mentor was a result of the stresses surrounding the events of 1572 and represented "an extreme case of the way in which even the most faithful followers of Calvin adjusted themselves to circumstances."[46]

The *Vindiciae* or *Defense of Liberty Against Tyrants* (1579) was less reticent about highlighting the religious dimensions of the contemporary struggle against tyranny. First translated from Latin into French in 1581, its probable author, the Calvinist Philippe du Plessis-Mornay (1549–1623), called upon kings and other officials to assure that the Church is rightly governed, while agreeing with Beza that lesser magistrates were duty-bound to resist a tyrannical monarch. But in an important departure, the *Vindiciae* allowed that on occasion other individuals might be called by God to lead a resistance movement in the name of the true faith. Two essential contracts governed the earthly pilgrimage, the first between God and the people, and the second between the temporal ruler and his subjects. The first always took precedence over the second, thus the king who violated his charge forfeited any claim to his subjects' obedience.[47] The *Vindiciae* even called for foreign intervention on behalf of the true religion or to protect the victims of official repression.

It was perhaps not coincidental that the volume of Huguenot resistance writing declined after the implementation of the Edict of Nantes in 1598. Indeed their support for the Catholic Bourbon monarchs remained strong as long as the general toleration continued. Only in the 1660s, when Louis XIV began to encroach upon the privileges enjoyed by dissenters did the literature of resistance once again find a receptive audience. By that time Catholic writers were firmly behind the absolutist agenda. But it had not always been the case. Indeed during the height of the civil wars in France, when the Protestant Henry of Navarre appeared to be the heir apparent, it was Catholics who advanced some of the most powerful arguments in favor of resistance. Jesuit theorists like Robert Bellarmine (1542–1621), Francisco Suarez (1548–1617), and Juan de Molina (1536–1624) cautioned against the dangers of living under a heretic king. According to Molina, tyrannicide was allowable for "any private person whatsoever who may wish to come to the aid of the commonwealth."[48] The discovery and advancement of religious sanction for regime change was an equal opportunity phenomenon.

John Locke, Christian contract, and the pursuit of property

The Oxford-educated physician, philosopher, and political theorist John Locke (1632–1704) was a student during England's mid-century civil wars and republican experiment. His middle-class father had fought on the side of parliament during the early stages of the war, and while the son professed strong royalist sympathies at the time of the restoration of the Stuart monarchy in the early 1660s, by the following decade Locke had become a harsh critic of royal prerogative. The transformation was influenced in no small part by his patron Anthony Ashley Cooper, Earl of Shaftesbury (1621–1683), a leading figure in the parliamentary opposition to the Stuart Court and a champion of religious toleration, individual freedom, and parliament's right to control the succession to the Crown. Locke was also from the non-noble background that had traditionally been excluded from power. During the Cromwellian ascendancy Locke's contemporary James Harrington (1611–1677) had argued, in a celebrated work called *Oceana* (1656), that property held the keys to political power, and that the English mid-century revolution could best be understood as the political coming of age of the mercantile middle class. Two centuries later, Karl Marx would arrive at a not dissimilar conclusion.

Efforts by Shaftesbury and his allies to exclude the Catholic James Duke of York from inheriting the throne led to a major clash with King Charles II (r. 1660–1685), James's older brother. Between 1679 and 1681, this opposition attempted to dislodge the heir apparent by introducing a succession of exclusion bills into parliament. Each time the king was able to rally his supporters and defeat the legislation, and in the end Shaftesbury was driven into exile. Locke, who was deeply implicated in the plan to exclude James from succeeding to the throne, also fled overseas and lived quietly in Holland from 1683 until 1688. The latter date marked the end of the brief reign of James II (r. 1685–1688), who had managed to antagonize most of the political nation in very short order by his efforts to end all disabilities against Catholics. When he was removed in a revolution led by his son-in-law, the Protestant William of Orange, Locke returned home and published a manuscript that he had originally composed during the height of the Exclusion Crisis of 1679–1681. That manuscript was the *Two Treatises of Government*, a major exposition of contract theory, natural rights, and the sanctity of private property.

The first of the treatises is largely ignored today, but in it Locke labored at great length to discredit the divine right theory of Sir Robert Filmer (1588–1653), whose ideas commanded great respect throughout much of the seventeenth century. At the outset of *Patriarcha* (1680), a work that had been written decades earlier, Filmer challenged what he described as a common misperception, the notion that "Mankind is naturally endowed and born with freedom from all subjection, and at liberty to choose what form of government it please, and that the power which any one man hath over others was at the first by human right bestowed according to the discretion of the multitude."[49] Locke was aware that patriarchal political theory aligned nicely with contemporary social theory, especially in its elevation of the father as head of household. The key challenge in the first treatise was to demonstrate convincingly how political obligation was both separate from family government and limited in its purview. He did this by stressing throughout the *Two Treatises* how humans were the workmanship and property of God alone. The Law of Nature, God's law, placed all parents "under an obligation to preserve, nourish, and educate the children" because they are the workmanship of God to whom they were to be held accountable for them.[50] Fulfilling a duty enjoined by a superior was for Locke at odds with the Filmerian attribution of unlimited and arbitrary authority in the household setting.

Having dispatched Filmer, Locke began the closely reasoned and now celebrated second treatise with an examination of the same hypothetical state of nature that for his countryman Thomas Hobbes had been an arena of constant conflict. Although he claimed to have never read Hobbes, Locke agreed that in the state of nature the Law of Nature was obscured by man's biases and general ignorance. Life in the pre-political state, where men had a natural right to their life, liberty, and property, lacked "a known and indifferent judge, with authority to determine all differences according to the established law." Unhappily, natural partiality led humans "to violate the rules of common equity and evaluate and punish the actions of others unfairly." Finally, the state of nature offers no "power to back and support the sentence when right, and to give it due execution."[51] Given these conditions, the freedom that each person enjoys within the bounds of the Law of Nature, and the property that they hold, is "very unsafe, very insecure." Only by entering into a voluntary contract and establishing formal government can each person hope to exercise their individual freedom and right to property unmolested.

Where Locke differed from Hobbes is in his refusal to grant absolute authority to the sovereign; indeed no one could transfer such power because the individual is not permitted the "liberty to destroy himself" nor to grant another the liberty to do so; for Locke only the Creator has a right to dispose of a person's life. Absolutism is invalid because people are not permitted to make themselves slaves. God requires of each person conduct that is incompatible with the surrender of freedom.[52] Under such a reading of human responsibility, the legitimate exercise of political power takes place only when the magistrate stays within the precise bounds set by the original contract. Just as parental authority was a God-ordained trust, so too political authority was a trust whereby the magistrate agrees to act within the limits set by the original contract. The right to resist, and to change the form of government, was inherent in the original contract, and could be interpreted as a defensive, conservative action to preserve God-given natural rights, including the right to hold and accumulate property. Locke's theory of responsible government by consent, unlike the model advanced by Hobbes, remained firmly allied to age-old theological concerns, but

with Locke theological sanction was deployed on behalf of plainly temporal ends. Individuals were endowed with inherent rights and freedoms,
including, most importantly, the right to acquire and accumulate personal
property, and any government that threatened these rights and freedoms
was acting against the God of reason.

Republics, rights, and religions

The unlikely emergence of Italian city-republics during the central Middle
Ages came against the backdrop of more than a millennium of monarchical theory and practice in Western Europe. Beginning in the city of Pisa
in 1085 and spreading to Genoa, Milan, Bologna, Padua, and Siena over
the next century, elective and self-governing systems, each with a written constitution and limited citizenship rights, stood as stark alternatives
to the feudal monarchies and ephemeral empires of the age. Writers like
Machiavelli defended the republic and the principle of popular sovereignty
as the ideal context in which the community could reach its highest collective goals. Only in a setting where citizens were empowered and obliged to
take an active role in common affairs, the *res publica*, would the qualities of
public spiritedness, courage, and honesty flourish. The focus in a republic,
at least in the minds of its most vocal champions, was on the moral dimension of governance, on the diffusion of power as a mechanism to foster the
human drive for excellence and improvement.

Building on its pre-Christian roots in the city-states of Greece and pre-
imperial Rome, early modern republican writers began with an ascending
conception of government where legitimate authority always originated
with the people. As we have seen with Locke, the idea that temporal
authority might be separate, both in origin and function, from the hierarchical assumptions that informed everything from the organization of
the family to the structure of the cosmos was of revolutionary potential.
Republicanism forwarded the possibility of an order that was shaped by
humans alone and that changed in response to circumstance. Constitutions
and political structures were human inventions, not theocratic dictates or
reflections of religiously inspired laws of nature.

Few writers in sixteenth- and seventeenth-century Europe agreed with
this analysis, preferring to view republics as curious aberrations on a continent dominated by ambitious, centralizing monarchies. Indeed most of the
Italian republics, long wracked by instability and selfish party rivalries, had
succumbed to the hereditary principle by the sixteenth century, with Venice
the lone hold-out until the dawn of the Napoleonic era (1797). In the early
seventeenth century the Venetians could look North to the Swiss cantons
and to the United Provinces of the Netherlands as the only other successful
republics. They were joined briefly by the Britain between 1649 and 1660,
and it was here that the largest and most radical body of republican literature was produced during and in the immediate aftermath of the English
civil wars. Led by writers who believed that their country was afflicted by

a pattern of political corruption and clerical interference in the affairs of state, new men of humbler origins entered the field of political discourse—in pamphlets, petitions, and books—to call for new models of governance and to inspire their contemporaries to action.

That action took a dramatic turn between December 1648 and March 1649, when King Charles I (r. 1625–1649), his forces defeated on the battlefield by a Puritan army loyal to parliament, was tried, convicted, and executed as a criminal. The army and its leadership viewed themselves as vehicles designated to carry out the will of God, and while theirs' was a minority position in the nation at the time, a large body of republican writing affirmed the essential justice of the action. In *The Case of the Commonwealth of England Stated* (1650) and in a series of editorials that appeared in the weekly journal *Mecurius Politicus*, Marchamont Nedham (1620–1678) defended the regicides and reminded his readers that many governments could trace their roots to acts of violence. The poet John Milton (1608–1674), a staunch opponent of the monarchy throughout the civil wars and an official propagandist for the republican regime during the 1650s was unequivocal in his endorsement of resistance to ungodly magistrates. In *The Tenure of Kings and Magistrates* (1649) and other works, Milton affirmed the natural freedom of all in the state of nature. Human liberty, he wrote in *A Defense of the People of England* (1651) "is not Caesar's, but is a birthday gift to us from God himself."[53] Milton always worried whether his countrymen were up to the demands of self-government, and in the *Ready and Easy Way to Establish a Free Commonwealth* (1660), when the return to monarchy was imminent, he acknowledged that only a select few embodied the moral qualities needed to maintain a state without a monarchy.

Radical democracy

For a brief moment during the English civil wars, a group of writers and pamphleteers derisively called Levellers by their enemies reached out to a popular audience and advanced a truly radical claim on political power. Addressing small tradesmen, artisans, soldiers, and poor urban laborers, between 1645 and 1649 the Levellers called for universal manhood suffrage without property requirements, a written constitution, freedom of religion, equality before the law, and an end to military conscription. They also demanded a representative assembly that held lawmaking and executive power, and defended the right to resist any magistrate who failed to carry out his delegated trust. In 1647, members of the army rank and file met with their officers to debate the overall objectives of the struggle against the king. One of their leaders, Colonal Thomas Rainsborough (c. 1610–1648), epitomized the Leveller outlook when he stated that "the poorest he that is in England has a life to live as the greatest he" and that every man "that is to live under a government ought first by his own consent to put himself under that government." Here was a revolution in political writing every bit as damaging to the centuries-old hierarchies in the social and political world as Copernican heliocentrism had been to the medieval picture of the physical universe.[54]

Yet certain of the Levellers did not think that this democratic program went far enough, claiming that political reform must be joined with a fundamental restructuring of English social and economic life. These were the Diggers or "True Levellers" as they sometimes referred to themselves, and led by the one-time clothing apprentice Gerrard Winstanley (1609–1676), they put forward plans for a communal government in England based on an understanding of the law of nature whereby everyone had a right to subsistence. For Winstanley the natural state was one in which all shared in the common ownership of the land; the sin of private ownership was the root cause of inequalities, social abuse, and immorality. Writing in 1649, Winstanley averred that under private property "some are lifted up into the chair of tyranny, and others trod under the foot-stool of misery, as if the earth were made for a few, not for all men."[55] The Diggers would root out this sin by removing opportunities for covetousness and greed, and in 1649 they proceeded to take up waste land at a number of sites outside London where they envisioned a primitive communist community. Ousted by irate local villagers, the squatter communities turned to national appeals. In his *Law of Freedom* (1652), Winstanley addressed his remarks to Oliver Cromwell (1599–1658), who was by this time the undisputed ruler of the republic. The government should erect a nation-wide communal economy where all are obliged to engage in productive labor, where the national church is recast as an educational organization, and where strict 1-year term limits are imposed on all officeholders. Of course nothing came of these proposals, but by connecting political equality and personal liberty with fundamental economic structures, the Diggers touched on an aspect of power relations that would be central to the later critiques of socialists and communists during the height of the Industrial Revolution.

New directions in natural law

The Levellers were among the first political thinkers to associate the ancient Law of Nature with innate and indefeasible individual rights whose preservation was the primary task of government. They were also innovators in claiming that this same Law of Lature located sovereignty in the people, who in turn delegated it to elected representatives who might be removed from their office of trust for cause.[56] In claiming the sanction of natural law for their position, they were working within a much longer tradition of natural law theory reaching back to the Stoics, but shaped by an environment where the unity once symbolized by the papacy had been shattered, and where emerging states were busy creating their own legal systems and instruments of enforcement. With the retreat of religious sanction for temporal authority during the mid-seventeenth century, theologically based explorations of natural law moved into new directions.

One of the most influential interpretations of natural law was advanced by the Dutch scholar and diplomat Hugo Grotius (1583–1645) in 1625. Grotius had first-hand experience of the power of intolerance when he was prosecuted for his anti-Calvinist beliefs in the early 1620s. Imprisoned with a life term, he escaped to France after serving 2 years and spent the rest of his life in exile. His *Law of War and Peace* (1625) was written in the midst of the horrific Thirty Years War, and its subsequent influence is reflected in the fact that at least 14 editions of the book appeared in print by 1680. Grotius returned to pre-Christian sources to establish a fundamental law that lay behind the civil law in every state, a law that would be acknowledged as binding on all. He sought to counter those skeptics who, in the wake of the Reformation wars of religion, could find no basis for belief in scholastic universals, and who instead anchored all law in changeable human convention.

Grotius began with Aristotle's principle that humans were social and rational by nature and added that the basic force shaping all human relations was the desire for self-preservation. From these two indispensable "laws of nature" he then inferred two more: neither people should injure others, nor should they appropriate another's possessions. Justice is achieved when all behave in conformity to their natural longing for society. For Grotius "right reason" tells us when an act is in conformity with our nature, and it is this source, not scripture or the creedal statements of divided churches, that alone can lead us out of the endemic violence of religious controversy. Laws of nature are obligatory, Grotius believed, even if there were no God; they are the dictates of our nature as rational and social beings. Like the natural philosophers and mathematicians of his day, Grotius made it his concern "to refer the proofs of things touching the law of nature to certain fundamental conceptions which are beyond question, so that no one can deny them without doing violence to himself." The principles of natural law, he was convinced, "are in themselves manifest and clear, almost as evident as those things which we perceive by the external senses."[57] The Law of Nature, once thought to be an expression of God's positive law, was now to be understood as a scientific principle as unbending as the Law of Gravity.

Hobbes was in agreement with Grotius' analysis, declaring in *Leviathan* that laws of nature are precepts "found out by reason, by which a man is forbidden to do, that, which is destructive of his life, or taketh away the means of preserving the same."[58] But it was the German scholar Samuel Pufendorf (1632–1694), writing after the end of the Thirty Years War, who most effectively advanced the non-theological argument for natural law. When he published *On the Law of Nature and Nations* in 1672, the age of the wars of religion was in recession, to be replaced by conflicts prompted by dynastic, commercial, and territorial interests. Like Grotius, Pufendorf wished to liberate his philosophy of society, law, and history from all sacred underpinnings and to align it with the regularities observed in physical nature. Translated into numerous languages and appearing in multiple editions, the book set out a primordial state of nature where a basic equality was threatened by the propensity of some men to impose their will and inflict harm on their fellows. Men entered into civil society in order to avoid the difficulties attendant upon life in the state of nature, a position strikingly similar to the one advanced by Locke, but this transition did not invalidate the force of the Law of Nature or Reason. It was not divine or civil law that offered the best hope for humankind, for these were limited to Christian duties and particular states, respectively. Only natural law was applicable to all nations and peoples of every condition, and its study and employment would repay dividends to all who would bring their lives into conformity with its dictates.

Exit divinity

In 1500, political thinking of every manner was informed by two critical assumptions: civil authority was a delegated trust from God, and effective government had to take account of the priorities of the universal Catholic Church. Indeed for centuries political thinking had been a minor branch of theology, one outcropping of a larger body of moral truth as interpreted by church authorities. Earthly kings remained essential personifications of the body politic, and their governments were designed to counteract the inexorable pull of sinful human nature. Church–State conflict was not unfamiliar, of course, but for centuries it was assumed that Europe's one transnational institution would continue to play a vital role in the day-to-day affairs of the subordinate temporal kingdoms. By the middle of the sixteenth century these two assumptions were being openly contested, and by 1700 both were on the verge of summary dismissal.

The gradual separation of political theory from theology was the work of many hands, and the road from confessional states, where belief was obligatory to one where civil authorities took no interest in the promotion of a particular path to heaven, was long and arduous. It involved new modes of thought because for some the latter position implied that truth was no longer unitary and that the rules for human behavior and the springs of political action were, after all, solely the result of human convention. Machiavelli and Hobbes reached this bold conclusion with equanimity; Grotius, Pufendorf, and Locke were loath to abandon the anchor of universalism and instead reinstated the pre-Christian concept of an immutable and knowable Law of Nature. Whatever theoretical option one chose, however, the result was the same: the emergence of separate and sovereign states whose claim on power had little or nothing to do with divine sanction. Instead that claim originated from inside the political community, from the people, and operated in pursuit of very mundane ends. By 1700, states were defined by institutional structures whose public power continued even as individual magistrates passed from the scene. Monarchy remained the preferred model of executive authority, but the monarch's higher purpose was no longer the fulfillment of God's eternal ordinance, but rather the continuous material advancement of the territory and its people.

The Protestant Reformation had begun with a call for individual autonomy and freedom of inquiry in spiritual discourse, but almost immediately devolved into sectarian infighting, new forms of dogmatism, proscription, and persecution, and in the end the formation of official, and officially intolerant, state churches. The resulting militancy and violence on behalf of respective orthodoxies served only to betray the foundational principles of Christian charity, but it took over a century—and much bloodshed—for Europeans to let go of the idea that religious uniformity was a prerequisite to civil order. "I saw throughout the Christian world a license in waging war that would shame barbarous nations" was how Grotius viewed the spectacle of the Thirty Years War.[59] Only in the second half of the seventeenth century did a profound reaction against the enforcement of a single faith take hold, and only then because toleration seemed not so much a virtue as a necessity.[60]

The 1599 Edict of Nantes had been a breakthrough declaration, but the toleration it afforded Protestants was later nullified by that supreme egoist King Louis XIV. In England the Puritan autocrat Oliver Cromwell offered a surprising degree of toleration for Protestants and Jews (Catholics were still beyond the pale) that, while brief, was unprecedented. Another famous Puritan, John Milton, issued what was perhaps the most eloquent plea for toleration during the conflict. In *Areopagatica* (1644) he insisted that truth needs but a fair field and no favors to triumph. After the restoration of the monarchy in 1660, some clergy within the official state church, called "Latitudinarians" by their detractors, sought to identify core principles that all Protestants shared in an effort to avoid the type of sectarian revulsion that was so much in evidence during the civil wars. John Locke was friendly with a number of these churchmen, and in 1695 he published *The Reasonableness of Christianity*, a work that reduced Christian doctrine to minimal statements about Christ's saving mission and the need for repentance. But it was King James II's ill-conceived plan to allow Catholics full civil rights that finally brought Protestants of every camp together. The futility of persecution had been demonstrated repeatedly, while evidence mounted that multiple religious perspectives did not lead to the type of moral decay and intellectual anarchy that so many feared.

As the state disengaged from the quest for salvation, the enhancement of centralized power became a recognizable feature of government across Europe. The colonial rivalries, territorial ambitions, and commercial competition that intensified throughout the seventeenth century led to higher taxes, the abridgement of local and aristocratic autonomy, larger military establishments, and a proliferation of officials and bureaucratic structures. There was plenty of resistance, especially among the aristocracy. In France, the backlash occurred just as the young Louis XIV assumed the throne. Between 1649 and 1652, widespread rebellions against the centralizing project occurred, but when the competing regional powers led to a situation of near chaos, the majority of Frenchmen turned back to the monarch as the bulwark of order. Political fragmentation and localism continued to hamper rulers in Germany, Italy, and parts of Eastern Europe, but elsewhere monarchs were able to consolidate their power and curb local autonomy. In France, it was done under Louis XIV's absolutist framework, while in England centralized power took the innovative form of a post-1688 partnership between the monarch and a parliament whose membership was enlisted in the key decisions of state.

At one level the French model of absolutism and English alternative of limited monarchy under the consent of the governed seem antithetical. But both were advanced as modern and progressive by their respective defenders. Both were engines of rapid centralization and both were held up as symbols of national unity in a period of disastrous religious conflict. In 1700, the future seemed to lay with the proponents and practitioners of the absolutist paradigm, while democratic theorists like the Levellers were subject to ridicule and the sword. Still, forceful arguments, many inspired by intense religious conviction, had been made on behalf of responsible, contractual government and the principle of consent. And the language of individual rights and government accountability were being heard for the first time as writers like Locke reduced the purview of state power to the safeguarding of life, personal freedom, and property. Corporate and status group interests, so long at the center of political life across Christian Europe, were at last being challenged by individual and private ones, where government now grounded its legitimacy in the promotion and protection of subjects who, regardless of status or association, were to be treated as equals before the law. This radical conceptual transformation of the purpose of civil society made its inaugural appearance in Britain and the Netherlands, but by the end of the next century it would become a widespread and infectious phenomenon.

Chapter 4 ....

From Subject to Citizen, 1700–1815

The eighteenth century is often referred to as the Age of Enlightenment, a wide-ranging movement of reform that began in Western Europe but whose influence extended across the Atlantic to Britain's North American colonies. What united most of the major thinkers of the period, irrespective of national or social origins, was a more confident attitude toward the human condition and a belief that progress was possible through the application of human reason to a wide range of activities. Although modest-sounding enough to us, this shift in perspective must be set against an intellectual backdrop in which Europeans had always looked backward for models of the good society and where few believed that the future could be appreciably better than the past. Important breakthroughs in seventeenth-century natural philosophy, not least of which was Newton's demonstration that a deep pattern of unity and law governed an essentially mechanistic physical universe at every level, helped to amend this outlook. It was one of the signal contributions of the Enlightenment to apply this critical, scientific habit of thought to the realms of social relations, religion, economics, and perhaps most importantly, to politics. For most political thinkers of the eighteenth century, then, reason provided the standard by which human social relations and civil authority were to be justified.

The most influential voices in the Enlightenment sought to construct a science of politics freed from traditional, age-old beliefs. As part of an assault against Europe's old regime they stressed the primacy of talent over inherited status, achievement over lineage, private conscience over public command, voluntarism, or consent over the mandate of tradition. By the close of the century, two great political revolutions, first in America and subsequently in France, gave birth to two enduring modern ideologies: liberalism and conservatism. The former stood for an end to "natural" political authority in its multiple forms, capricious restrictions on human freedom, and monopolistic economic practices, while the latter descried abstract *a priori* theorizing and championed the sustaining values of custom and tradition. The French Revolution spurred Europe's monarchs into action against the spreading influence of liberal republicanism, plunging the continent into almost two decades of unrelenting military conflict. Out of the cauldron of war emerged conflicting views of the significance of the Enlightenment, but all sides were agreed that the power of ideas on common people had galvanized the revolutionary movement and forged a new political culture where legitimacy was allied with moral autonomy, with individual consent.[1]

The old regime and the *philosophes*

If seventeenth-century England, with its protracted struggle between king and parliament, its mid-century civil wars, and its end-of-century "Glorious Revolution" produced some of Europe's most significant political writing, then France must be accorded that distinction during the eighteenth century. While the *philosophes* viewed themselves as citizens of the world who shared a common intellectual heritage, the incontestable intellectual center of Enlightenment thought was Paris. The leading voices there were not of philosophers in the time-honored sense of the word. Instead of writing formal treatises or associating themselves with universities, they were men of affairs, experimenters who wrote plays, novels, pamphlets, letters, journal and encyclopedia essays, and histories. The writer and critic Denis Diderot (1713–1784) exemplified this approach, editing over the course of many years a multi-volume *Encyclopedia* that featured articles from a number of the leading *philosophes* and proved to be a key vehicle in the dissemination of enlightened thought. Through their work the *philosophes* provided a series of rallying cries on a wide range of contentious issues, believing that the reform of society, of manners and morals, would, in the end, both inform and reform politics.[2]

Just as the English worked out the implications of Lockean contract theory, the parameters of civil liberty and religious toleration for Protestants, and the relationship between London and the ruling elite of Britain's North American Empire, French writers began to investigate the claims—and the wisdom—of royal absolutism and reform from above. The reign of Louis XIV had begun with much promise, but by the close of the seventeenth century the monarch's inability to distinguish between narrow dynastic and broader national interests resulted in a series of costly and unsuccessful wars that reduced the kingdom to the verge of bankruptcy. Louis had effectively undermined the power of the independent nobility, assigning provincial administration to salaried, crown-appointed *intendants* and military commanders, and in the process the main source of potential opposition to the Crown was purged. The elaborate court at Versailles may have been the envy of European royalty, but by the turn of the eighteenth century the king had made enemies of most of his neighbors abroad and many of his subjects at home, especially members of the country's commercial and business communities. As the political aspirations of the bourgeoisie were blocked and the economy languished, calls for fundamental reform increased and plans for a new political order became more radical.[3]

Voltaire and reform from above

Perhaps the best-known of the French critics of unreconstructed monarchy was the satirist, novelist, historian, poet, and dramatist François Marie Arouet, known to his contemporaries as Voltaire (1694–1778). Having lived in England between 1726 and 1729 (after a short imprisonment in the Bastille for the crime of insulting an aristocrat), Voltaire was deeply impressed by that country's relative freedom of thought and religious practice. Notable English jurists like Sir Edward Coke (1552–1634) in the early seventeenth century and Sir William Blackstone (1723–1780) in the eighteenth attributed this to a constitutional structure that balanced the respective powers of the Crown, parliament, and the judiciary. Voltaire was also influenced by Newton's efforts to explain the behavior of physical objects in terms of general mathematical rules and by Locke's theory of learning that stressed the role of environment and experience. In his *Letters Concerning the English Nation* (1733) Voltaire introduced French readers to the benefits of religious toleration, a comparatively free press, the rule of law, and constitutional government. By the time of his residence in England, the Crown had conceded the power of the purse to the House of Commons, while the leader of the majority party in the Commons, the prime minister, worked in partnership with the monarch to set government policy. Perhaps most importantly, the Crown conceded the principle that no man could legally be taxed without the consent of his duly elected representative. This English "system," thanks in no small part to Voltaire's exposition, became the envy of a number of reform-minded Frenchman during the mid-eighteenth century.[4]

Voltaire was born late in the reign of Louis XIV, and despite his own bourgeois origins and unwavering support for religious toleration, he retained an admiration for the "Sun King" and the thesis that the government of France, if it were to be effective, must be centralized, absolute, and wise— the position adopted by Bodin and Bossuet during the previous century. Although he had written approvingly of the English House of Commons, Voltaire did not view France's provincial *parlements*, headed by the titled nobility, as in any respect analogous to the lower chamber of parliament. Nor did he think that the medieval Estates-General, which had not met since 1614, represented a viable solution to France's many problems, since it too had been dominated by self-interested nobles and clergyman, the two estates detested by Voltaire as bigoted and oppressive. Every nation had a distinctive character forged in history, and in the case of France energetic monarchy remained for Voltaire the best instrument of reform, if only it could be freed from the malevolent influence of the first two estates.[5]

Although John Locke was the philosopher who he praised most frequently, Voltaire did not accept Locke's doctrine of parliamentary sovereignty as appropriate for France given its history. Nor did he endorse the Lockean contract theory of the origins of the state. He believed instead that all governments originated through conquest, but the force that had originally shaped the dominion or one man over another could be tempered with the passage of time and under the leadership of an enlightened prince.[6] Voltaire spent long periods at the Court of Versailles during the 1740s and was appointed royal historiographer in 1745. But Louis XV showed little promise as a reformer, and for a brief period Voltaire turned to Frederick II of Prussia (r. 1740–1786) as the ruler who offered the greatest potential as an enlightened ruler. A long correspondence, initiated by Frederick while he was still crown prince in the 1730s, resulted in Voltaire relocating to the royal court at Potsdam between 1750 and 1753, but in the end the relationship soured as the king's militarism, contempt for international agreements, and failure to carry through on promised reforms demonstrated the high-risk nature of support for autocratic regimes. Still, Voltaire could not bring himself to an endorsement of republicanism. In his *Philosophical Dictionary* (1764) he observed that the reason most of the whole world is governed by monarchs "is that men very rarely deserve to govern themselves."[7] The masses, in Voltaire's view, deserved freedom to practice their religion of choice and to enjoy civil liberties, but they were not yet prepared for self-government.

Montesquieu and the balance of power

Although a wealthy French aristocrat, Charles-Louis de Secondat, baron de Montesquieu (1689–1755) had, like Voltaire, spent time in England and praised the English constitutional system for enhancing individual freedoms without sacrificing order and prosperity. Both men overlooked the fact that an oligarchy of landed and commercial elites dominated the political order through the House of Commons, but in comparative terms England did represent the aspirational ideals of the enlightened reformers. Montesquieu had first come to the attention of the reading public in 1721 with his highly successful *Persian Letters*, fictional travelers' tales that combined biting social criticism with candor and wit. But his most influential work, *Spirit of the Laws* (1748), sought to anchor its conclusions in the firm ground of empirical evidence and comparative analysis. The author spent more than a dozen years composing the work, appraising the unique customs, religion, laws, and social practices of peoples from many different cultures and conditions, classifying governments into types, and analyzing the results within the context of such factors as geography, climate, and social milieu. Acutely aware of the influence of history, law, and place on a society's capacity for change, the author's massive attempt at a general science of social phenomena, a set of universal laws informing social organization and political structure, was informed by a diffuse sense of confidence growing out of the scientific revolution, where Newtonian methodology revealed the mathematical harmony at the core of creation.[8]

In true Enlightenment fashion, Montesquieu took for granted a universe regulated by a series of laws governing the material world, spiritual beings, humans, and animals. To understand these laws or "necessary relations arising from the nature of things" one must acknowledge the existence of invariable principles of justice discoverable through reason.[9] If only positive laws were brought into alignment with eternal law, he observed, social relations would be productive and harmonious. Montesquieu analyzed all political institutions from a relativistic perspective, arguing that culture, climate, customs, and beliefs must be taken into account before one can identify the form of civil society that "best agrees with the humor and disposition of the people in whose favor it is established."[10] Republics, for example, were only workable in small states, whereas limited monarchies are appropriate in large countries like France. The tendency of monarchs to aggregate power to themselves was best prevented through a series of checks and balances, together with a separation of powers into executive, legislative, and judicial functions.

In its overarching aim to analyze the constitutional architecture best fitted to advance liberty, the *Spirit of the Laws* was an instant success, appearing in 21 editions within the first 2 years of publication.[11] Montesquieu adopted the traditional threefold classification of governments that originated with Aristotle: republican, monarchical/constitutional, and despotic. Each pure form is animated by a guiding principle. Republics are successful in geographically small city-states and require high degrees of civic virtue or public spiritedness; monarchies, which depend on rectitude and honor, are appropriate for the large states now emerging across Europe; while despotism is sustained by fear and the slavishness of the subject population. He denounced absolute monarchy for its destruction of intermediate authorities such as the nobility and called for a balance of power between the legislative, executive, and judiciary. It was one of Montesquieu's signal contributions to advance the novel idea that virtue or public spiritedness is not an essential prerequisite to well-ordered government. The same end, he claimed, might be achieved through the correct organization of the state, the right balancing of forces, always taking into account the environmental and cultural circumstances of a given people.[12]

The idea of the separation of powers, influenced no doubt by the ancient idea of the mixed constitution that informed the work of thinkers from Plato and Cicero to Aquinas and Locke, distinguished *Spirit of the Laws* as a central text of the Enlightenment. Other Enlightenment figures, including David Hume (1711–1776), Jean Jacques Rousseau (1712–1778), and Edmund Burke (1729–1797), were generous in their praise for the work.[13] At its core was a claim that would have its greatest impact in the United States, the idea that freedoms are best insured when laws are enacted by an elective legislature, implemented by a separate executive, and interpreted by an autonomous judiciary. In his warnings against the ill effects of disproportionate centralization, Montesquieu reminded his readers of the frailty of human nature whenever one person or corporate body, no matter how well-intentioned, wields singular authority in the state. But in his belief that all social phenomena could be studied objectively, and in his search for a set of scientific laws, "necessary relations which derive from the nature of things,"

Montesquieu pointed toward a central feature of Enlightenment thought, the conviction that humans might master their environment, better order their relations with one another, and assure the march of progress.

Rousseau, contract, and community

Although an original and deeply influential writer, Jean Jacques Rousseau was the eternal outsider: a troubled and aimless youth in Calvinist Geneva, a provincial rustic living amidst the sophisticated salons of Paris, the irresponsible parent whose serial relationships never translated into concern for the well-being of his offspring. He was never accepted by the French *philosophes* with whom he quarreled incessantly, and he lived most of his adult life in a state of neurotic wariness and suspicion of those around him.[14] But his confidence in human nature never wavered, and his creative study of the role of social conventions in shaping human character placed him solidly within the larger community of Enlightenment thinkers. His most important political works, *A Discourse on the Origin of Inequality* (1755) and *The Social Contract* (1762), probed the negative impact of modern civilization—including the arts and sciences—on human behavior and offered a theory of the origins and role of government that turned away from Lockean individualism and stressed instead the value of the collective action and community good.

Like Hobbes and Locke, Rousseau accepted that people in the state of nature seek first and foremost their own self-preservation. But he demurred from their estimate of the likelihood of confrontation in the pre-political state and emphasized instead the human capacity for pity and compassion. This innate restraint on selfish tendencies "is a natural feeling which, moderating in each individual the activity of love of oneself, contributes to the mutual preservation of the entire species ... in the state of nature, it takes the place of laws, morals, and virtue ...."[15] Companionship, mutual affection, collegial action, and self-respect lay at the core of "savage" society. Humans, for Rousseau, were by nature good and while living in primitive innocence engaged in none of the anti-social behaviors that were common in allegedly civilized societies. In a sweeping indictment, he claimed that human nature had been corrupted by the productive capacity of humans in society, by the arts and sciences, the institution of marriage, the falseness of organized Christianity, and, most disturbingly, by the invention of private property. "The first person who, having fenced off a plot of ground, took it into his head to say *this is mine* and found people simple enough to believe him, was the true founder of civil society. What crimes, wars, murders, what miseries and horrors would the human race have been spared by someone who, uprooting the stakes or filling in the ditch, had shouted to his fellows: Beware of listening to this imposter; you are lost if you forget that the fruits belong to all and the Earth to no one!"[16]

With Rousseau the Lockean natural right to property is firmly identified as the main source of social instability, and the existing social and political order is betrayed as nothing more than a conspiracy of the rich and power-ful against the poor and humble. Far from being a partnership of all citizens, the state "gave new fetters to the weak and new forces to the rich, destroyed natural freedom for all time, established forever the law of property and inequality, changed a clever usurpation into an irrevocable right, and for the profit of a few ambitious men henceforth subjected the whole human race to work, servitude, and misery."[17] In the words of historian Roland Stromberg, Rousseau's radical message, thanks in no small part to the power of his prose, constituted "the most electrifying social message the European world had ever received since the days of primitive Christianity."[18]

The Social Contract offered an unlikely pathway out of the unhealthy con-ditions that resulted from the false start of civilization. Whereas one might expect a call for anarchism or very limited government given the critique of civilization contained in the *Discourse*, Rousseau instead called for a new contract, not between rulers and ruled, but between free and equal members who understand the value of unity and cohesiveness, and who commit themselves to active public service in a reconceived—and markedly statist—political order. Civilization cannot be undone at this late stage, but by reconstituting the social contract in a manner that elevates and ennobles humanity, he argued that the principal qualities of the pre-political state can be realized under a collective or "general will." For Roussseau, the concept of the general will was more than the sum of atomistic individual choices, but recalled instead the pre-individualism of antiquity.[19] Modern political life distracted individuals who were encouraged to pursue the morality of private interest as the highest good at the expense of the common welfare. Rousseau admired the Spartan city-state, where an idealized simplicity, dis-cipline, and civic religion drew citizens outside of themselves to share in the authentic pleasures of communal concerns. As a practical matter he acknowledged that laws must be administered by an elected elite charged with executive powers. But lawmaking, he insisted, is the function of the sovereign people who act in popular assemblies, and the majority decisions of individuals educated into enlightened citizenship were, he believed, always in conformity with the general will. In unreservedly conforming to the general will—a public, moral collective person—we obey ourselves and affirm our sovereign freedom as individuals.

Rousseau believed the essential prerequisite to the successful operation of the general will involved the drawing down of class distinctions based on wealth and the implementation of a common system of education. In the ideal society "No citizen shall ever be rich enough to buy another, and none be poor enough to be forced to sell himself."[20] How social and economic inequalities were to be mitigated is left uncertain, but it was the call for the inculcation of common educational ideals and the transcendence of self-ish interests that led some later critics to equate the concept of the general will with indoctrination and, more harshly, with the seeds of modern total-itarianism. The state envisioned by *The Social Contract* included an office of official censor who would encourage people to act in accordance with the norms of popular morality. In addition, Rousseau called for a civil religion that all must subscribe to as the foundation of good citizenship, and those who demurred were to be dealt with severely. Unconventional behavior and the voice of the dissenter were to be disallowed on the assumption that the general will, as the source of social virtue, provides appropriate standards of conduct that everyone would assent to if they were thinking correctly, were they fully rational. Rousseau was convinced that the "mere impulse of appetite is slavery, while obedience to a law we prescribe to ourselves is liberty," but later observers detected an anti-liberal and repressive proclivity in the general will, an ungenerous refusal to acknowledge the legitimacy of minority viewpoints and the authenticity of the individual dissenter.[21]

The American contribution

The colonial revolt against British rule that took place in North America between 1776 and 1783, and the subsequent formation of a new republic, would have been of minor significance to Western history had it not been accompanied by the successful implementation of a set of political principles, born during the Enlightenment, over a wide geographical area. The few extant republics in Europe—in The Netherlands, in Geneva and the Swiss cantons, and in Northern Italy—were either city-states or small territorial entities that experienced more than their fair share of factional infighting and political instability. Montesquieu was not alone in reminding his contemporaries that republics had to be both small and homogeneous in character. One had to journey back to Rome to find precedent for a functional large republic, and even that bold experiment eventually devolved into empire and imperial autocracy.[22] The Americans sought to defy the lessons of history, to weld 13 colonies into a single large republic, balancing state autonomy with federal responsibilities, and erecting the entire structure on the foundation of responsible government and the principle of regular elections.

As historian Gordon Wood has written, the lead-up to the Revolution of 1776 was a period rich in political thought, but no single great text, or cluster of major works, emerged from the American colonies during the Enlightenment. Instead the most important contributions were made by practical men of affairs, lawyers and legislators, most of whom were deeply engaged in the struggle against perceived imperial abuses.[23] In the heat of debate they produced an extensive pamphlet literature, polemical tracts, and occasional essays that incorporated many of the new ideas at the center of Enlightenment thought. Together this literature produced a set of potent arguments on behalf of representative government, the limits of executive authority, the role of the judiciary, and the capacity of citizens to construct institutional mechanisms for the regulation of the darker elements of human nature.

Until very late in the controversy with the government of King George III (r. 1760–1820), the majority of Americans viewed themselves as proud members of the British Empire. They celebrated Britain's victories in European wars and cherished its balanced constitution. In addition to commercial privileges and the protection of the world's largest navy, Americans enjoyed freedom of speech and press, trial by jury and the right of habeas corpus, security of property, and the absence of standing armies. For more than a century colonial legislatures had passed laws without hindrance from the imperial capital, and subjects of the Crown pursued their business and personal affairs with minimum interference from London. Social stratification was most obvious in the continent's few emerging urban areas, but a titled aristocracy and an official church were nowhere to be found, and this contributed to a sense of social fluidity (for free whites) that was unimaginable in Europe. The Lockean language of rights and liberties was familiar to a wide spectrum of the colonial population, even in the face of an expanding slave system in the Southern colonies. Respect for the institution of Monarchy in general and of the British Crown in particular was sincere, but royalism was tempered by the fact that until the middle of the eighteenth century the employment of Crown authority in the colonies was intermittent and selective.[24]

Conditions changed dramatically in the aftermath of the Seven Years War, known in the colonies as the French and Indian War (1754–1763). There had been earlier conflicts involving British and French interests in North America dating back to the 1690s, but the costs associated with this final showdown were enormous. The national debt had doubled between 1754 and 1763, and when combined with the fiscal implications of administrating the new territories East of the Mississippi won from the French, the government of Prime Minister William Pitt (1759–1806) felt obliged to tighten imperial controls and increase revenues through new forms of indirect taxation. His actions were built on the argument, advanced by the great eighteenth-century jurist William Blackstone in his *Commentaries on the Laws of England* (1765–1769) that in every state there must be one acknowledged, final law-making authority. But parliament had never before attempted to by-pass the colonial legislatures, and the British claim that all members of parliament represented the whole British nation was soundly rejected by the colonists. When the revenue enhancement program began with the Stamp Act in 1765, colonial resentment and resistance was immediate and triggered a severe crisis of empire.

To British eyes the American reaction to the new tax schemes was both selfish and disloyal. The war, after all, had been fought on behalf of colonial interests, removing once and for all French and Native American aggression on the Western frontier. The colonial position, on the other hand, was informed by almost a half-century of polemical opposition literature in England. At its heart, this so-called radical Whig or Country ideology alleged a long-term and systematic effort by the Crown and its agents in parliament to undermine the balanced constitution that had been established in 1688. In particular, it was asserted that the king's ministers were employing their patronage powers to corrupt members of the House of Commons with Crown appointments, commissions, bribes, favors, and jobs. For Americans steeped in this opposition viewpoint, recent hostile decisions with respect to the North American colonies could only be explained as the product of a massive conspiracy on the part of the Crown to create servile colonial assemblies, destroy the balanced constitution, and follow the path of continental despotism. American efforts to resist this alleged conspiracy were framed in terms of preserving the balanced constitution, with defending hard-won liberties under attack both in England and now in the colonies.[25]

In a conciliatory speech delivered to the House of Commons in 1775, the Irish-born MP from Bristol, Edmund Burke, appealed to his colleagues to accept the American "fierce spirit of liberty" as an English inheritance, a proud reflection of the finest qualities of English political culture." Few in the House were prepared to accept Burke's interpretation of American motives, however, and in the end, after a protracted and expensive war, the Americans won the opportunity to create their own model of enlightened self-government.[26] What they eventually erected, after a troubled period under the Articles of Confederation (1781–1789), where the central authority was no more than a weak league of independent states, was a strong national government that derived its power from the consent of a sovereign people, and whose structure and powers were detailed in a written constitution.

An extensive republic

Prior to 1776, constitutions were normally associated with the full range of governmental powers, including laws, institutions, and even the customs that buttressed political decision making. Historic rights were also folded into the idea of the English constitution, especially the rights that were affirmed in the wake of the Revolution of 1688. The Americans took the innovative step, so common in the modern world, of crafting written constitutions that were distinct from the operations and offices of government. Thomas Paine (1737–1809), whose 1776 pamphlet *Common Sense* had done so much to vilify King George III and galvanize support for independence, wrote in 1791 that a constitution is "a thing antecedent to a government, and a government is only the creature of a constitution."[27] The practice began with the new state constitutions drawn up during the war against Britain, culminating in the national constitution drafted by a special convention in Philadelphia in 1787, and finally ratified by a majority of the states in 1789.

Supporters of the new instrument of national government were known as Federalists, and their challenge during the ratification process was twofold: to convince their opponents, the Anti-federalists, that the new enlarged republic was feasible; and to reassure skeptics that a strong central government would neither abridge the power of the states nor descend into an arbitrary and tyrannical regime. They addressed the first challenge through an innovative approach to the issue of political factions. In a series of newspaper essays gathered together in *The Federalist Papers* (1788), James Madison (1751–1836), Alexander Hamilton (1757–1804), and John Jay

(1745–1829) derided the established notion that republics could only flourish where homogeneity of interests existed. Turning this notion on its head, Madison in particular argued that every society, irrespective of size, was made up of a myriad of conflicting interests and parties. The key to preventing any single interest from dominating was to expand the size of the republic, multiply the number of interest groups, and thereby afford elected officials the opportunity to rise above the clash of party and govern in a neutral manner for the common good. Using the analogy of the multiplicity of religious sects in America, the Federalists pointed to the inability of any one religious tradition to dominate the state. According to Madison in *The Federalist*, "the security for civil rights must be the same as for religious rights. It consists in the one case in the multiplicity of interests, and in the other, in the multiplicity of sects."[28]

The second challenge was met in an equally revolutionary manner. In their dispute with Britain the colonists had opposed the sovereignty of parliament with the sovereignty of the individual colonial legislatures. Anti-federalists now contended that sovereignty would be usurped by the consolidated national government, especially in light of the Constitution's claim to be the supreme law of the land. The intellectual deadlock was broken by transferring the idea of sovereignty, absolute and supreme power, from a legislative body to the people at large who merely delegate elements of sovereignty to such bodies as they find appropriate. Some power would be accorded to state government and additional powers would be designated as appropriate for the federal government. Within both systems a further separation of legislative, executive, and judiciary power would check inordinate ambitions. With this move both state and federal authorities represented the people, and political power was always revocable by a sovereign people who no longer accepted prerogative powers in any configuration. The distinction between rulers and subjects had dissolved; a status society had given way before an equal citizenry that temporarily and conditionally granted some of its sovereign power to agents who were stewards of the public trust—and who had no right to encroach the rights and liberties that were retained.[29]

Revolutionary ideas in Western Europe

In the first of the *Federalist Papers*, Alexander Hamilton observed "that it seems to have been reserved to the people of this country, by their conduct and example, to decide the important question, whether societies of men are really capable or not, of establishing good government from reflection and choice, or whether they are forever destined to depend, for their political constitutions, on accident and force."[30] Hamilton was writing in 1788, just prior to the adoption of the new federal Constitution of the United States and one short year before the outbreak of the French Revolution. As we have seen, the American secession from the British Empire was an important precursor to the great upheaval that began in France in 1789, but the revolutionary demand for equality of rights and the sovereignty of the people had much more profound implications for old regime Europe as a whole.

Perhaps the most pronounced dissimilarity between the revolutions in America and France had to do with social structure. In America, the revolutionary movement was led by existing elites and it was they who inherited the levers of power after independence. The situation was quite different in France. There the first two semi-feudal estates of clergy and nobility enjoyed special privileges and exemptions that were denied to the wider population of 26 million people. The Catholic Church controlled education, collected tithes, censored books, and avoided most taxes. The nobility also exploited the majority, collecting manorial dues and exacting labor services, monopolizing the highest offices in Church and State, and like the clergy circumventing most taxation. Some members of the nobility supported reform and patronized the *philosophes*, but most were interested solely in preserving the socially exclusive and repressive *status quo*. The leaders of the Third Estate, on the other hand, the bankers, merchants, manufacturers, doctors, lawyers, and other professionals who enjoyed growing financial success, were left without the social prestige and access to political power monopolized by their titled superiors.

Fiscal mismanagement, an inefficient and corrupt bureaucracy, arbitrary justice compounded by the absence of a uniform system of law, and a tax system that was both unjust and badly administered put the French Crown in a precarious situation by the 1780s. Debt service alone constituted a major portion of the national budget. When King Louis XVI's (r. 1774–1792) ministers recommended that the first two Estates forego their tax exemptions, resistance was immediate and framed in terms of opposition to arbitrary government. As a final recourse, the king called a meeting of France's medieval assembly, the Estates General, in May 1789, with the expectation that under pressure all three estates would compromise to address the ballooning financial crisis. Not anticipated was the impact of Enlightenment reform thought on the bourgeoisie who took their places as the representatives of the Third Estate. Together with sympathetic aristocrats, some of whom, like the Marquis de Lafayette (1757–1834), had fought alongside the Americans in the early 1780s, the members of the Third Estate demanded constitutional change in France modeled after the American example.[31]

During the period 1789–1791, a series of sweeping constitutional changes were made in France that seemed to affirm the possibility of reform through peaceful means. The Third Estate, supported by peasant unrest in the countryside and by politicized workers in Paris, successfully brought an end to the feudal privileges of the aristocracy, while a newly formed National Assembly began work on a written constitution for the country. A "Declaration of the Rights of Man and Citizen" was drawn up by the National Assembly and approved by the king in October 1789. The document called for the liberty of the individual, careers open to talent, freedom of thought and religious toleration, equality under the law, and the sovereignty of the people. In the fall of 1791, the new constitution was finally issued. In a few short years the ancient political order of France had been transformed, remarkably, into a limited monarchy with a unicameral legislative assembly composed of members elected by a franchise open for the first time to the bourgeoisie.[32]

On the basis of the core principles set forth in the "Declaration of the Rights of Man and Citizen"—especially the alleged sovereignty of the people—none of the monarchies in Western Europe could lay claim to legitimacy. When war erupted in 1792 between revolutionary France and its neighbors, the French government declared a *levee en masse* that put the entire nation on a war footing and engaged the masses in the affairs of state for the first time. Understandably, the Revolution was interpreted by Europe's political elites as a lethal threat to existing assumptions about political leadership and social order. In their call for "liberty, equality and fraternity," France's revolutionary armies provided a level of ideological motivation for popular action comparable to Europe's earlier wars of religion.[33]

The question of natural rights

The American and French Revolutions were products of disparate forces, with colonial resentment over imperial consolidation driving the former and bourgeois demands for political empowerment compelling the latter. But there is no avoiding the influence of broader Enlightenment principles on both upheavals. The language of natural rights, contract theory, and the sovereignty of the people permeated learned treatises and popular discourse alike during the final quarter of the eighteenth century. But what, specifically, were the laws of nature in the social and moral realms? What constituted natural rights under those laws, and how did the faculty of reason arrive at them? Were "the laws of nature and nature's God" really as "self-evident" as Thomas Jefferson (1743–1826) claimed in the Declaration of Independence (1776)?

During the Enlightenment, the age-old concept of natural law applicable to all humans was increasingly identified with the language of individual natural rights that preceded and were independent of the wider community. Over the past quarter century, there has been much debate respecting the origins and development of the concept of natural rights, with some scholars claiming precedents as far back as the twelfth and thirteenth centuries, in the work of medieval canon lawyers.[34] A more traditional approach has been to emphasize the early modern roots of natural rights talk, beginning with religious dissenters, both Protestant and Catholic, who pressed for freedom in the discreet area of confessional practice. But whatever the extent of medieval influence on later developments, something more than tonality had changed by the late seventeenth century. Instead of rights as the embodiment of the community that in some sense had the right to choose its rulers and to participate at some level in the governmental process (the medieval understanding), rights and consent theory assumed a different posture.

It was Hobbes who, with his anarchic state of nature, is often seen as the first to advance the notion that individuals had inherent rights outside of civil society, especially the right to use their own power for personal protection and preservation. Under such fluid and uncertain conditions, rational individuals enter into a compact to transfer individual power to a ruler who can maintain security.[35] Locke subsequently argued famously in *Two Treatises* that certain rights pertain to individuals as human beings, including the right to life, liberty (freedom from arbitrary rule), and property (the product of one's labor).[36] For Locke, humans were rights-bearing agents, and the transition from the state of nature to civil society did not—indeed could not—negate these rights; in fact, the primary purpose of establishing the state was to better insure and protect the rights that existed prior to the formation of civil society. Consent now referred to voluntary individual acts, not the decisions of communities that informed medieval and early modern political thought. Free and equal humans in the pre-political state of nature chose civil society and imposed new rules on themselves not because they were naturally sociable in an Aristotelian and Thomistic sense, but out of rational calculation and a desire to protect both their persons and their property from harm. Most people are "no strict observers of equity and justice" according to Locke, making the enjoyment of rights in the state of nature precarious at best.[37]

Edmund Burke, natural rights, and the advent of conservatism

Many across Europe and America applauded the early stages of the French Revolution. For men like Jefferson, the American standard of responsible self-government was now being exported back to the old world. But another early defender of American resistance to the Crown was less sanguine. Although he had come to the defense of the colonists in their struggle against King George III, Edmund Burke doubted whether the newly elected French assembly could control the forces of change that it had unleashed. In his *Reflections on the Revolution in France* (1790), Burke denounced the revolutionaries for their careless rejection of national precedent and tradition. Society was a complex organism, but the revolutionaries, in "a great departure from the ancient course," have fashioned abstract blueprints for the good society, hastily implemented them without regard for a nation's unique experience, and set the stage for disaster.[38]

Burke was no reactionary opposed to reform for the sake of a capricious *status quo*; he wrote that "a state without the means of some change is without the means of its conservation"[39] and in parliament he supported Catholic emancipation, colonial rights, and value of emerging party politics. The English in 1688, and the Americans in 1776, however, had fought on behalf of time-tested custom and an existing constitutional consensus, whereas the French in 1789 had embarked on a course of total political and social reorganization, discarding all tradition for the impatient promise of abstract principles like natural rights and doctrinaire platitudes. Nothing productive and lasting could issue from such sources, for humans were flawed and complex creatures with a limited capacity to act reasonably under an *a priori* model of the good society. For Burke, there was a natural order in human affairs, but it emerged not from "constructed" notions of natural law and natural rights but instead from historical experience; rights attached to people not in a state of nature but within the texture of human needs and what he called the "partnership" of society. Government, Burke insisted, was "a contrivance of human wisdom to provide for human wants."[40]

Burke's *Reflections* had an immediate and profound impact, especially in Britain where public opinion was already beginning to turn against the French Revolution. Multiple editions appeared across the continent, with Louis XVI personally translating the work into French. But by 1793 the royal translator was dead, executed by radicals who were intent on moving France into the republican camp. For a moment Burke's prescience seemed on the mark, as the French radicals, known as Jacobins, consolidated their power and implemented a reign of domestic terror in pursuit of their "republic of virtue." But even in the face of these disturbing events Burke's *Reflections*, with its penetrating exploration of the historicity of societies, was not without its powerful critics, impatient for the dawn of the equalitarian world.

The first international revolutionary

Two years after the appearance of *Reflections on the Revolution in France*, and in the midst of a radical and destructive turn in the Revolution, the former artisan and excise officer Thomas Paine issued his polemical *Rights of Man*. An important figure in the transition to a brand of political thought that was accessible to a mass audience, Paine had left his native England for America in 1774 after the failure of his business and the break-up of his second marriage. With letters of introduction from Benjamin Franklin (1706–1790), Paine was able to rebuild his life and career in Pennsylvania, working as a printer and contributing editor for *The Pennsylvania Magazine*. Soon after his arrival in America he was engaged in the debate over colonial autonomy, and within 2 short years he had become a celebrated intellectual leader of the revolutionary movement.[41]

When *Common Sense* was published in January 1776, few in the colonies were prepared to challenge the sovereignty of King George III. The most radical proposals denied the right of parliament to legislate for the colonies directly, allowing the king to retain his title of head of the State. Paine rejected this compromise and laid America's ills directly at the doorstep of the Monarchy. With exceptional rhetorical skill, this recent immigrant made republicanism acceptable to the pamphlet's wide readership. Over 100,000 copies of *Common Sense* were sold during the first year of publication, an

enormous achievement for the time.[42] After the Declaration of Independence, Paine enlisted in the colonial army and was present at the loss of
Fort Lee to British forces in the winter of 1776. He was employed by several
wartime congressional committees and continued to write essays in support of the war effort, making him an engaged theorist whose writings,
and especially a series of tracts published between 1776 and 1783 known
as *The Crisis*, communicate the type of authenticity associated with lived
experience.[43]

Paine remained in America after independence, retiring to a house in
New Rochelle, New York, that had been confiscated from a British loyal-
ist. But his radical egalitarianism, perhaps a product of his humble roots
and resentment of social elites, earned him the enmity of many conservative gentry within the new national government. In 1787, he returned
to England in hopes of pursuing some commercial interests, and it was
there that he first met Edmund Burke. When the French Revolution began
Paine traveled to Paris in hopes of offering his services to the reformers in
the National Assembly. He wrote to George Washington (1732–1799) that
"A share in two revolutions is living to some purpose."[44] While in France
he learned of Burke's intention to attack the Revolution in print, and he
vowed to answer the critique. The publication of *Reflections on the Revolution in France* in November 1791 touched off a robust pamphlet war and
contributed to the growth of reform societies in London. Paine's *Rights of
Man* was the most popular rejoinder to Burke, with sales exceeding 100,000
copies during the first 2 years. Fearing social disorder, the British government attempted to suppress the book and prosecuted Paine for libel. He
departed for France before his conviction and was received as a hero by
the revolutionary leadership. Although he supported the abolition of the
French monarchy, he spoke in favor of sparing the king's life, a position
that earned him the enmity of the radical Jacobins in the French National
Assembly.

In addition to his powerful indictment of the institution of Monarchy in
Common Sense, Paine advanced the claim that humankind's natural sociability would eliminate all need for intrusive government, which "even in
its best state is but a necessary evil."[45] Returning to this theme in the
Rights of Man (1791–1792), he connected the progress of civilization with
the dwindling of government action in the lives of ordinary citizens and
the enhancement of social cooperation over wider spheres of human activity. For Paine "A greater part of that order which reigns among mankind
is not the effect of government. It had its origin in the principles of society and the natural constitution of man."[46] The author's hopes for limited
government in France were dashed, however, as Jacobin radicals under the
leadership of Maximillian Robspierre (1758–1794) vilified their enemies and
forced their countrymen to embrace the will of the nation as the embodiment of their better selves. A semblance of order was only restored in 1795
under an authoritarian government with Napoleon Bonaparte (1769–1821)
as First Consul in 1799 and, after 1804, as emperor. But before the revolution

came full circle with the establishment of the imperial office, Paine chose to return to the United States, where he lived his final 6 years in relative obscurity.

By adopting the view that human sociability in a revolutionary age will make government redundant, Paine captured the essence of the radical Enlightenment. The future security and prosperity of people were tied to the growth of trade and commerce, what Paine took to be Laws of Nature with respect to economic exchange. "The landholder, the farmer, the manufacturer, the merchant, the tradesman, and every occupation prospers by the aid which each receives from the other, and from the whole."[47] As these mutual connections mature, the absurdity of power based on hereditary title and the accident of birth propels those engaged in trade and commerce to throw off the shackles of inequality. "The more perfect civilization is, the less occasion has it for government, because the more does it regulate its own affairs and govern itself."[48] An essential first step in that process is the dismantling of hereditary government, "an assumption of power for the aggrandizement of itself," to the adoption of the republican model, "a delegation of power for the benefit of society" where taxes are minimal, personal freedoms are extensive, and commerce uninhibited by arbitrary regulations. A representative system offered the best expression of the popular will in a large republic, but even representatives were at times liable to violate their trust. As a remedy Paine took the astonishing step to end the property-based franchise and embraced universal manhood suffrage. Only then could a representative system claim to be "parallel with the order and immutable laws of nature, and meet[s] the reason of man in every part."[49]

The utilitarian turn

Going even further than Paine in his prescription for the ills afflicting monarchical Europe was the utopian anarchist William Godwin (1756–1836). His *An Enquiry Concerning Political Justice* (1793) called for the replacement of conventional governments with small, self-subsisting communities where individual freedom, guided by reason, would be strengthened and emancipated. "Monarchy and aristocracy would be no evils," he wrote, "if their tendency were not to undermine the virtues and the understandings of their subjects." For Godwin, the promise of the Enlightenment was that reasonable actors would pursue their individual interests in a manner that would contribute to the collective good of the whole. There was no place for the heavy hand of paternalist Monarchy, or indeed any formal institutions of government, in such a vision of social organization.[50]

Godwin's philosophical anarchism attracted few admirers, but his argument that the general good naturally emerged out of the individual's enlightened self-interest reflected a powerful strain within late eighteenth-century thought. As we have seen, the majority position within Enlightenment political thinking tirelessly underscored the doctrine of inalienable rights, Laws of Nature, and the power of reason to discover universal truths. But residual doubts about these broad abstractions, especially in light of the failure to reach consensus respecting their "self-evident" meaning, contributed to the emergence of another, more plain-spoken approach to human motivation, the definition of the good society, and the origin and purpose of government. Not everyone agreed about respecting the reasonableness of republics, for example, or the irrationality of hereditary nobility. But consensus might be reached at a less abstract level. Jefferson's reference to the pursuit of happiness in the Declaration of Independence was written from the standpoint of the natural rights school, but the reference could as easily be associated with simple, elemental human desires like the search for pleasure and the evasion of its opposite.

A number of ancient Greek philosophers, including Aristotle, had written that the ultimate good is happiness, but they discussed this state with reference to the gratification of the rational soul, the desires a perfect man would have. Few eighteenth-century rationalists would have disapproved of actions which led to general happiness, but the consensus still centered on the existence of natural laws. The Scottish philosopher David Hume initially embraced the proposal that a "science" of politics could be constructed through the careful use of reason, but his investigations into the emotive side of human behavior led him to conclude that political phenomena were not akin to laws of mathematics. Scientific knowledge even of the natural world consisted only of conjecture as to laws based on observed regularities, but the causes of such regularities remain unknowable. Similarly government cannot be viewed as a mechanism for preserving natural law since neither reason (which is passive) nor God (whose existence is not demonstrable) can provide us with the unambiguous content of an alleged natural order or natural law. Instead the function of government, whatever its configuration, exists to uphold agreed social institutions (peace, civility, property, legality) that are felt to be just, a widespread "sentiment of approbation."[51]

Hume found no compelling sanction for government in divine right theory, hereditary claims, or, most damaging of all, in Lockean social contract theory and the assumption of tacit consent. In his final essay, "Of the Origin of Government," Hume observed that the comparison of regimes always involved consideration of relative merits instead of reference to any "fixed unalterable standard in the nature of things."[52] He reasserted that government was the practical issue of felt human needs, typically the product of force and violence at the outset but subsequently accepted as advantageous in an increasingly complex social setting. In other words, we obey government because it is useful to us; when it becomes oppressive we may employ the language of abstract natural rights to justify acts of resistance, but in reality we cannot agree what these rights are and instead fight back because the state has lost its utility for us.

Joseph Priestley's (1733–1804) *An Essay on the First Principles of Government* (1768) made a similar argument and called for a limited government whose success is measured by its effectiveness in securing the welfare of individuals. Priestley held that human progress demanded the maximum level of freedoms in the areas of speech, religious practice, and education, and that government was to be evaluated on its ability to forward these objectives. In France, the timeless and universal interplay between pleasure and pain became the organizing principle of human motivation for Claude-Adrien Helvetius (1715–1771) in his controversial *De l'esprit* (1759). Like the majority of the *philosophes*, Helvetius was a thoroughgoing rationalist who embraced a hedonistic ethic that equated the good with pleasure. Government, he contended, should leave men alone to pursue their individual interests. If those interests harmed others, then the state was responsible for society's redress. But even here the principle of utility dictated that steps be taken to insure the maximum benefit to society. The just ruler blends "the light of knowledge with the greatness of soul. Whoever assembles within himself these different gifts of nature, always directs his course by the compass of the public utility." Nascent utilitarianism even informed thinking about the causes and treatment of criminal behavior. The Italian Cesare Beccaria's (1738–1794) *On Crimes and Punishments* (1764) challenged the traditional view of incarceration as simple retribution and instead called for the establishment of prisons that stressed remediation and training, with the goal of reintegrating the offender into the mainstream of society. "If we open our histories," he alleged, "we shall see that laws which are, or should be, pacts between free men, have for the most part been only the instruments of the passions of the few . . . ." Opposed to both torture and capital punishment, Becarria detailed the economic and social roots of criminal behavior and counseled legal reform measures that would promote the greatest happiness for the greatest number.[53]

Back in England, the legal theorist Jeremy Bentham (1748–1832) was strongly influenced by the work of both Priestley and Helvetius. Like David Hume, Bentham dismissed talk of abstract natural law as beyond rational demonstration and instead emphasized the function of the man-made law in advancing concrete individual freedoms. In the initial stages of the French Revolution, Bentham sent to Paris a host of practical reform plans, not least of which included a blueprint for a penal system based on deterrence rather than punishment. The effectiveness of government, he was convinced, should be measured solely in terms of its ability to advance the happiness of the whole. He insisted that "Nature has placed mankind under the governance of two sovereign masters, pain and pleasure. It is for them alone to point out what we ought to do, as well as to determine what we shall do." None of Bentham's ideas was taken up by the revolutionary government, but through his friendships with a number of leading figures he was made an honorary citizen of France in 1792.[54] His influence over the next generation, and in particular his disciple James Mill (1773–1836) and his son John Stuart Mill (1806–1873), was enormous, with the major impact of utilitarian thought coming in the nineteenth century.

Adam Smith and the minimal state

The advent of responsible, limited government whose main charge is the protection of property and individual freedoms had implications for spheres of activity beyond the organization and demployment of state power. A new view of economic activity, first expressed by a group of French thinkers known as Physiocrats, emerged alongside liberal theories of the State. Physiocracy meant the "rule of nature" and its exponents, led by Francois Quesnay (1694–1774), personal physician to Louis XV, were convinced that a universal law of economic relations, centering on rational self-interest and the free play of supply and demand, was as certain as Newtonian laws of physics.[55] The Scottish moral philosopher Adam Smith (1723–1790) put forward the classical expression of this position in *An Inquiry into the Nature and Causes of the Wealth of Nations* (1776). For Smith the old mercantilist system of government protection, regulation, and restriction had been predicated on the assumption that international trade was a zero-sum game, that the world's aggregate wealth was finite, and that a key function of the state was to secure the largest possible portion of the world's fixed assets by regulating economic activities at home and employing military power to extend economic interests abroad.[56]

In place of this inherently combative paradigm, Smith wrote that politicians and civil servants should recognize and respect the self-regulating natural laws of economic activity by ending all tariffs, monopolies, and price fixing. They should also accept that the world's wealth was limited only by the entrepreneurial acumen of free citizens. In the midst of unhindered economic transactions, men will pursue their individual interests and are "led by an invisible hand to promote an end which was no part of his intention." That end was the enhanced material well-being of every citizen. Since the business person cannot serve himself without serving others, selfishness and benevolence are harmoniously joined under a natural regulatory law over which no human legislation must interfere. "Every man, so long as he does not violate the laws of justice," should be free to pursue his own material interest in his own manner. For Smith there were three core functions of the state: protecting society from outside aggressors; protecting every citizen from injustices perpetrated by fellow citizens; and building and maintaining public functions and institutions that are essential to the implementation of the first two responsibilities.[57] It had no business interfering with natural laws of supply and demand.

The limits of enlightenment

The rhetoric of the Enlightenment may have been inclusive, but none of the *philosophes* took seriously the claims of women to be included in the political life of kingdoms and republics. "If men are born free," queried the Englishwoman Mary Astell (1666–1731) in 1706, "how is it that all women are born slaves?"[58] Throughout the eighteenth century, male and female authors explored what became known as the "woman question," analyzing the origins of sexual inequality in a variety of works that were mainly concerned with other topics.[59] Still, the historic domination of the male householder remained unimpeachable during the eighteenth century. Married women had few property rights, and legal recourse for acts of domestic abuse was severely limited. Academies and universities excluded women, thus any formal education that took place was provided in the home.

A few male writers began to interrogate some of these age-old assumptions. Locke, for example, questioned the biblical grounds for the ascendancy of the father, but this was very much a minor issue in *Two Treatises* and none of those who later celebrated his achievement took any interest in the digression. Montesquieu was suspicious of the claim that there were permanent intellectual differences between the sexes and supported the right of divorce. And Thomas Paine, writing in the *Pennsylvania Magazine*, wrote that society "instead of alleviating [women's] condition, is to them the source of new miseries."[60] But most of the *philosophes* ignored the cultural argument and affirmed male privilege and domination as a law of nature. The German philosopher Immanuel Kant (1724–1804) thought that education for women would prove too strenuous, while Rousseau, the most retrograde of the Enlightenment figures in this regard, belittled women as natural inferiors and admonished them to stick to childbearing and child-rearing duties. In his best-known didactic works, *Julie; or, The New Heloise* (1761) and *Emile; or, Education* (1762), he drove home the thesis that women's education should be in preparation to serve men in the domestic setting.

Despite the weight of such prejudice and the abundance of literature in favor of sexual hierarchies, there were two examples of female political leadership that called into question the anti-feminist certitudes. The reigns of Maria Theresa in Austria (r. 1740–1780) and Catherine the Great in Russia (r. 1762–1796) demonstrated the capacity of female monarchs to navigate the dangerous waters of political intrigue in male-dominated courts. A few aristocratic women managed to play a pivotal role in discussions about social reform while others, largely from the middle class, published works of social criticism that pointed up the hypocrisy of natural rights rhetoric. In France—a country that excluded women from succeeding to the throne—a number of aristocratic and bourgeois patronesses facilitated the republic of letters by hosting private salons in their homes, where critiques of current institutions and cultural values were commonplace. In the setting of the salon, class and gender distinctions were blurred, as talented male commoners intermingled with affluent female patrons. Occasionally even establishment insiders participated. For example, Madame de Pompadour (1721–1764), the mistress of Louis XV, played a key role in deflecting some of the harsh official criticism of the multi-author *Encyclopedia* project. And Emilie du Chatelet (1706–1749), the mistress of Voltaire, was keenly interested in the new science and published a highly respected translation of Newton's *Principia*. Salons were most widespread in Paris, but London, Berlin, Vienna, and Warsaw also featured gathering places organized by influential women.[61] While these patronesses did not specifically challenge the inequality of the sexes, their activities stood as a powerful refutation of the nature argument and raised the issue of gender as a social construction.

During the early stages of the French Revolution, women spoke out directly about their enforced disabilities. The anonymous *Petition of Women of the Third Estate to the King* (1789) demanded that the monarch address women's lack of access to education, profitable employment in the trades, and vulnerability in the marriage market. Asking "to be enlightened, to have work, not in order to usurp man's authority, but in order to be better esteemed by them..." the pamphlet triggered a large outpouring of printed petitions and grievances authored by women and calling for protection of female-dominated trades and even representation in the Estates General.[62] Direct action was also a feature of this call for political empowerment. Responding to food shortages and price hikes in the capital, in October 1789 some 6000 women, accompanied by members of the National Guard, marched to Versailles and obliged the king to return to Paris and address the crisis. Soon after this event, another anonymous pamphlet was addressed to the National Assembly, excoriating its members for having "decreed that the path to dignities and honors should be open without prejudice to all talents; yet you continue to throw up insurmountable barriers to our own."[63] The petition went unheeded; in December of 1789 the National Assembly determined that women would be "passive citizens" who, like propertyless males, were ineligible to participate in the electoral process.

Over the course of the next year, as the Constituent Assembly began work on a new constitution for the country, two powerful appeals on behalf of citizenship rights for women were published. The first, *Plea for the Citizenship of Women* (1790) was authored by the Marquis de Condercet (1743–1794), one of the few *philosophes* to participate in revolutionary politics. He bravely defined natural rights in gender inclusive terms, arguing that "Either no individual of the human race has genuine rights, or else all have the same; and he who votes against the right of another, whatever the religion, color, or sex of that other, has henceforth abjured his own."[64] The second text was issued by Olympe de Gouges (1748–1793), the daughter of a provincial butcher. Her *Declaration of the Rights of Woman and Citizen* (1791) was a frontal assault on the better-known document of 1789. Demanding equality before the law and in property relations, de Gouges brought to the public square the aspirations of laboring women across France. They "should be equally admissible to all public offices, places, and employments, according to their capacities and with no distinctions other than those of their virtues and talents."[65] She thought that Louis XVI and Queen Marie Antoinette (1744–1792) could be converted to the cause, but when the Constitution of 1791 was promulgated it invoked the principle of public utility to deny women the right to active citizenship. Both Condorcet and de Gouges fell victim to the Jacobin terror: Condorcet voted against the king's execution and died in prison in 1794 while de Gouges, having turned her pen against the radical leader Maximilien Robespierre (1758–1794), was arrested,tried for sedition, and executed in 1793.

The cosmopolitan moment

Just as admiration for early eighteenth-century British constitutionalism contributed to the Anglophilia of *philosophes* like Montesquieu and Voltaire, so too the democratic implications of the French Revolution engendered a strong wave of Francophilia in late eighteenth-century Britain and the United States. And women writers played a significant, if only lately discovered, role in this phenomenon, transforming admiration for events in France with a wider commitment to revolutionary cosmopolitanism based on universal human rights. In 1790, Helen Maria Williams (1761–1827) expressed the hopes of many British reformers when she wrote from Paris that the Revolution "was a triumph of humankind; it was man asserting the noblest privileges of his nature; and it required but the common feelings of humanity to become in that moment a citizen of the world."[66] The claim of intellectual kinship with revolutionaries in France was all the more remarkable in light of the historic antipathy between Europe's two major powers. Britain and France were at war repeatedly throughout the eighteenth century, over the territorial ambitions of Louis XIV, over colonial possessions and maritime prerogatives, and finally over the spread of revolutionary principles.

Enlightenment cosmopolitanism received its earliest formulation in Montesquieu's *Persian Letters* (1721) in which provincial national prejudices are exposed by Muslim visitors to France. In *The Citizen of the World* (1760–1762) Oliver Goldsmith (1730–1774) used a fictional Chinese visitor to England to examine, among other topics, the relationship between law and freedom in a constitutional monarchy. The cosmopolitan ideal won its most prestigious endorsement from the philosopher Immanuel Kant, whose 1795 pamphlet, *Toward Perpetual Peace*, called for an association of states that would embrace a legal system dedicated to the protection of universal rights. Like Hobbes, Kant accepted that the state of nature "is not a state of peace among human beings who live next to one another but a state of war" and that a state of peace "must be established." The goal, he insisted, was best achieved under a republican form of government, where citizens "would consider very carefully whether to enter into such a terrible game, since they would have to resolve to bring the hardships of war upon themselves."[67]

Embracing pacifism over militarism, secular over religious perspectives, and universal over gender-specific rights of citizenship, Mary Wollstonecraft (1759–1797) was the best-known of the British female cosmopolitans of the 1790s. Her *Vindication of the Rights of Woman* (1792) conceded the frivolity and narcissism of aristocratic women was a social ill that was not to be remedied and directed her appeal to members of the emerging middle class. In what one recent author has described as "the intellectual manifesto of western feminism," Wollstonecraft affirmed that the purported intellectual inferiority of women was the direct result of unequal education and unhealthy social values.[68] Afford women the same educational and career opportunities as men, and the tone and substance of both domestic and public life will be enhanced. Wives would become partners, tyranny in all of its manifestations would be destroyed, and the betterment of humanity assured. Reserving some of her harshest criticism for Rousseau, whose attitudes exemplified the worst of the disparaging stereotypes, Wollstonecraft was nonetheless careful to frame her call for reform within the context of strengthening the nuclear family.[69]

Although the *Vindication* underlines the public utility of educating women, Wollstonecraft never overtly championed the aspirations of the working poor, and never mentioned the protests of working women in Paris that played such a large role in bringing down the Monarchy. As one prominent scholar has observed, Wollstonecraft "was no democrat and watched with trepidation the increasing pressure exercised by the Paris sections over the politicians."[70] Her call for women to emerge as rational and independent beings, "whose sense of worthiness came not from the looking glass but from their inner perception of their self-control,"[71] was ridiculed by a wide array of counter-revolutionary and Francophobe contemporaries. The *Memoirs* of her life published by her husband William Godwin, with their revelations of her affairs and suicide attempts, served up additional fodder for hostile conservative writers.

A modern agenda

Out of the Enlightenment's search for a definitive science of politics and the experience of revolution in America and France, the West's first modern ideology, classical liberalism, established itself in the political discourse of the nineteenth century. The new ideology jettisoned the status society, attacked the closed "mercantilist" economy, disputed age-old religious sanctions, and undercut metaphysical explanations of the origin and function of government. In place of these guideposts—allegedly born of privilege and prejudice—liberals asserted individual "negative rights" against the state, including the right to association without reprisal, economic autonomy, and intellectual freedom in speech and print. Liberals embraced a secular and rational outlook, although their rationalism was combined with a dramatic leap of faith concerning God's purposes for humankind. That faith allowed them to assert a belief in natural rather than prescriptive divine laws, a simple trust that society functioned best, and material progress was realized, when individuals were allowed to compete and pursue their social and economic interactions in an unhindered fashion. Classical liberalism demanded responsible government by elected officials, written constitutions and judicial review, careers open to talent and social mobility, and religious affiliation based on personal choice, not state fiat. Lastly, liberals sought to balance the maximization of personal freedom with regard for security against the potential predations of their neighbors. The minimal state, in the end, was to function as an impartial arbiter in the affairs of this world, allowing the natural laws of social and economic interaction to operate as effectively as possible.

These were ambitious goals, and as we have seen they were not extended to women or to propertyless males. Most of the liberal thinkers of the Enlightenment were champions mainly of the literate, property-owning middle class, the class that they were from. They had little trust in the political acumen of the majority, fearing mob rule and the redistribution of wealth should the poor gain the franchise. Their plans for the amelioration of society faced strong opposition, and not just from irredentist monarchs and inflexible aristocrats, but more importantly from exponents of a second, and equally influential, modern ideology: conservatism.

Born in the wake of the French Revolution and the excesses of the Jacobin terror, conservatism was more than a panicked backlash ideology of traditional status elites. Its proponents claimed that their analysis was shaped by a deep sense of moral order in history, by an understanding of human nature informed by experience. When the former revolutionary and second President of the United States, John Adams (1756–1826), referred to classical liberalism as "the science of idiocy . . . taught at the school of folly," his harsh language was aimed squarely at his own generation's penchant for abstract theorizing.[72] For political figures like Edmund Burke and John Adams, the overemphasis of individualism undercut critical social units like the family, the local church, the immediate community. It invariably dislodged public-regarding actions and instead privileged narrow self-interest. Most perniciously, it mistook rights as agreed universals instead of distinctive products of a particular history and set of customs.

Conservatives allowed a role for rational discourse, but insisted that societies were akin to organic entities, and that habits, customs, and even prejudices were important variables in the fabric of healthy civil society. Reason and idealism were no substitute for experience and wisdom in the work of governance, just as the singular pursuit of personal happiness in a market environment could not compare with the intangible rewards of relationships that are enjoyed for their own sake. By the time the armies of Napoleon Bonaparte had been defeated in 1815, the conservative worldview had been vindicated, at least momentarily. But as the new century began, Europe's restored monarchs sat uneasily on thrones that had been contested in fundamental ways by a liberal vision that was not easily extinguished. The nineteenth century would see the broad extension of that vision, with the issue of equality taking on more ominous tones for classical liberals and conservatives alike. As a new revolution in industry took its hold across Western Europe, the propertyless began to call the question on the rhetoric of Enlightenment equalitarianism.

Chapter 5 ....

Ideology and Equality, 1815–1914

The nineteenth century gave birth to our modern political vocabulary, our association of politics with institutionalized bargaining for power, and our embrace of written constitutions, parliaments, electioneering, and a popular press. The great political "isms" of the modern era—liberalism, conservatism, socialism, communism, and nationalism—all took root between the French Revolution and World War I, as millions of men won the right to vote. Indeed most of the governments that plunged Europe into the cataclysm of global war in 1914 had been popularly elected on the basis of a franchise that afforded the ballot to all adult males.[1] Monarchy remained an important fixture of national political life in 1914, but major constitutional changes effected during the course of the century brought the representative principle to the foreground. Democracy, which had been the object of much opprobrium in 1789, was welcomed and celebrated by most politicians and pundits alike in 1914. Even hereditary heads of state were careful to brandish their credentials as stewards of democratic, and not just dynastic, interests.

By 1900, political thought and practice had moved well beyond the Enlightenment vision of the state as defender against foreign aggressors, neutral arbiter between free individuals, and enforcer of agreed contracts. Both elected and hereditary rulers now acknowledged political power as a delegated trust and moved to employ state resources for the advancement of the collective well-being of citizens irrespective of social class and economic circumstance. The vastly enhanced power of the state thus paralleled the march of citizen democracy. It was a momentous change in the political culture of the West over a very short period of time, and as the drive toward popular rule and the activist state proceeded, most political thinkers embraced and advanced the new age of mass politics and emerging nationalism. There were others, however, who voiced deep concern over the ability and willingness of citizens to assume the responsibilities of self-government, calling instead for dynamic authoritarian rule in a world of competitive nation-states. It was this latter perspective that would successfully contest the liberal democratic paradigm in the aftermath of World War I.

Material transformation

The historic move toward a more responsible and inclusive politics—and the acceptance of state intervention in social and economic activities—can be traced to the continuing influence of revolutionary ideals and to sweeping changes in the fabric of material life. Europe's population more than doubled in the nineteenth century, from approximately 200 million in 1800 to 460 million in 1900. And this figure does not include the almost 40 million who departed the land of their birth for the promise of better opportunities on other continents. Parallel with the population boom was an unprecedented shift in labor patterns. In 1800, most Europeans lived in rural villages and worked under conditions that would have been familiar to their great-grandparents. Human intersections with the natural world and work patterns were shaped by the seasons, the weather, and the soil. Subsistence farming, or at most production for a local market, still accounted for the bulk of each person's economic activity. One century later the majority of men and women lived in places and under conditions that were markedly different. As the social landscape was transformed by the rise of a new middle class or bourgeoisie, the continent's economic underpinnings were increasingly defined by the growth of commercial enterprise, long-distance trade, and industrial manufacture.[2]

Beginning first in Britain in the 1760s, industrialization spread to the German states, Northern Italy, Belgium, and France by the mid-point of the nineteenth century, accelerating dramatically after German unification in 1871. By the latter date the industrial middle class, including new white-collar professionals in affiliated fields like banking, insurance, law, and property development, had secured the vote and were playing an increasing role in political life at the national level. They carried forward the Enlightenment banner of equality of opportunity, uniform justice, the sanctity of contract, and property ownership, but as a class they vigorously opposed voting rights for the workingman and disparaged most state intervention in the private sector as a new form of despotism, inimical to meritocracy and the enemy of both personal freedom and the principle of a fair field and no favors.

For the hundreds of thousands of rural laborers who flocked to Europe's urban centers and mill towns in search of a better standard of living, the Industrial Revolution offered some initial promise. Economic output doubled from 1800 to 1900, and the results were palpable for everyone. Large-scale manufacturing enterprises proliferated, rail and ocean-going transportation networks facilitated the movement of goods and people around the globe, and telegraph and telephone communications shrunk distances between individuals, businesses, and governments. Near the close of the century, state provision for public education at the elementary and secondary levels put an end to illiteracy in Western Europe, and this in turn contributed to the birth of the newspaper-reading public. Not surprisingly, the popular press was filled with stories chronicling the imperial exploits of national armies, adventurers, and Christian missionaries. On the domestic front, Europeans benefited from the relative absence of military conflict and enjoyed the advantage of longer and healthier lives, thanks to remarkable advances in medical science.[3]

But even with these unprecedented changes, the vast majority of common people continued to live under very difficult conditions. Rural life remained arduous and oppressive, with landowners exacting rents that took no account of forces other than market demand. Some progress occurred after a wave of continent-wide revolutions in 1848, when the remnants of serfdom were swept away across central Europe. But rural poverty remained a distressing constant in the midst of industrial plenty. Even greater levels of misery and degradation were to be found in the bourgeoning cities, where working conditions in the giant factories, and housing in the overcrowded industrial slums, rarely fulfilled workers' hopes for a better life. This new urban social reality fueled the creation of the modern working class. In the second half of the century, the propertyless workers who were entirely dependent upon wage labor for their survival began to claim a political voice and petitioned the state for action on a wide range of social and economic concerns.

The accelerating demand for working-class political empowerment and economic justice also galvanized efforts to extend political rights and professional opportunities at the national level to women. Like the movement for universal manhood suffrage, feminism traced its roots to the eighteenth-century Enlightenment. But the middle-class feminists of the industrial age, most of whom resented the cult of domesticity that denied them any public role outside the home, were prepared to take direct political action to advance their vision of gender equality. They called for universities and the professions to end their male-only admissions policies, and they insisted on equal property rights and economic independence for married women. While the franchise at the local level was conceded in most states, prior to World War I the right to vote at the national level had been achieved only in Finland (1906) and Norway (1907).

Parallel with the emergence of working class and female political consciousness and the gradual extension of the franchise to propertyless males, a new, more spontaneous and more foreboding theory of nationalism emerged across industrial Europe. Initially associated with the enlightened self-determination of peoples during the era of the American and French Revolutions, late nineteenth-century nationalism took on a more chauvinistic tone as its supporters infused the idea of the nation-state with imperialist and Social Darwinian language. Political leaders both on the left and the right increasingly appealed to ethnic, racial, and linguistic identities as a mechanism to advance colonialism or to highlight the inequalities of peoples around the globe. Europe's imperial advances into large sections of the habitable earth, made possible through industrial supremacy, provided fodder for jingoistic journalism and distracted the working class from myriad domestic discontents. Stories of imperial destiny offered the poor and dispossessed a muscular narrative of national power and cultural superiority that would carry forward to the outbreak of World War I. On the eve of that disaster, the cosmopolitan spirit of Enlightenment rationalism was back on the defensive, and its fate would remain in the balance throughout the bloody crucible of the twentieth century.

Conservatism and liberalism

The egalitarianism at the heart of the American and French Revolutions continued to shape much of the political theory and practice of the nineteenth century. Age-old inequities based on birth and inheritance, social hierarchies built around freedom from physical labor, and political authority paired with dynastic and noble privilege—each of these practices had been dealt significant blows during the revolutionary years. The meteoric ascent of Napoleon Bonaparte, a commoner from the island of Corsica, was due in part to the principle of meritocracy at the core of the French Revolution. Even after consolidating power and crowning himself Emperor of the French in 1804, Bonaparte called for plebiscites to ratify the core elements of his domestic reform agenda, thus allowing him to maintain the fiction of rule by popular will. Many of the reforms, including the ouster of parasitic ruling families, the abolition of serfdom, equality before the law, careers open to talent, and religious toleration, were extended across Europe by victorious French armies between 1804 and 1810. One final, and inadvertent, export product—nationalist sentiment—ultimately served as a catalyst to the collapse of the Napoleonic regime and a reaction against the entire Enlightenment project.[4]

When Napoleon was defeated in June 1815 at Waterloo, Europe's military and aristocratic elite sought to quash the revolutionary impulse once for all and reclaim their leadership prerogatives. At an extended international congress in Vienna in 1814–1815, delegates from Britain, France, Russia, Prussia, and Austria-Hungary declared for the rights of dynastic families, not peoples, and redrew the borders of European states in pursuit of a balance of power that would prevent future international upheaval. Popular revolts were quashed in Southern Italy in 1821, in Spain in 1823, in Russia in 1825, and in Poland in 1830. Convinced of the superiority of dynastic over national states, and of personal allegiance over abstract nationalism, Europe's traditional leaders regarded the revolutionary principles of liberty, equality, and fraternity as a mortal danger to the future well-being of the continent. Constitutional republics, or states ruled by the people themselves through elected representatives and written constitutions, were associated reflexively with mob rule, despoliation of property, the overturning of public morality, and Jacobin terror tactics.[5] For these men, a quarter century of war, revolutionary terror, and Napoleonic dictatorship had demonstrated the intrinsic malevolence of efforts to supplant the status society.

The conservative case

Conservative political thinkers invariably looked back to Burke's *Reflections on the Revolution* for inspiration and direction. In the aftermath of the French Revolution and the Napoleonic wars, they pointed to Burke's contention that social engineering and constitution-making based on abstract principle always led, in the end, to bloodshed and disaster. One of the most influential, if controversial, voices of mid-century conservative thought was the Scottish-born essayist and social critic Thomas Carlyle (1795–1881). Much admired by the American transcendentalists for his rejection of materialism and *laissez-faire* economics, Carlyle early on in his career attacked universal suffrage. He worried that with democratic and popular governments, the guiding and regulatory role of the state would atrophy, leaving masses of newly enfranchised citizens directed exclusively by corrosive wealth-seeking under the guise of the pursuit of happiness. The modern equivalent of Hell, Carlyle averred, had become "The terror of not succeeding; of not making money, fame, or some other figure in the world . . . ."[6]

Claiming that skilled political leadership was just as much a fundamental natural right as the right to property or to equality before the law, Carlyle argued that the regulation of human conduct in accordance with the principles of natural law demanded that leadership roles be reserved for trained and inspired elites. In contentious works like *Sartor Resartus* (1838), *Chartism* (1840), *On Heroes, Hero Worship, and the Heroic in History*, (1841), and *Past and Present* (1843), Carlyle emphasized the salutary dimensions of heroic and paternalistic leadership, especially in an era of industrialism, urbanism, and economic disorder. For Carlyle, the dehumanization of society that was associated with rapid material change was not to be addressed through the political empowerment of masses preternaturally disposed to make bad decisions. Only under the guidance of the ablest men, the few who could harness the energies of the common people and channel those energies into communal and morally integral ends, would social progress be assured. He insisted that "the history of what man has accomplished in this world, is at bottom the history of the great men who have worked here."[7] Truth, he believed, was not to be found in the votes of the majority but instead under the guidance of the autocratic hero.

Similar concerns were expressed by the French nobleman Alexis de Tocqueville (1805–1859). Author of the enormously influential *Democracy in America* (1835, 1840), de Tocqueville held that conservatism's rearguard action against Enlightenment rationalism was futile: egalitarianism and political democracy were inevitable in the West. But rather than bemoan this future, he interrogated the conservative claim that the democratic imperative was the natural precursor of despotism. Gathering evidence from his travels in the United States (ostensibly to study the prison system), de Tocqueville found no basis to the allegation that popular, representative government invariably degenerated into anarchic mob rule, the destruction of property, and disrespect for principled leadership. In Andrew Jackson's America he found that private property was respected, traditional religious forms prospered, and political power at the local, state, and federal levels was exercised in a responsible manner. He further observed that the extension of the franchise and opportunities for social mobility actually strengthened allegiance to the established order and deepened patriotic sentiment. Engaged citizens were, by and large, loyal to the political *status quo*.[8]

But this perceptive early sociologist also detected some less sanguine trends in democratic culture that validated the reservations of Europe's traditional conservative elite. If the people are truly sovereign, de Tocqueville asked, what counterweight exists to curb the collective power of the majority? "The majority exercise a prodigious actual authority, and a power of opinion which is nearly as great; no obstacles exist which can impede or even retard its progress, so as to make it heed the complaints of those whom it crushes upon its path."[9] According to de Tocqueville, the uncommon man, the creative artist, the solitary, and unconventional genius all were overlooked and discounted in America's rapidly democratizing culture. Sadly, the democratic majority always tended toward a stultifying conformism, celebrating mediocrity and creating its own pernicious version of intellectual tyranny. Old-style European monarchs, according to de Tocqueville, had "materialized oppression," but democratic republics "have rendered it as entirely an affair of the mind, as the will which it is intended to coerce." In the United States, he lamented, "the body is left free, and the soul is enslaved."[10] How, he wondered, might political liberty be protected as social conditions across the West are leveled and political centralization advances? These challenges would be taken up again, under circumstances where industrialization played a larger role in shaping social conditions, by the Englishman John Stuart Mill during the second half of the nineteenth century.

Intercessory conservatism

With their strong belief in the moral propriety of hereditary leadership and the Christian vision of the meaningful life, conservative writers often were sympathetic to the idea of using government to undertake socially ameliorative action. Such a position, of course, stands in blunt opposition to our twenty-first century understanding of conservatism, with its suspicion of expansive state power. Writers like Joseph de Maistre (1753–1821) in France and Samuel Taylor Coleridge (1772–1834) in England applauded state intervention to assist the poor and buttress traditional values, if only to avoid the oppressive social and economic conditions that drove people to revolution in the first place. Rejecting the notion that one ideal form of government exists for all people, de Maistre echoed the utilitarian principle that the only viable standard is when government secures "the greatest possible sum of happiness and strength, for the greatest number of men, during the longest possible time." Coleridge believed that the positive ends of the state included efforts "to make the means of subsistence more easy to each individual" and "to secure to each of its members the hope of bettering his own condition and that of his children."[11] Appropriate intercessory actions, especially in the degrading and crime-ridden cities, included aid to church-controlled educational establishments, targeted financial relief and skills training for the poor, and, most controversially, national regulation of trade and manufactures.

Growing out of a paternalistic sense of *noblesse oblige* and disturbed by the materialism and greed of early industrial society, conservatives affirmed the need for state engagement to improve the blighted lives of the urban poor. Burke had written during the very earliest stages of the Industrial Revolution and could not have anticipated the harsh conditions of the factory towns, but his successors challenged the *laissez-faire* principles of the industrial bourgeoisie as inimical to social cohesion and political stability. Taking into consideration the historic national character of a people, traditional rulers had a responsibility, albeit a limited one, to soften the community-eroding impact of massive social and economic change. For conservatives, the "social question" had changed dramatically with the advance of commercial culture and atomistic individualism, with the shift from a status to a contract society, and its attendant problems could not be addressed absent thoughtful political action under the direction of men of wisdom and experience.

Conservative statesmen

As the full impact of industrialization became clear during the second half of the century, conservative political leaders like British Prime Minister Benjamin Disraeli (1804–1881), French Emperor Napoleon III (r. 1852–1870), and German Chancellor Otto von Bismarck (1815–1898) skillfully positioned themselves as sympathetic allies of the working class. Beginning in the 1860s, Disraeli combined an appeal to the country's increasingly democratic electorate through targeted social reforms with an aristocratic paternalism that stressed the value of traditional leadership. In 1867, while serving as Chancellor of the Exchequer and leader of the House of Commons, he introduced a landmark reform bill that roughly doubled the national electorate, bringing the franchise to the working man for the first time.[12] A man of letters as well as an accomplished political figure, Disraeli's 1844 novel *Sybil* offered a realistic critique of England's growing chasm between rich and poor that was as powerful as the better-known protests of his famous contemporary Charles Dickens. During his final ministry (1874–1880) Disraeli took aim at some of the more egregious conditions that blighted so many lives. His conservative government passed two important measures of social reform: the 1875 Artisans' Dwellings Act that began a concerted attack on slum housing, and an 1876 Trade Union Act that legalized peaceful picketing.[13]

In France, a new form of conservative and authoritarian political thought—driven by fears of worker radicalism and popular democracy—gained credibility after 1848. The vast social changes that had taken place in the wake of industrialization had been overlooked by the government of King Louis Philippe (r. 1830–1848). A mere 200,000 Frenchmen out of a total of 35 million held the right to vote in 1848. Public banquets and petitions demanding reform were ignored by the government, and when rioting broke out in the capital and the barricades went up, the king opted for abdication over massive military repression. A republic was declared and universal suffrage adopted, reformist political clubs reminiscent of 1789 burst onto the scene, and the new government included noted socialists who briefly established national workshops to provide food and employment for the poor of Paris. It was all too much too fast for the country's more conservative rural majority. When a socialist rising occurred in June 1848 the government acted with brutal dispatch, killing and subsequently deporting thousands of citizens. A new constitution was drawn up which placed executive power in the hands of a president elected by universal manhood suffrage.[14]

The man elected to the presidency was Prince Louis-Napoleon (1808–1873), nephew of Napoleon Bonaparte. He enjoyed broad support from the socially conservative rural peasantry and France's landed elites, who thought, in the words of de Tocqueville, "he would be a tool for them to use at will and break at any time they wanted. In this they were mightily deceived."[15] Within 4 years Bonaparte had dispensed with the combative National Assembly, crushed all resistance in a military *coup d'etat*, and declared himself Emperor of the French. Newly enfranchised French voters overwhelmingly supported these unilateral actions through plebiscite. Over the next decade, there was little resistance to the government's curbs on the press, the erosion of legislative power, or the harsh measures taken against working-class political opponents of the emperor. Instead, as Bonaparte positioned himself as a populist figure dedicated to stability and prosperity, attention turned to industrial expansion, wealth creation, and the rebuilding of Paris on a scale fit for an autocratic ruler.[16]

The regime was influenced by the ideas of August Comte (1798–1857), whose six-volume *Course of Positive Philosophy* (1830–1842) and four-volume *System of Positive Polity* (1851–1854) jettisoned metaphysical and abstract thought in favor of a realist or "positivist" analysis of society. "The present condition of political science," he lamented "revives before our eyes the analogy of what astrology was to astronomy, alchemy was to chemistry, and the search for the universal panacea to the system of medical studies." Comte viewed Napoleonic dictatorship as an appropriate antidote to revolutionary disorder, and he applauded the regime's repeated use of the plebiscite as a means of building legitimacy.[17] Although neither a great general like his uncle nor a great administrator, by the 1860s Bonaparte felt confident enough on the domestic front to allow many political exiles to return to France, to grant the national assembly more fiscal authority, and to relax press censorship. In a bid to attract broader support to his regime, ministers were made responsible to the legislature and laws forbidding labor unions were relaxed to accommodate the resurgent demands of urban workers.[18]

A comparable trend in conservative leadership characterized German political life. After the unification of the country in 1871 and suppression of a Marxist-influenced Social Democratic Party, Otto von Bismarck introduced significant social legislation that included accident, disability, and old age insurance for workers. Provision for state-supported education was expanded and former liberals eagerly embraced the nationalist rhetoric that animated a highly authoritarian state. In making the new benefits the product of joint contributions from workers and employers, Bismarck defended private property while also positioning himself as the political conscience of the nation-state in the wake of the Industrial Revolution. By criticizing *laissez-faire* economic principles, the smug conflation of private interest with public good, and the squalor and philistine tendencies of unregulated material civilization, conservatives like Bismarck successfully migrated from opposition to revolutionary principles to defenders of forms of the Enlightenment project that had been abandoned in unregulated industrial society: humanitarianism and the emotional bonds of community. Earlier in the century the intellectual current called Romanticism had rejected the cold rationalism of eighteenth-century thought and emphasized in its place the value of emotion and the mystical power of the state. Conservatives appropriated key elements of this outlook in an effort to maintain their relevance in the industrial age.[19]

Classical liberalism: Equality before the law

Except for the years immediately after the defeat of Napoleon I in 1815, conservative writers often were caricatured as apologists for the past and defenders of undeserving privilege. They were opposed by the growing ranks of the bourgeoisie, the businessmen, bankers, traders, manufacturers, and lawyers who championed a strong individualist ethic and found much to admire in the universal rights language of the Enlightenment. The first half of the nineteenth century saw the gradual political empowerment of this bourgeoisie, who carried forward the Enlightenment's faith in the full autonomy of the rights-bearing citizen, in constitutional government, and in the limited state where each man, equal before the law, was free to succeed or fail after his own efforts. The Italian nationalist and republican Giuseppe Mazzini (1805–1872) captured the spirit of this outlook when he wrote that "true association is only possible among equals in rights and duties." For Mazzini all are born morally equal and whenever equal distribution of rights is not universal "there are castes, domination, privileges, superiority, helotism, and dependence."[20] Calling for representative assemblies that were more than advisory estates and diets, liberals interpreted the representative principle in terms of vigorous and open debate in national assemblies, the power to question ministers and evaluate their performance, and a constitutionally guaranteed role in fiscal matters.

Most early nineteenth-century liberals were steeped in the writings of Adam Smith and eagerly embraced the notion that rational self-interest was the unfailing guide to the collective well-being of society. This "classical" school of political economy became the reigning orthodoxy by mid-century, leaving those who failed in the capitalist environment, who experienced poverty and unemployment, with little public recourse. Such failure in the liberal world-view was inevitable. The British economist Thomas Malthus (1766–1834) cast the blame for poverty directly on the poor themselves. Unwilling to practice the type of strict moral discipline essential to family planning in an environment where population would eventually outstrip food supply, the poorest were condemned to suffer even greater natural woes. England's poor laws, although designed to alleviate hardship, had in Malthus's view "spread the general evil over a much larger surface."

Fellow economist David Ricardo (1772–1823) described how wages ineluctably drop to subsistence levels due to the same demographic reality. With too many workers chasing a fixed number of jobs, the "iron law of wages" insured the impoverishment of the many.[21] Both men counseled against government action that would interfere with these harsh natural laws, advice that was followed with tragic results in Ireland after the failure of the potato crop in 1845. An estimated 1 million Irish subjects of the British Crown perished as a result, while those who were fortunate enough to emigrate did so in large numbers. To better inform and execute the few state actions that were necessary, British liberals favored a modest extension of the franchise, a goal realized under the so-called Great Reform Bill of 1832. It brought the kingdom's powerful industrial elite into national politics, but carefully excluded those whose lack of property marked them as inherently distrustful and improvident.

The industrial state

As we have seen, those who wrote on behalf of political democracy or greater access to the vote were few in number during the first half of the nineteenth century. There were numerous champions of liberty, for certain, but for most liberals it was one thing to universalize rights and quite another to afford uneducated, propertyless men access to the ballot. By the second half of the nineteenth century, however, the political aspirations of the industrial working class finally began to claim the attention of political leaders. The 1840s was a decade of acute food shortages and economic hardship. Across the continent rising unemployment and attendant distress contributed to the outbreak of revolutions in 1848 that threatened to topple governments and remake the social and political order. As noted above, universal manhood suffrage was achieved in France in 1848, although Napoleonic dictatorship blunted its full impact. Working men were awarded the vote more gradually in Britain through the parliamentary reform acts of 1867 and 1884. And in Germany, the franchise was extended to all males after national unification in 1871. Across the Atlantic, amendments to the US Constitution enfranchised newly freed black males, but effective enforcement would be delayed for another century. By the outbreak of World War I in 1914, Spain, Belgium, Norway, Italy, Switzerland, Austria, and the Netherlands joined the other major powers in adopting universal manhood suffrage.

John Stuart Mill and liberalism reconceived

Early nineteenth-century liberals focused on economic man and constructed their vision of the State in relation to the "natural laws" of the marketplace. Whether accepting the Lockean notion that these natural laws could be discovered through reason or proceeding on the assumption, most famously advanced by Kant, that man's limited understanding must assume such laws exist in order to make possible other values that humans wish to hold, liberals defined "freedom" as an absence of external restraints. But the industrial working class and the trades union movement saw little benefit in supporting traditional liberal values; what use, after all, was the maximization of personal freedom if one's life became dependent upon an unscrupulous factory manager or landlord? Increasingly, urban workers began to use their newly won ballots to support political parties that were committed to advancing the interests of the laboring class.

And as the negative implications of the unfettered market society took its debilitating toll on the lives of the working poor in mills, mines, and factories, some liberal theorists began to reconsider the ameliorative value of state action and the proposition that legal equality and quality of life had to be engaged together.[22] One of the leading figures in this evolutionary process was the Englishman John Stuart Mill (1806–1873).

Mill was educated by his father James Mill (1773–1836), an official of the East India Company and an associate of Jeremy Bentham. During these formative years the younger Mill embraced the central premise of the utilitarian school, that the measure of all moral rules and social arrangements was their effectiveness in advancing the happiness of the greatest number. He later recounted how this eminently practical education, which considered humanity in narrow and mechanical terms, plunged him into a severe mental crisis at the age of 20. Finding relief in the prose and poetry of the English Romantics, Mill came to discard the harsher elements of Bentham's utilitarianism and instead drew a distinction between the higher pleasures of reflection and creativity and lower pleasures associated with the mundane and material. He was also deeply affected by de Tocqueville's arguments in *Democracy in America*, particularly by the author's warnings against the conformist, leveling, and illiberal tendencies inherent in majority rule. With Mill, classical liberalism's emphasis on economic man and the public benefits of private selfishness was transformed into a conspicuously humane habit of mind, a readiness to consider divergent viewpoints, a healthy skepticism of all rigid creeds and ideologies, and a willingness to consider collectivist action to advance human well-being in an industrial age.

Mill was a prolific author, but a number of his main ideas are captured in the provocative *On Liberty* (1859). Here he reminded his readers that democratic societies have a tendency to practice a social tyranny "more formidable than many kinds of political oppression, since, though not usually upheld by such extreme penalties, it leaves fewer means of escape, penetrating much more deeply into the details of life, and enslaving the soul itself."[23] In order to protect individual freedoms, Mill declared that "the sole end for which mankind are warranted, individually or collectively, in interfering with the liberty of action of any of their number, is self protection."[24] Even if one's neighbor is patently foolhardy, misguided, or engaged in activities that will undermine their chances for individual happiness, it is not the business of government or society to intervene. More provocatively, Mill insisted that all opinions must be engaged in a free society if the cause of truth is to advance. Even patently wrong opinions are of value, he wrote, if only to sharpen our skill at defending true ones. The sole condition under which state interference is permitted is if a person's thoughts or actions result in harm to another.

But while always a passionate defender of the need to protect individual freedoms, Mill recognized that collective state action was sometimes necessary if the utilitarian objective of achieving his expansive notion of the greatest good for the greatest number, the object of all moral action, was to be realized. In *Considerations on Representative Government* (1861), he asserted that an important criterion of good government was "the degree in which it tends to increase the sum of good qualities in the governed, collectively and individually."[25] As a result he was willing to consider specific areas of public action that could be shown to address social needs as a whole while still allowing one's individuality to develop. Provision for minimal public education, prohibition of child labor, minimum wage, and old-age insurance all qualified as areas where state action was imperative if human freedom were to advance. In his *Principles of Political Economy* (1848), he also acknowledged a role for the state in devising an equitable tax system, in funding infrastructure projects and basic research. And it was under a representative form of government that the objective of progressive human development was to be met most effectively, not least because it encourages increased participation in political life.[26]

Governments typically stress obedience, but for Mill it was equally important that the state serve as an instrument of progress and freedom for everyone. Because of this conviction Mill supported the enfranchisement of the working class, but he tempered his embrace of political democracy by indicating that votes should be "weighted" to favor the educated and the financially independent. Perhaps more famously, Mill spoke out boldly on behalf of women's suffrage. In *The Subjection of Women* (1869) he challenged the prevailing notion that women were not to be trusted to exercise the franchise in a responsible manner. He argued instead that there was no empirical evidence to support this long-standing prejudice, a position that earned him the enmity of both the political right and left.[27]

Liberalism and human potential

Mill was by no means the only descendant of the utilitarian school who reframed liberalism in response to the massive social changes wrought by the Industrial Revolution. Thomas Hill Green (1836–1882), a professor of moral philosophy at Balliol College, Oxford, articulated the theoretical underpinnings of the new liberalism in a series of lectures delivered in 1879 and posthumously published under the title *Principles of Political Obligation* (1882). Green retained liberalism's deep concern for the dignity of the individual and, like Mill, supported efforts to enfranchise the working class. But instead of emphasizing how the state must be restrained, as was common in classical liberal thought going back to Locke, Green stressed the value of communal threads within society and the advancement of human freedom through public action.

Each citizen, irrespective of class or income, was entitled to live under conditions that were conducive to the development of one's full potential. And for Green, human development in the industrial age, where market-based capitalism created enormous disparities of wealth, necessitated the limited and targeted intervention of the state. He firmly rejected the old liberal consensus respecting the self-regulating nature of economic interests, the assumption that all would be well so long as the state did not hamper the free play of individual economic activity. He also took issue with the utilitarian conception of human nature where psychological hedonism and a rough material version of happiness tended to predominate. Genuine happiness, he believed, transcended the boundaries of what one happened to want at the moment, of mere getting and spending. It was also to be found in robust civic engagement and democratic activism, qualities that were best cultivated when the state promoted the social, cultural, and intellectual improvement of everyone.

Green took active citizenship, citizenship with a broader end in mind, seriously. He was a member of the Oxford School Board and the first don elected to represent residents on Oxford town council. A champion of compulsory, state-financed primary education, Green also supported the admission of women to university and the employment of scholarships to make university education available to the working class. He encouraged his own students to champion democracy through participation in the governance of their communities and in the education of their neighbors. Freedom for Green involved not simply negative rights against the actions of others, including the state, but the right and opportunity to influence and shape public policy with the objective of enhancing self-development. The collective action of groups and group politics was becoming an inescapable fact of modern culture, and Green insisted that individuals join together in the work of ruling and being ruled and, in the words of J. S. McClelland, "to be able to agree among themselves what it is to be a good citizen and even a good man."[28]

Another influential Balliol don was the economic historian Arnold Toynbee (1852–1883). Toynbee's field of academic interest was the Industrial

Revolution, and it was as a student of political economy that he came to dissent with the notion of immutable natural laws of economics. Free trade and *laissez-faire* capitalism had fueled innovation and generated enormous wealth, but free competition did not automatically foster social progress. He refused to equate the Social Darwinian struggle for daily existence with the unbroken human search for a particular quality of existence. The latter phenomenon demanded that the marketplace be regulated according to circumstances, but always with the primary goal of protecting the weakest members of society. Toynbee took his philosophy into the poorest neighborhoods of East London, where he was instrumental in establishing public libraries and encouraging his students to offer instruction to working-class inhabitants. An ardent supporter of the trades union movement, Toynbee maintained that associations were crucial to the economic and social advancement of the industrial proletariat. After his untimely death, a university settlement named Toynbee Hall was established to champion social reform in this depressed section of the capital, engaging upper- and middle-class university students to instruct and to live amongst the working poor, advocating on their behalf and empowering them through educational outreach.[29]

Many liberal politicians were quick to assimilate the ideas of Green and Toynbee. John Morley (1838–1923), a member of Prime Minister William Gladstone's (1809–1898) liberal cabinet, wrote in 1883 that he was beginning to doubt "whether it is possible to grapple with this enormous mass of evil in our society by merely private, voluntary, and philanthropic effort." According to Morley "we shall have to bring to bear the collective force of the whole community, shortly called the state, in order to remedy things against which our social conscience is at last beginning to revolt." Gladstone's government had already begun to extend the regulation of labor to include adult males, passing an Employers' Liability Act in 1880 allowing workers to sue employers in the aftermath of an industrial accident, and tentatively supporting the 8-hour work day. And David Lloyd George (1863–1945), who became Chancellor of the Exchequer under a liberal ministry in 1908, outlined to an audience in Wales that liberalism must be about more than the establishment of personal freedom and civil equality. The Liberal Party, he insisted, must "promote measures for ameliorating the conditions of life of the multitude." In referring to a just-enacted and precedent-setting Old Age Pensions Act, Lloyd George observed that inasmuch as poverty is due to circumstances beyond an individual's control, "the state should step in to the very utmost limit of its resources, and save the man from the physical and mental torture involved in extreme penury."[30]

Women and democracy

With the exception of outliers like Mill and Mazzini, neither classical liberalism nor its interventionist successor offered much in the way of addressing

Mary Wollstonecraft's charge that female inferiority was solely the product of social, intellectual, and political constraints imposed on women. Most socialists, on the other hand, embraced the equality of the sexes, and later Marxists made a strong appeal to women as members of the working class. In his *Origin of the Family, Private Property, and the State* (1884), Friedrich Engels (1820–1895) argued that women in bourgeois society were considered property, and that their liberation was part of the larger struggle against all forms of private ownership in property.

Only in the final decades of the nineteenth century did women gain the right to enter universities, sue for divorce, and control their own property in most Western European states. There were a handful of women lawyers and physicians, but on the whole the professions were still off limits to one half of humanity. Suffrage organizations emerged in the 1860s, but political militancy came rather late and was largely restricted to Britain. There "suffragettes," as their opponents called them, organized public demonstrations and marches in the 1890s, while after the turn of the century more extreme figures interrupted political speeches, vandalized property, chained themselves to the House of Commons, and staged hunger strikes while under arrest. A local government act of 1894 extended the right to vote at the local level to women who held property in England and Wales, but in general liberals were opposed to the national vote for fear that affluent women would support a conservative agenda.[31]

Equality of condition

As we have seen with changes in liberal ideology, by the 1860s the attention of political writers moved beyond the origins, structure, and relationship of the individual to the state. Access to political power remained a deep concern for members of the industrial working class and for women, but a broader concern over social and economic relationships took a more prominent role in political thought. Questions concerning economic fairness, right of entry to participate in the bounty of industrial productivity, and the potential function of state power in the workplace, all drew the attention of writers and elected officials. For the first time, as the productive capacity of Western Europe's industrialized nations surged ahead, the status of a people's economic condition emerged as a central responsibility of the state. Equality before the law, long a pivotal feature of Enlightenment political thought, was now expanded to include equity of outcome, a more evenhanded distribution of the nation's economic goods.

Utopian socialism

This cooperative theme was very much at the center of early socialist thought. Neither the paternalism of Restoration conservatives nor the natural law claims of liberals satisfied those who believed in a version of the Enlightenment project that emphasized a less individualistic form of moral renewal and social transformation. For this movement, referred to as "associationalism" in the 1820s and subsequently labeled "utopian" socialism by its detractors, the logic of eighteenth-century rationalism demanded a decent standard of living for all, a dignified work experience, and maximum personal freedom. And these goals, it was argued, could be attained only through a reconstituted social and economic order that was antithetical to the selfish, property-centered, and competitive material culture of the industrializing West. Influenced in part by Rousseau's critique of property in the *Essay on the Origin of Inequality*, and in part by Romanticism's focus on the emotive and creative side of human personality, the utopian socialists believed that the fulfillment of individual happiness occurred within a community that planned production and distribution for maximum fairness. Solidarity and sharing, not the egotistic scuttle of commercial culture, offered the only humane way forward in a protean industrial age.[32]

Seeking to break with the assumption that human nature was essentially self-regarding, the utopian socialists offered blueprints that ranged widely from Christian communalism to secular collectivism. The latter solution to society's ills was recommended during the most radical period of the French Revolution by the Englishman William Godwin. His *Inquiry Concerning Political Justice* (1793) called for an end to all coercive arrangements, including government, law, property, and even marriage. Godwin's anarchism, strangely enough, shared the liberal's anti-statist posture and conviction that society will order itself if left free from the meddling of government. The book was predicated on the intrinsic rationality and sense of justice that all humans exhibited once freed from the distorting lens of contemporary culture. Anarchism would return at the end of the nineteenth century, often employing violence in an effort to destroy the hated bourgeois state and promoting alternative, if often incoherent, schemes for organizing social power.

Godwin attracted few followers in England, but the case was different north of the border in Scotland, where the former textile laborer and successful businessman Robert Owen (1771–1858) purchased cotton mills in New Lanark and instituted a series of dramatic reforms. Owen raised wages, built cooperative residential villages adjacent to the factories, and set up schools for adults and children all in an effort to demonstrate that a decent standard of living for workers was not antithetical to good business practice. In 1824, he established the utopian community of New Harmony in the American state of Indiana, a venture that sought the elimination of ignorance though the provision of education for all and a rejection of competition in the marketplace. Although his innovative schemes gathered considerable interest (Owen was invited to address a special session of the US Congress), his New Harmony venture failed within a few short years.[33]

Some of the early socialists, like the Frenchman Henri Comte de Saint-Simon (1760–1825), were inspired by a combination of Christian communitarian thought and faith in the power of science and technology, rightly managed, to ameliorate the human condition. Just as early Christianity had provided humans with a sense of earthly and transcendent order, so too in the modern world science and technology, under the beneficent direction of trained experts, industrial managers, and social engineers, could organize human and material capital in a way that would assure a better quality of life for all. In his final, posthumously published work, *New Christianity* (1825), Saint-Simon called for a social religion that rejected a clergy-dominated faith in favor of the associational values of the early church. His countryman Charles Fourier (1772–1837) recoiled from the giant scale of Saint-Simon's technocratic society and called instead for the creation of small communities called "phalanstries" where simplicity would guide decisions regarding the products of labor. In his *New Industrial and Societal World* (1829), Fourier stressed the overriding value of communal partnership in the phalanstries and forecast the withering away of the traditional family unit, to be replaced by new models of sexuality and the collective care and education of children. Another Frenchman, Pierre-Joseph Proudhon (1809–1865), echoed Fourier's suspicion of large-scale states managed by technocrats. Turning instead to worker cooperatives, Proudhon antagonized the bourgeois establishment by encouraging the working class to rise up against their oppressors. A number of utopian communities based on Fourier's principles were established in the United States during the 1840s, the most notable of which was Brook Farm in Massachusetts, but all were extinct soon after their founding.[34]

Marx and "scientific socialism"

The handful of utopian communities established in Europe and America during the 1830s and 1840s were unsuccessful for a variety of reasons, but in large measure their founders were unable to curb the self-regarding instincts that corroded all social systems built around principles of mutuality. Despite these setbacks, the search for alternatives to a capitalist world order that left the majority wanting for life's basic material needs did not end with the experimental utopian cooperatives. Other theorists, deeply influenced by Enlightenment rationalism, sought to anchor the communal paradigm in scientific laws of progress that were every bit as compelling as the purported laws of classical economics. The German philosopher Hegel provided what was perhaps the strongest intellectual grounding for the idea of progress as an intrinsic force in history.

As part of his larger system of metaphysics, Hegel claimed that absolute reality or spirit was both knowable and dynamic, in the sense that it evolves over time, always moving toward greater perfection. This reality is present in history through a dialectical process whereby opposing ideas come into conflict at critical junctures but resolve themselves through a creative synthesis. The synthesis always guides civilization into a higher state of truth, but not before planting the seeds of a new and more dynamic clash of opposing ideas. The ongoing struggle between thesis and antithesis in every compartment of human life—politics, art, religion, social relations—accounts for the positive trajectory of humanity's self-awareness of freedom. Rejecting individualist definitions of freedom, Hegel embraced the political community as the optimum setting for the realization of human potential in all its forms. The rational state, through its institutions and its laws, embodies the higher goals of absolute reality or spirit and allows for the progressive development of the individual.[35]

Karl Marx (1818–1883) was first introduced to Hegel's ideas as a university student in Berlin. Conservatives had appropriated Hegel's philosophy of history as a justification for the *status quo* under the authoritarian Prussian state, but Marx identified with a group of self-styled "Young Hegelians" who were eager to take the concept of dialectical change in a radically new direction. Completing a doctoral dissertation on the ancient Greek materialists Democritus and Epicurus, Marx began his career as a journalist and editor, quickly earning the unwelcome attention of Prussian authorities. He relocated to Paris in the 1840s where he came into contact with French socialist thought and established what would become a lifelong friendship and collaboration with fellow German Friedrich Engels. In terms of their background, it was an unlikely alliance on behalf of the unskilled working class: Marx was the son of a middle-class lawyer, while Engels was part owner with his father of a textile factory in England. In 1844, Engels wrote a powerful description and critique of the industrial landscape titled *The Condition of the Working Classes in England* based on his experiences in the city of Manchester. The profits of the family-owned factories, ironically, together with the inheritance of other family industrial concerns, enabled Engels to become Marx's key financial patron and allowed the latter to concentrate his time and energy on writing.[36]

The bourgeois leaders of the 1848 revolutions and their student and working-class supporters had called for an extended franchise, written constitutions, and national unity. Initially successful, the fragile alliance between the middle-class revolutionaries and the laboring poor broke down amidst class divisions and bourgeois suspicion that the workers, if successful, would prefer equality to liberty and demand substantive economic change. In the end, Europe's established governments employed superior military force to crush the uprisings, but not before Marx and Engels had published a brief call to direct action titled *The Communist Manifesto*.[37] The pamphlet had a negligible impact on the events of 1848, but it would become the most cogent statement of Marxist thought and have a far greater impact on European and world history than the failed mid-century revolutions. Marx's later writings, including the massive, multi-volume *Capital*, never strayed from the core premise of the *Manifesto* regarding the inevitable triumph of the working class over the repressive system of market capitalism and private ownership of the means of production.

Like his Enlightenment forebears, Marx believed in the existence of scientific laws operating in history. Hegel's error had been to identify the causal aspect of change in the world of ideas, whereas Marx identified material factors, in particular the means of production, or the way goods were produced and wealth distributed in society, as the key to intellectual and cultural formation. At every stage in history those who controlled material power determined the shape of society's institutions and the content of conventional ideas. For Marx this meant that religious systems were no more than distracting myths devised to keep the masses in line; moral codes and political systems were mere constructs that affirmed the privileges of the commanding elite. And at the center of human history was the unceasing dynamic of class conflict, with the dispossessed in an "uninterrupted, now hidden, now open fight" against the minority whose interests were served by the *status quo*. From the master–slave relationship in the ancient world, to the medieval lord and serf, and ending with the collision between the modern factory owner and the humble proletariat, Marx's materialist philosophy affirmed that in an unceasing dialectical struggle, the group in control of economic power always shaped human consciousness.[38]

Once these laws of historical causation were understood fully by the industrial working class, they could take charge of their destiny, align themselves with the progressive forces of history, and accelerate the overthrow of the bourgeois order. The workers would then claim for themselves what would become the final stage of human history—the classless society. Despite his emphasis on violent class conflict, Marx was at his core an optimist whose secular faith in the inevitability of the communist revolution, ushering in the end of the dialectical process, was held as firmly as any apologist for the Christian narrative. His critique of the exploitative factory owner was combined with a grudging admiration for the transformative power of modern industrial capitalism, its capacity to topple centuries of retrograde aristocratic hegemony. But the triumph of the industrial bourgeoisie, its recent capture of the economic and political commanding heights, was also the signal for its imminent demise at the hands of a politically awakened proletariat. This new type of man—a new human nature really—would break the chains of false nationalism and individual selfishness and usher in the world of social and economic equality.

Unlike his utopian contemporaries, Marx did not believe that bourgeois property owners would ever address the problem of economic inequality in a rational manner. Industrialization would inevitably issue in social conflict. As the ranks of the proletariat grew and their self-awareness as an exploited class intensified, their physical proximity in overcrowded cities and on the factory floor would enable them to form a disciplined and unified force against an ever-shrinking number of capitalist oppressors. Rarely was a faith, complete with its own version of the judgment day in the great revolution and an earthly Eden after the workers' triumph, held with such tenacity. In a sense Marx too was a representative Romantic, a new age prophet and moralist who captured the suffering of the industrial worker and who offered hope and the promise of a new heaven here on earth. After the failed revolutions of 1848 Marx settled in London with his family and there, living in relative obscurity and supported by Engels, he continued to write and prepare for the great workers' revolution that would never come.

His message, however, did not go unheeded, and this was especially the case for the very class that Marx had concluded would never compromise the rigors of the capitalist system or move to ameliorate the lives of the proletariat.

The advent of the welfare state

As the franchise was extended to ever larger numbers of male citizens, politicians from across the ideological spectrum came to embrace, some more grudgingly than others, unprecedented levels of state intervention in social and economic affairs. Political parties evolved from private clubs into large organizations with professional staff. Politicians took advantage of the rail network and print media to reach out more effectively to their growing constituencies. Mass meetings and political rallies became standard fare by the 1880s.[39] Fiscal support for education, state-sponsored initiatives in the areas of public health and workplace safety, and the expansion of social services to the poor all featured prominently in the domestic legislative agenda of major political parties. By 1900, there remained only a handful of writers and political figures still defending the minimalist view of the state as an enforcer of contracts and guarantor of public safety. Socialist political parties grew in strength in Germany, Italy, France, Britain, and even in the United States, championing legislation targeted at improving the lives of working people and their dependents. Instead of adhering to the Marxist alternative to capitalism, these socialist leaders sought to reform capitalism peacefully by working through the existing political system. The establishment of comprehensive systems of public education, the promotion of union membership, and stricter regulation of the workplace all became priorities for these writers and political actors.

In Germany, the socialist movement found one of its most articulate champions in Ferdinand Lassalle (1825–1864). Accepting the Marxist interpretation of history but demurring from Marx's critique of democratic politics under capitalism, Lassalle urged the formation of working-class political parties to effect immediate change. One year before his death he assumed leadership of the Universal German Workingman's Association, whose chief purpose was to end class antagonism through the extension of voting rights in each of the German states. Other German socialists were unwilling to jettison the language of class conflict, and in 1891 leaders of the Social Democratic Party drew up the so-called Erfurt Program, emphasizing the monopolistic character of capitalism and the immediate need for a transition to socialism through equal suffrage, the right to legislate through popular initiative and referenda, the secularization of schools, progressive income taxes, the 8-hour work day, and the abolition of all child labor.[40] The Erfurt Program, replete with its language of class conflict, remained the official position of the SDP until the 1920s.

But Lassalle's vision of cooperation and peaceful change through democratic politics was not entirely lost in the SDP's embrace of the more confrontational Erfurt Program. One of the leading theoreticians of what became known as the revisionist movement within German socialism was Eduard Bernstein (1850–1932).[41] He first joined the Social Democratic Party in 1872, but Bismarck's harsh anti-socialist laws forced him and many others into political exile. Settling first in Zurich and subsequently in London, Bernstein was acquainted with Friedrich Engels and began publishing books and articles dedicated to the proposition that a social-ist society could be created without violent class conflict and revolution. Marx had been incorrect, Bernstein insisted, in his belief that the com-petitive dynamic inherent in capitalist enterprise would preclude peaceful reform. Thanks to the expansion of the franchise, Bernstein argued that fundamental social and political change could be accomplished in a legal manner through the parliamentary process. As evidence he pointed to the fact that significant factory legislation had improved the lives of work-ers and that even conservative politicians were acknowledging the just demands of the proletariat. When he was at last allowed to return from exile in 1901, Bernstein was elected to the Reichstag under the banner of the SDP.

In France, a strong and sometimes violent trades union movement, known as "syndicalism," gathered momentum in the final decades of the nineteenth century. Beneath the organizational umbrella of the General Confederation of Labor, syndicalists championed expansive and inclusive industrial unions over fragmented craft or trade unions, and retained the Marxian language of class struggle and direct action against capitalists through strikes, boycotts, and sabotage. They also rejected the Third French Republic (1871–1940) and the existing political process as oppressive tools of the ruling class. One of the movement's leading interpreters was Georges Sorel (1847–1922). He refused to compromise with those who believed that the socialist vision could be achieved without the destruction of the rul-ing class. Instead, Sorel held up the prospect of the general strike, where workers bring an end to capitalist production, as the essential step in the transition to socialism through revolutionary action.[42]

British socialism after Marx attracted a range of leading intellectuals, including H.G. Wells (1866–1946), George Bernard Shaw (1856–1950), and Sidney (1859–1947) and Beatrice Webb (1858–1943). In 1883 (the year of Marx's death), the Fabian Society was formed to advance the reorganiza-tion of society through the abolition of private property and "the transfer to the community of the administration of such industrial capital as can be conveniently managed socially."[43] Collecting and assembling useful data on patterns of economic inequality, the Fabians were more aligned with the revisionist perspective of Eduard Bernstein and eschewed the stri-dently confrontational rhetoric of French syndicalism. The moral critique was always at the core of Fabian writings: authors like the playwright Shaw, for example, censured those who enjoyed a legal claim to wealth by virtue of their ownership of property without having contributed to the production of that wealth. At its heart the Fabian position centered on the corrosive power of competitive capitalism, its tendency to undermine community and social morality.

The radical journalist Robert Blatchford (1851–1943), author of the enormously popular *Merrie England* (1894), communicated something of the spirit of the Fabian movement in layman's terms. The land, the factories, the mines, the railways, and the machinery of England are not deployed for the general good of the people, "but are used to make wealth for the few rich men that own them. Socialists say that this arrangement is unjust and unwise, that it entails waste as well as misery, and that it would be better for all, even for the rich, that the land and other instruments of production should become the property of the state, just as the post-office and the telegraphs have become the property of the state."[44] A million copies of *Merrie England* were sold in the first 2 years after publication, but perhaps a more practical outcome of Fabianism was the emergence of so-called "gas and water" socialism. Even prominent conservative politicians like Joseph Chamberlain (1836–1914), the mayor of industrial Birmingham from 1873–1876, began to recognize that a modern industrial economy produced problems that could not be effectively addressed by traditional nostrums regarding hard work and individual responsibility. During his tenure the city took over the private gas and water works and razed dilapidated homes in slum areas, replacing them with new worker-occupied properties. The city also built and operated a street railway system and took charge of providing lighting on municipal streets. Chamberlain even called for the formation of state-led public health agencies to address problems associated with urban living.[45]

The growing recognition of the need for state intervention on behalf of the industrial working class transcended political parties. The Roman Catholic Church, for example, was for decades one of the most inflexible opponents of socialist thought. But it dramatically shifted its position during the pontificate of Leo XIII (r. 1878–1903). In a major encyclical of 1891 titled *Rerum Novarum* (Of New Things), the Pope upheld the right to private property while simultaneously calling on the state to champion the cause of social justice. Nineteenth-century materialism and unfettered capitalism had compromised the well-being of all social classes, he wrote, but the poor had suffered the most. Although the encyclical acknowledged that "It is hard indeed to fix the boundaries of the rights and duties within which the rich and the proletariat—those who furnish material goods and those who furnish work, ought to be restricted in relation to each other," the Pope observed that in recent decades "a very few rich and exceedingly rich men have laid a yoke almost of slavery on the unnumbered masses of non-owning workers."

Turning to Aquinas for direction, the Pope maintained that natural justice dictated the provision of a living wage. While private property is supported by the principles of natural law, humans must not think of their possessions as their own, but employ them for the advancement of all. The secular state exists to serve the common good, and "since it would be quite absurd to look out for one portion of the citizens and to neglect another, it follows that public authority ought to exercise due care in safe-guarding the well-being and the interests of non-owning workers." Breaking with the church's earlier position, Leo supported the establishment of labor unions and the right to collective bargaining as legitimate means to improve the condition of the working class. *Rerum Novarum* was widely discussed and contributed to the emergence of a Christian socialist movement across Western Europe. By the early twentieth century, Christian democrat political parties, emphasizing conservative cultural and moral views but supporting moderate social and economic change, gained support in France, Germany, and Italy.[46]

Nationalism and disquiet

There were no major military conflicts in Western Europe during the final quarter of the nineteenth century. Military alliance systems involving Germany, Italy, and Austria-Hungary on one side, and France, Russia, and eventually Britain on the other, provided some measure of assurance that diplomacy would pre-empt violence, although in the end the rigidity of the commitments helped lead to the great conflagration of 1914.[47] Imperial rivalries intensified during these decades, however, as the leading powers laid claim to trade and territorial privileges in East Asia and partitioned sub-Saharan Africa into colonies. On more than one occasion strenuous diplomatic efforts were needed to avert clashes overseas. In an environment where industrialization and the cash nexus fueled a strongly individualist ethic, and where organized religion was losing its centuries-old directive power, people still longed for a sense of communal well-being and higher collective purpose. Nationalism, with its forceful mythmaking capacity, provided that essential purpose and focus of allegiance for ever larger groups of people.[48]

Early nineteenth-century nationalism in the hands of anti-colonial writers like the Italian Giuseppe Mazzini galvanized patriots around the idea of independent states that embraced liberal and equalitarian principles. But after mid-century, nationalism assumed a more troubling posture. One of the more representative apologists for a new, more bellicose nationalism was the German historian Heinrich von Treitschke (1834–1896). A liberal in his youth and the son of a soldier-father who harbored a deep distrust of Prussian ambitions, von Treitschke became a passionate supporter of Otto von Bismarck's authoritarian style of leadership. In a series of lectures and books he celebrated Prussia's expansionist posture, its military victory over the Austrian-led German Confederation in 1866, and its decisive defeat of France in 1870. In 1874, he was awarded the chair in history at the University of Berlin that had previously been held by the great scholar Leopold von Ranke. But where Ranke had always endeavored to be critical of sources and understand the past on its own terms, Treitschke sought to influence the course of history by stressing the values of militarism, patriotism, and the ethical autonomy of the state over civic freedom and social justice.

Treitschke authored a five-volume survey of German history up to 1848 that was eagerly embraced by the German middle class. But it was his posthumously published *Politics* (1898), consisting of his academic lectures, that wielded the greatest influence in Germany down into the 1930s. Challenging liberalism's contract theory, separation of powers, and celebration of the individual, Treitschke contended that the state "is primordial and necessary . . . as enduring as history, and no less essential to mankind than speech." There was, he insisted, no natural condition of man, no state of nature anterior to the state, and therefore no substance to the Enlightenment's claim that government "should be treated only as an instrument to promote the aims of its citizens." The modern state operates most efficiently when the monarch is fully empowered with executive, legislative, and judicial powers, when church interference in public affairs is prohibited and Christian morality has no influence over official government actions. In times of military conflict especially, each subject must rise above petty individualistic concerns. "The grandeur of war," he wrote, "lies in the utter annihilation of puny man in the great conception of the State, and it brings out the full magnificence of the sacrifice of fellow-countrymen for one another."[49] With Treitschke, the rights of the individual against the state, the historic focal point of liberal thought, were decisively eclipsed by reasons of state on the assumption that the state is its own corporate, ethical personality without superior.

Democracy interrogated

Considered in a global context, Western Europe had undergone an astonishing transformation by the turn of the new century. Rapid industrialization, with all of its attendant social disruption, had taken place—peacefully for the most part—in tandem with political democratization. Imperialism and nationalism bolstered self-confidence, and technology combined with expanding educational opportunities seemed to augur well for a future of limitless possibilities. The conquest of night with electric lights, the shrinking of distances with trams, trains, and steamships, and the assault on pain and disease by medical science all testified to the power of Western Europe.[50] The growth of the state, accepted by liberals, conservatives, and socialists alike was framed increasingly in terms of social justice and national security. And broad-based support for the idea of the nation as an object of allegiance separate and distinct from elected or hereditary rulers tempered some of the class divisions that had been at the core of revolutionary activity since 1848.

Yet for all of the material advancement and the trending toward responsible, democratically elected government, for all of the self-satisfaction that enlightened ideas long in the making were at last put into practice, there was a strong undercurrent of doubt and misgiving about some of the practical implications of representative democracy and majority rule. At one level the very rapidity by which Enlightenment political ideas had been incorporated into the majority political culture by 1900 seemed to speak well for the decisions of rational human actors. But two of the intellectual giants of the century, Karl Marx and Charles Darwin (1809–1882), had each in his own way pointed to the insignificance of discreet human agency in historical change—both natural and social—over time. And Sigmund Freud (1856–1939), with the publication of perhaps his most important work, *The Interpretation of Dreams* (1899), called into question the essential rationality of the human mind and its ability to think critically and function uniformly across cultures. Some of these insights had already been explored in practice by symbolist writers, modernist composers, and *avant garde* artists who took a strong interest in the power of untutored instinct, will, and irrationalism. Their approach was rooted in multiple intellectual sources, but the general backdrop, especially in its more pessimistic leanings, owed an enormous debt to the work of Friedrich Nietzsche (1844–1900).[51]

The "assault on reason" that is so often associated with Nietzsche's writings was driven by the author's quest to live authentically in a culture where, in his view, Enlightenment conventions had fostered complacency and decadence. According to Nietzsche, the *philosophes* had attacked Christian theology but retained its conformist slave morality. The idea systems emerging from Enlightenment thought, including belief in the essential goodness of human nature and the value of parliamentary government, were in fact life-denying and perverse. For Nietzsche a godless universe lacking absolute standards of good and evil demanded a new type of man, one who rejected established conventions and forged new values based on an instinctual, heroic will to power. Western Europe's future, he claimed, lay not along the path of "progressive" science and representative government, but under the direction of a higher type of leader who sees through the myth of rationalism and bourgeois moral conventions. The new leader rejects historical determinism and boldly sets his own standards, untrammeled by the life-denying precepts of Christian metaphysics and Enlightenment rationalism.[52]

This late nineteenth-century assault on rationalism involved a renewed critique of mass democracy. The Italian sociologist Vilfredo Pareto (1848–1923) lamented the tendency of parliamentary democracy to descend into statism, where the governing class panders to the electorate with empty promises of a better life under state centralization. Elites in power employ the rhetoric of serving the people, but in reality commit themselves to preserving and enhancing their own power. His contemporary Gaetano Mosca (1858–1941) criticized democracy and popular sovereignty along similar lines. In his *On the Theory of Government and On Parliamentary Government* (1884), Mosca claimed that popularly elected representatives dedicate the majority of their time toward keeping themselves in power, employing bribery and corruption, and demonstrating little statesmanship or interest in the general welfare. Despite the spread of education and increased rates of literacy in Western Europe, newly enfranchised voters showed scant commitment to or capacity for self-government. Public affairs in an ostensibly democratic age, Mosca wrote, remained securel in the hands of political elites whose skill at manipulating the public, when combined with the public's failure to engage the leading issues of the day, discredited the promise of Enlightenment rationalism.[53] Even the future architect of the Bolshevik Revolution in Russia, Vladimir Lenin (1870–1924), in a pamphlet titled *What is to be Done?* (1902), observed that "there can be no talk of an independent ideology being developed by the masses of the workers" and called for the formation of a small, disciplined leadership elite.[54]

By the start of the twentieth century, then, writers on both the left and the right were calling into question the efficacy of representative democracy. The confidence that had earlier in the century associated political democracy with the course of progress and enlightenment was now giving way before a deeper sense of uncertainty. One thing alone was for certain: any hope that democratically elected governments would eschew the ancient ways of fratricidal warfare, and that Western Europe's industrial and technological superiority was a sign of intellectual and moral superiority over colonial peoples, was proven demonstrably false in the late summer of 1914 when the continent descended into the abyss of total war.

Chapter 6 . . . .

Breakdown and Uncertainty, 1914–2010

In the political thought of the twentieth century, the intellectual landscape was marked by strong continuities and by one massive, and massively destructive, dissent. Many of the seminal ideologies of the 1800s, including liberalism, democratic socialism, nationalism, and Marxian communism, were further developed and put into practice, sometimes imperfectly and at other times grotesquely, with consequences that directly affected the lives of millions not just in Europe but the world over. And between the third and fifth decades of the century, a new type of absolutism came to the foreground as capitalist economies faltered and democratically elected governments struggled to address the material needs of citizens who had sacrificed—and been promised—so much during the crucible of World War I. The "war to end all wars" settled little other than to confirm to colonial peoples the hubris of Europe's self-proclaimed superiority. Four years of colossal mechanized carnage in the trenches, together with the incapacity of the victors to accept collective responsibility for 1914's descent into darkness, allowed opponents of liberal democracy and constitutional government to claim the high ground.

The rise of European Fascism, and in particular its German instantiation, stood in defiant opposition to the entire Western rationalist tradition, to the Enlightenment's vision of universal rights and human equality, and to the liberal consensus on the nature of responsible government. It would take another global war, which in the end contributed to making the twentieth century the bloodiest in recorded history, before liberal democratic values were vindicated, but not before another ostensibly rationalist and scientific ideology, Marxian communism, had taken a cruelly despotic turn in the Soviet Union. It too would be discredited and dismantled by the early 1990s, but for four decades after World War II the discord between liberal, capitalist democracies and the collectivized and bureaucratized workers' state would implicate developing countries worldwide and, on more than one occasion, risk an unthinkable nuclear exchange.

Toward the close of the twentieth century the spotlight shifted again, this time in a markedly particularist direction where identity politics, ethnonationalism, religious fundamentalism, and a postmodern repudiation of universal ideologies developed in tension with greater globalization on the economic front and calls for transnational cooperation on common environmental threats. After the collapse of Europe's colonial empires and the end of the Cold War, new voices entered the discussion to investigate whether Western political ideals were any longer global in application. The Enlightenment project, after all, with its dedicated rights language, had been emphatically universalist in orientation. But were Western political ideals truly applicable to all peoples irrespective of culture and material circumstance? Or were they merely the detritus of lingering colonialism, the preferred model of social order for acquisitive, secularized civilizations at a particular time and place?

The consolidated national state remained the focal point of political thinking during this latter period, but in the final two decades of the twentieth century increased attention was paid to the roles of religion, history, ethnicity, language, and culture in the formation of identity and political thought. The rise of international business, non-governmental organizations or NGOs, a global environmental movement, and a renewed focus on human rights similarly influenced political thinking, raising important questions about the ability of states to move beyond the inherent provincialism of nationalism—the politics of difference *par excellence*—in a meaningful manner. The events of 9/11 and the subsequent "war on terrorism" did not auger well for the spirit of international cooperation and universalism, but as the planet's resources were depleted and its climate imperiled by the very industrialization that had brought so much affluence to the West, the alternatives to greater internationalism seemed, sadly, on track to nowhere.

Repudiating liberal democracy

Europeans went to war in 1914 and they would go to war again in 1939. The interwar years were not unlike the briefer intervals in the religious wars of the seventeenth century, the so-called Thirty Years' War (1618–1648). In both centuries these intervals became preliminary to the resumption of fighting, for the fundamental issues dividing the parties were never resolved in a comprehensive manner. Religion was not at issue in what some have labeled the Second Thirty Years' War, but the breakdown in the international order that began in 1914 led directly to the collapse of four empires (Habsburg, German, Russian, and Ottoman), the triumph of communism in Russia, and the rise of Fascism in Italy and Germany. The final period of general European conflict (1939–1945) was characterized by an unparalleled level of ruthlessness and mass murder, and in its wake Europe's status as a global military and economic authority was shattered.[1]

Few expected this frightful outcome when enthusiastic volunteers marched off to battle in August 1914. Nationalist ideology had done its job well, as strong support for the war—and the rightness of the nation's claims—was shared by artists, university students, intellectuals, and the recently enfranchised working class. Even socialists turned in their internationalist and anti-war credentials and rallied to the flag in 1914. There was every expectation that the conflict would be brief, that the latest military technology would limit the scale of damage on all sides. Indeed many viewed the prospect of a general war as cathartic and cleansing. War would renew each nation's sense of purpose while liberating factory workers, farmers, office clerks, and students from their dull workaday activities, the complacency of bourgeois existence. Only a small number were as prescient as British foreign secretary Sir Edward Grey (1862–1933), who on the eve of the fighting observed laconically that "the lamps are going out all over Europe. We shall not see them lit again in our lifetime."[2] Not until 1945, and only then under the military and financial protection of the United States and in the shadow of Soviet expansion, would Western Europe begin its slow, chastened return to democratic politics. Earlier notions of inevitable progress now seemed tragically misplaced, and as governments committed themselves to a broader notion of social well-being, they enlarged the purview of the welfare state knowing more than a little about humanity's collective capacity for inhumanity, and about the challenges involved in trying to create a society informed by rational cooperation.

The rise of Fascism and Nazism

Even before World War I, as we noted at the end of the last chapter, numerous intellectuals had come to question the merits of democratic politics and mass culture. Although conservatives were pleased that the advent of democracy had not led to the seizure of property that had been feared, radicals were dismayed by the fact that an expanded franchise had not translated into greater civic engagement. Critics lamented the forfeiture of reasoned argument in political debate and the tendency of emotion, prejudice, crude self-interest, and mythmaking to infest the parliamentary process. By the start of the twentieth century, anti-democratic politicians were exploiting the democratic electoral process in order to undermine liberal values. Militant nationalist, anti-Semitic, and ethno-centric arguments resonated with many voters, especially during periods of economic hardship. Representative assemblies were derided as talk shops for the weak and indolent built on the erroneous assumption of human goodness and rationality. And abstract notions of human equality served only to hamstring the exceptional leader. What was needed in the West, according to those disillusioned by democratic practice, was the empowerment of a minority of action-oriented statesmen entrusted with supreme power. The true unity of fellow citizens rested not on enervating myths about equality, but in and through the crucible of combat, the power of common ancestry, and the distinctiveness of racial identity. These sentiments provided much of the backdrop to Fascism in Italy and Nazism in Germany, whose supporters could point to additional evidence in the failure of liberal regimes during the war years.[3]

One of the earliest casualties of World War I had been truth. Governments on both sides harnessed the power of print and new film propaganda to vilify the enemy, a strategy that served to intensify belligerency on the domestic front while making future diplomatic compromise harder to achieve. When the victors met in Paris in 1919 to draw up a peace treaty, idealistic notions of "a world made safe for democracy" and the "self-determination of peoples"—both phrases originating with the American president Woodrow Wilson—neither the French nor the British were sympathetic. New states did emerge—Poland, Hungary, Czechoslovakia, Romania, and Yugoslavia—as part of the overall settlement, but treatment of Germany reverted to the centuries-old pattern of punishment and humiliation. The fiscal and territorial penalties imposed on Germany, which had never been invaded during the war, left citizens of the new Weimar republic dispirited and resentful. Ironically, the Weimar constitution was one of the most democratic in Europe, affording the vote to women at the national level. It was exactly the type of political order that the victorious powers had envisioned for a peaceful Europe, yet in the final treaty Weimar was saddled with accepting a humiliating "war guilt" clause and a crushing reparations burden.[4]

Disgruntled ex-soldiers like Adolf Hitler viewed the Weimar democracy with contempt, and many, including Hitler, joined the German Worker's Party, which was renamed the National Socialist (Nazi) Party in 1920. The following year the 32-year-old Hitler rose to the presidency of the party and advanced the argument that wartime Germany had been politically betrayed and economically undermined by Jews, liberals, Marxists, and other internationalists. Jailed in 1923 after a failed coup attempt to overthrow the Weimar state, Hitler spent his year of imprisonment writing *Mein Kampf* (My Struggle), a combative and unsystematic political testament that captured the spirit of ethnocentric ultra-nationalism in post-war Germany. The book also outlined a future political program anchored in pseudo-scientific racial theory and aggressive expansionism at the expense of inferior peoples located to the east of Germany.

Hitler believed in the inherent irrationality of the masses and extended the pre-war attacks against parliamentary democracy. After his release from prison in 1924 he employed propaganda in a masterful fashion to advance the aims of the Nazi Party under charismatic, "great man" leadership. "All propaganda must be popular," he wrote in *Mein Kampf*, "and its intellectual level must be adjusted to the most limited intelligence among those it is addressed to." The art of propaganda, he insisted, "lies in understanding the emotional ideas of the great masses and finding, through a psychologically correct form, the way to the attention and thence to the heart of the broad masses." His crude interpretation of history as a protracted struggle between racially superior Aryans and the carriers of degenerate culture, in particular the Jews, appeared to a growing segment of the German population that could not accept the outcome and aftermath of the Great War. His emphatic rejection of contemporary Western values, including democracy, pluralism, and liberal humanitarianism, became hallmarks of twentieth-century totalitarian thought.[5]

Italian Fascism

Italy had been in the victor's camp in 1918, but its military had not performed well during the war and its influence at the Paris peace conference was minimal. Diplomatic efforts to secure the Adriatic port city of Fiume were rebuffed by negotiators at Paris, while the transition to a peacetime economy proved difficult. Returning veterans faced sharp inflation and poor job prospects, and fear that the country, in the grip of widespread industrial strikes, might be vulnerable to a communist takeover modeled after the Bolshevik Revolution in Russia prompted many to support politicians who championed economic and political nationalism. It was in this general climate of uncertainty that the ex-soldier, former school teacher, newspaper editor, and pre-war socialist Benito Mussolini (1883–1945) built his political base. Abandoning his earlier socialism, Mussolini guided the nascent Fascist (derived from the term "combat groups") organization to power using a combination of intimidation and skillful propaganda. The combat groups or Fascist gangs regularly disrupted socialist meetings, attacked striking workers, and posed as defenders of order and international respectability.[6]

In 1922, promising to deal firmly with the menace of communism and the enervating influence of do-nothing parliaments, Mussolini's black-shirted followers led a symbolic march in Rome. Speaking to the Fascist congress in Naples just days before the March, Mussolini proclaimed that "every time in history deep clashes of interest and ideas surface, it is force which finally decides the issue."[7] When King Victor Emmanuel III (r. 1900–1946) refused to call out the army against the Fascists, the cabinet resigned in protest and Mussolini was asked to become prime minister. Months of intimidation finally paid off. Over the next few years, Mussolini increasingly ruled by decree while employing corporatist rhetoric that emphasized the collective will of the Italian people and the need to compel cooperation between capital and labor. Opposition parties were dissolved in 1926, and those who spoke out against the regime were either jailed or bullied into silence by Fascist operatives. Despite the intimidation and violence, Italian Fascism had many supporters among the country's leading intellectuals in the 1920s. Even international literary figures like George Bernard Shaw and Evelyn Waugh admired the Italian ruler. In 1929, Mussolini solidified his domestic authority and gained international respectability when he negotiated an accord with the Roman Catholic Church, ending decades of tension between the papacy and the Italian state.[8]

Uncertain democracies

The ascent of leaders like Mussolini and Hitler confirmed the worst fears of liberal democrats. Yet in the two major states that had emerged victorious after World War I, France and Britain, parliamentary democracy seemed adrift, incapable of inspiring the level of engagement requisite for the healthy functioning of civic life. Between the end of the war and 1933, more than two dozen different cabinets governed in France and the only thing that they had in common was a desire to keep Germany weak. In Britain the post-war franchise was extended to women who were aged 30 or older and in 1928 women voted on the same terms as men at age 21. But the nation's economy remained in the doldrums throughout the 1920s with never fewer than 10 percent of the workforce chronically unemployed. Even the formation of the first Labour ministry under Ramsey MacDonald (1866–1937) did little to create new jobs. A nine-day general strike brought industry to a standstill in 1926, but while the government prevailed it was ill-prepared to deal with the crushing impact of the Great Depression in the 1930s. Conditions were worse in the successor states of Eastern Europe. National self-determination may have been achieved through the Versailles Peace Treaty, but in Poland, Hungary, Romania, Czechoslovakia, and Yugoslavia disgruntled minority populations felt cheated in their quest for autonomy. Lacking any history of parliamentary practice and the economic resources to bring about a fundamental change in material conditions for the majority, all but Czechoslovakia devolved into self-imposed authoritarian rule by the early 1930s.[9]

Tragically, Europe's leading intellectuals appeared largely resigned to the apparent failure of the democratic project, and of Western values generally. The German historian Oswald Spengler's (1880–1936) *The Decline of the West* was published just before World War I but appeared in a number of translations after 1918. Its main thesis, that Western civilization had peaked long ago in the midst of the Middle Ages, had little good to say about modern liberalism and mass culture. In England Arnold Toynbee (1889–1975) published a multi-volume *Study of History* between 1934 and 1939 that praised creative minority leadership and disparaged secular democracy and its crass materialism. Cultural critics lamented the role of motion pictures, commercial advertising, and popular journalism as by-products of democracy. The censorious tone was reflected in much of the literature and poetry of the post-war period, perhaps no more powerfully than in T.S. Eliot's (1888–1965) *The Waste Land* (1922), a trenchant indictment of the pre-war West's misplaced optimism and pride. Even leading theologians came to reject the confidence of nineteenth-century liberalism. Influential voices like Karl Barth (1886–1968) in Germany and Jacques Maritain (1882–1973) in France reintroduced the notion of a fallen world where inveterate sinners must rely on unmerited divine grace in order to find purpose in modern life. It was certainly not to be found in popular mass culture, with its embrace of the lowest common denominator. The psychiatrist Sigmund Freud (1856–1939), whose own experience of the Great War led him to identify a naturally aggressive streak within human nature, wrote in *Civilization and Its Discontents* (1928) that the main task of civil society was to curb, but sadly never conquer, the innate anti-social and destructive proclivities within each person. The rational actor, the very predicate of Enlightenment thought, was for Freud nowhere to be found in the modern West, no matter how remarkable the technological advances of the age.[10]

When the American stock market crashed in October 1929, the repercussions affected every capitalist country. Massive unemployment in the Western democracies lent greater credibility to authoritarian parties. In Germany, the National Socialists gained strength in every election and in 1933 Hitler secured the chancellorship. His ascent was generally praised by the country's intellectual and business leaders who saw in Nazism a way out of the economic morass of the day, a situation compounded by the ineffectiveness of parliamentary democracy. In denouncing communism, capitalism, pacifists, liberals, internationalists, and degenerate modernists, Nazi propaganda allowed for an uncomplicated message of national restoration based on racialist ideology. It even had force at the international level. The American historian Carl Becker (1873–1945), writing in 1932, wondered whether liberal ideals had run their course, now to be eclipsed by more corporatist views of the good society. British and French public opinion began to shift on the subject of war guilt, no longer confident that Germany was solely to blame for 1914 and willing to accept German arguments about the need to restore the country's "natural" borders. "Appeasement" was not a dirty word in the late 1930s, despite the odious core of the Nazi message.[11]

Moscow's Marxism

There was another response to the catastrophe of World War I that did not involve, at least initially, the full abandonment of Enlightenment rationalism or belief in the progressive unfolding of history. In November 1917, a dedicated and tightly organized minority of Marxist revolutionaries overthrew a short-lived provisional government in Russia. The autocratic Tsar Nicholas II had abdicated in March of that year, having led a woefully under-prepared country into a modern, mechanized war in 1914 with disastrous results. Massive casualties at the front, widespread hunger, urban strikes, and peasant unrest all combined to destroy the credibility of Tsarist autocracy. The decision of the provisional government to continue the war effort enabled a radical wing of Russia's Social Democratic Party, the Bolsheviks, to organize workers and peasants and to stage an uprising that led to the unlikely formation of a new government under the leadership of V.I. Lenin (1870–1924) and Leon Trotsky (1879–1940). As the least industrialized of the great powers, with a tiny working class or proletariat, Russia seemed an unlikely candidate for Marxist Revolution; as historian J.M. Roberts has observed, what transpired in November 1917 "was as much a collapse of an old as an insurrection of a new order."[12]

But Lenin was convinced that Russia in 1917, like undeveloped colonial countries around the world, was poised for greatness if only the shackles of capitalist control were broken. He also believed that a genuine

Marxist Revolution could be successful despite the fact that Russia had not undergone a bourgeois, capitalist, and industrial phase of history. Once in power, the Bolsheviks signed an armistice with Germany and repudiated the international debts incurred by the Tsarist state. They proceeded to nationalize large estates, banks, church property, and the country's few industries, prompting resistance and precipitating a major civil war that lasted until 1921. Lenin held that successful Marxist Revolution demanded an intellectual leadership elite—an oligarchy of single-minded professional revolutionaries—that would guide (or compel) the uneducated Russian peasant and the numerically tiny proletariat along the ineluctable paths of history. This was one of the main themes in *What is to be Done?* (1902), a pamphlet composed in exile, and was reiterated in *"Left-Wing" Communism: An Infantile Disorder* (1920), written after the Bolsheviks took power. The masses, Lenin insisted, lack the requisite discipline and clear sense of direction needed to overthrow the bourgeois state; typical worker "trade union consciousness" merely seeks to do a deal with the ruling class and engage in "pompous projects for miserable reforms, so miserable that much more has been obtained from bourgeois governments." The victory of the proletariat could only be assured, he wrote, under conditions of absolute centralization and unwavering party discipline. With Lenin, the Marxist creed became a sort of religious fundamentalism with its cadre of true believers indisposed to acknowledge any divergent reading of the hallowed text.[13]

Unlike so many socialists, Lenin had been opposed to the war from the outset, declaring that it represented the crisis stage of capitalism where, lacking further lands and peoples to exploit overseas, Europe's bourgeois leaders turned against each other's assets. In order to bring the Russian masses around to this view of history, the Bolsheviks silenced all opposition groups and built a secret police apparatus, the *Cheka*, to pre-empt dissent. With the apocalyptic revolution poised to envelop all of Europe after World War I (worker revolutions had broken out in Germany, Austria, and Hungary immediately after World War I), and with capitalist states actively intervening in the Russian civil war on the side of the reactionaries, the Bolsheviks felt justified in maintaining their grip on power by all means at their disposal. Internal state power therefore was wielded ruthlessly; when mutiny broke out at the Baltic naval base at Kronstadt in March 1921 with a call for the secret ballot, free speech and press, and the release of all political prisoners, the government first broke the resistance and then massacred the mutineers on the spot. As with the Jacobins in revolutionary France, the Bolshevik leadership was convinced that only repression and terror tactics could save the revolution from its bourgeois enemies. Proletarian consciousness and the ultimate transition to communist society would come later.[14]

The devolution of this theory of elite leadership into raw dictatorship occurred under Lenin's eventual successor, Joseph Stalin (1879–1953). In his *Problems of Leninism* (1926), Stalin abandoned the prospect (advanced by his rival Trotsky) of revolution in the bourgeois West and called for "socialism in one country," the quasi-nationalist notion that the Soviet Union must build its own industrial resources and military might in order to defend the revolution at home and project communist power abroad. Inaugurating the first of what became a series of 5-year plans to expand Russia's economic and military capacity, the apparent success of the programs under full employment, in stark contrast to the unemployment occasioned by the Great Depression in the West, won the attention of sympathetic foreign observers. Of course the Stalinist state did its best to mask the human costs of rapid industrialization. The show trials and the forced labor camps of the 1930s exposed something of the vicious nature of the regime, but few in the West were aware of the larger horrors like the collectivization and orchestrated famine in Ukraine in 1932–1933 that led directly to the deaths of millions—more, perhaps, than the total number of deaths for all countries during World War I.[15] With Stalin, the communist "new man" could not be forged absent totalitarian control over media, education, culture, and the arts. A cult of the leader was enforced as the purges and the internal terror tactics intensified during the 1930s. No one was safe—not old Bolsheviks, not the military high command, not the industrial engineer who proposed changes in the 5-year plans, and not the artist who questioned socialist realism.

Irrespective of their claims on behalf of the oppressed working class and peasantry, neither Lenin nor Stalin had much confidence in the rationality or equality of their countrymen. A new consciousness, they believed, could only be delivered to them from above. The Enlightenment faith in the improvability of the human condition remained standing in their worldview, but political pluralism, the autonomy of the individual, and the marketplace of ideas all were dismissed as instruments of bourgeois manipulation and deceit. With Stalin, the communal foundations of the Soviet state had to be set by a single revolutionary party, and a leader who embodied the highest ideals of the party. In pursuit of the Marxist utopia, Stalin murderously forged its antithesis. It was, perhaps, the final tragic irony of the dialectical view of history.

A tempered faith: Democracy after 1945

The Fascist and Nazi assault on liberal democracy was defeated in 1945, and the Soviet caricature of Marxian communism ran its course by 1990, but larger questions regarding human nature and the ability of humans to act in community remained unsettled in the West. Europe's global preeminence had come to an end, its military and economic might eclipsed by the principal Cold War adversaries, and its colonial empires untenable both in terms of power relations and, more importantly, in terms of the democratic principles that so many had fought and died for in World War II. Many of the continent's industrial cities had been severely damaged by the war, with overall manufacturing capacity in 1945 at approximately 20 percent of pre-war levels. Relief agencies struggled to feed hungry populations, while millions of refugees displaced by the fighting or fleeing persecution awaited resettlement. The war had demonstrated beyond any doubt that even in the world's best educated, most technologically advanced, and (despite the Great Depression) wealthiest civilization, the human penchant for cruelty equaled its capacity for kindness, the predilection to objectify others every bit as strong as the motivation to empathy and compassion.[16]

And whither reason in the aftermath of two world wars in the space of 30 years? How was it possible to reconcile Enlightenment values with firebombing raids over civilian-occupied cities, with atomic weapons incinerating non-combatants, and with extermination camps pushing racism to new depths with scientific efficiency? "It must be emphasized that we create tragedy after tragedy for ourselves," observed the historian Herbert Butterfield in 1949, "by a lazy unexamined doctrine of man which is current amongst us and which the study of history does not support...it is essential not to have faith in human nature."[17] But even if those of little faith were to engage in the rebuilding of European civilization after 1945, what approach, and what model of political order was best fitted to come to terms with the new anthropological reality? Little choice was available to the peoples of Eastern Europe who lived in one-party states under the watchful eye of Soviet troops, but in the allied-controlled Western portion of the shattered continent, and in Britain, a chastened reaffirmation of democratic practice resulted in a measured approach to the great ideological conflict of the post-war world.

Noel O'Sullivan has made the case for an essential unity to the period through to the first decade of the twenty-first century. According to O'Sullivan, in 1945 there was general agreement in countries like Britain, France, West Germany, and Italy that the costly defeat of totalitarianism must be followed by a renewed commitment to liberal democracy, making it more inclusive and responsive to all citizens. This consensus in turn led to four key undertakings. First was the need to configure the nation-state and the law in a manner consistent with the preservation of individual rights and freedoms. As Karl Popper (1902–1994) wrote during the war in *The Open Society and Its Enemies* (1945), the critical use of reason must be employed to defend the liberty of individuals and groups by means of democratic institutions.[18] Second—and in dynamic tension with the first—was the felt need to defuse protracted class friction by expanding the welfare capacity of the state and thereby afford citizens the conditions under which human flourishing could occur. Finding the proper balance between individual and social rights therefore became the key to the first two tasks.

The third undertaking—also in tension with the first and coming to the foreground in the 1960s—involved a heightened recognition of the rights and plural demands of groups that had been historically marginalized or excluded from civic life: women, ethnic and racial minorities, and persons whose sexual identity did not align with the majority culture. Finally, Europeans East and West had to come to terms with a world in which Europe was no longer dominant and, especially after the collapse of communist Eastern Europe, where efforts at integration and transnational union took on new significance.[19] The need for greater integration, and international cooperation, was apparent on many fronts, but nowhere more urgently than in the area of preserving the earth's natural resources for the long-term sustainability of life on the planet. From the late 1940s through the 1980s, the fundamental threat to the earth's ecosystems appeared in the form of nuclear winter; after the end of the Cold War the threat was more amorphous and involved the very economic model, market capitalism, that had apparently triumphed as the Berlin Wall came down.

Rights reconceived

In stirring preambles, official constitutions, and basic laws, the post-war governments of West Germany, France, and Italy boldly reclaimed their devotion to the Enlightenment faith. The fundamental duty of democratically elected governments, all agreed, was to protect and advance the universal human rights of citizens, to embrace the humanity of all persons, and to reject all forms of totalitarian thinking. The 1946 Nuremberg trials attempted to make this point emphatically, convicting Nazi war leaders on the principle that duty to humanity trumped duty to country, and that crimes against humanity could be prosecuted even though the conduct in question was condoned, even encouraged, by sovereign states. The foundational assumption of the United Nations Organization, established immediately after the war, was the conviction that universal standards and principles are objectively real and universal irrespective of culture or place. The 1948 Universal Declaration of Human Rights, with its assertion in Article I that "All human beings are born free and equal in dignity and rights" was the most cogent embodiment of this freshly restored Enlightenment philosophy.[20]

Unlike the situation after World War I, when a retributive peace settlement was imposed on the vanquished, both the Western half of Germany and the island nation of Japan were quickly integrated into the circle of democratic states and were assisted in the transition by a massive infusion of American aid in the form of the Marshall Plan of 1947. And unlike the climate after 1918, when European intellectuals harshly criticized democracy, ridiculed mass culture, and flirted with "good" dictatorships, there was after 1945, and particularly after the beginning of the polarizing Cold War in the late 1940s, a sober recognition of the virtues of an open society that were first articulated during the eighteenth-century Enlightenment. The French novelist Albert Camus (1913–1960), speaking for many of his generation, opined that "none of the evils that totalitarianism claims to remedy is worse than totalitarianism itself." Both Camus and fellow Existentialist Jean Paul Sartre (1905–1980) wrote of the absurdity of the modern condition, but they nonetheless insisted that one must strive to create purpose, meaning and moral order in a world where humans are left to their own devices.[21]

The restored Enlightenment language or discourse effectively framed the majority of political thinking in the immediate post-war years. It involved a constellation of related ideas that were assumed to be true by all parties, from communists on the left to conservatives on the right. Broadly speaking, these included a belief that progress and human emancipation were transcendent forces in history, and that humans were obliged, by virtue of their rationality, to advance democratic principles of social organization. For liberals and conservatives both progress and emancipation were inextricably tied to the nation-state and to the development of a market economy, while for Marxist thinkers the repudiation of both provincial nationalism and the competitive market represented a higher state of human consciousness and the necessary prelude to social harmony. Left and right together assumed that the earth's natural resources were limitless and that the exploitation of those resources would entail few, if any, negative consequences for life on the planet. Both sides fully embraced the master narrative of progress, freedom, and development, but with conflicting diagnoses of current ills and antithetical paths to civic and social health.

Communism discredited

The United States, Britain, and the Soviet Union had been allies through much of the war, and in occupied France and Yugoslavia, the acknowledged leaders of the anti-Fascist resistance movement were associated with the Communist Party. Immediately after the war the leading political groups in France and Italy included both Christian social democrats and communists. The French communists won 28 percent of the vote in elections to the national legislative assembly in 1945, bolstered by their long-standing commitment to greater economic justice and their dogged anti-Fascist activities during the years of Nazi occupation. Many prominent European and American scientists and intellectuals expressed sympathy with the Soviet struggle against Germany, with a handful of scientists and intelligence officials even assisting Stalin's regime in its quest for nuclear weapons technology.[22]

By the late 1940s, however, a combination of Soviet heavy-handedness in Eastern Europe and revelations about Stalin's megalomania and the brutalities inflicted on his own people led to a widespread revulsion against what had become a communist dystopia replete with its own concentration camps. Spy scandals prompted a communist witch hunt in the United States while in France, the Communist Party's denial that official purges or prison camps existed in the Soviet Union deeply undermined its electoral strength. When the new Soviet premier, Nikita Krushchev (1894–1971), acknowledged the crimes of Stalin in 1956, the reality of Marxism's descent into dictatorship chastened erstwhile supporters and emboldened dissenters to speak and write about the failure of the Marxist ideal in Russia. Successive Soviet leaders blandly affirmed the rightness of the basic structure and principles of the bureaucratic and alienating state that had been forged by Lenin and Stalin, but as the repression continued it was increasingly difficult for outside observers to make the case for any measure of similarity between Marxist theory and Soviet practice.[23] George Orwell's (1903–1950) best-selling *Animal Farm* (1945) and *1984* (1949), together with Arthur Koestler's (1905–1983) *Darkness at Noon* (1940), were three of the more notable works of fiction that captured the emerging consensus on dystopias predicated on the scientific organization of society. The loss of individual liberty, suffocating statism, and the manipulation of the majority by power elites all characterized the fictional critiques of communist society. Western democratic practice in the post-war era never inspired the level of enthusiasm characteristic of the late eighteenth and nineteenth centuries, but by the 1950s the luster that had been briefly attached to its Marxist alternative was all but eradicated. Pluralist, multiparty democracy seemed to offer the best check against the lure of ideology, the totalizing answers to questions of social organization. Many now shared Winston Churchill's (1874–1965) laconic observation that democracy was the worst form of government, except for all the others that have been tried.

The post-war welfare state

There was, however, one common thread connecting each of the competing political ideologies of the post-war era. The war had served as a great equalizer for many, when bombing raids and the rationing of food drew no class distinctions. Many Europeans had discovered a new sense of community during wartime and expressed hope that state power could be deployed to forge an era of social justice and economic equality. The opportunity to mute historic class divisions once and for all while preserving the broad outlines of a market economy was a powerful driver of new welfare legislation. But precisely what responsibility did democratically elected governments have in assuring a purposive community where all citizens enjoyed the fruits of material advancement? What role should the state play in setting public policy to ameliorate some of the social costs of extraordinary change in the fabric of daily life?[24] Should there be a "guarantor state" that ends poverty in all its forms and assures every citizen of equal opportunity for self-development, and what would be the implications of such concentrated power for both the ideal and practice of personal freedom and responsibility?

In Britain, these important questions had been engaged for decades prior to the end of World War II. Old-age pension schemes, together with limited accident insurance, had been enacted into law in response to the social dislocation resulting from industrialization. The 1911 unemployment insurance program brought together employers, workers, and the state to guarantee a minimum standard of material well-being within a sometimes unpredictable market-driven economy. That same year, social philosopher L.T. Hobhouse (1864–1929) expanded T.H. Green's idea of social well-being through the state's involvement in the economic and physical well-being of all citizens. In *Liberalism* (1911), Hobhouse argued that every person should have the opportunity to explore the full range of their creative and intellectual potential. Pursuant to that goal, the state must adopt a more expansive notion of rights to include the "right to work" and the right to a "living wage." The purpose of civil society, Hobhouse argued, was not to support the creation of enormous personal wealth by a few, but rather to educate the young, support the aged and infirm, and assist the majority who struggle to find a living wage.[25]

The economist Richard Henry Tawney (1880–1962) was similarly influenced by Green's work. A faculty member at the London School of Economics, Tawney advanced a model of Christian socialism that defined "equality" not in terms of abilities and potential, but as a natural corollary of common humanity. All persons share a fundamental moral equality and their "freedom" is defined by much more than the classical liberal's negative conception of "absence of coercion." People are free, Tawney wrote in *Equality* (1931), only insofar as they recognize mutually supportive social duties and obligations. The radical individualism and rights language of earlier liberal thought, which he traced back to the religious reformers of the sixteenth century in his *Religion and the Rise of Capitalism* (1926), were neither socially sustainable nor consistent with the idea of a common humanity. Even capitalist activity must be disengaged from earlier notions of individual aggrandizement and embrace the notions of optimum human development and social solidarity. Accumulation as an end in itself, according to Tawney, was a moral and spiritual blind alley.[26]

These were enormously influential ideas. Even before the end of the war, both leading political parties accepted the broad outlines of Tawney's social vision by endorsing the conclusions of a special government-sponsored report issued in 1942 under the leadership of the veteran social reformer William Beveridge (1879–1963). The Beveridge Report called for a comprehensive system of social insurance that would assure all citizens security from birth to death from ills over which they had no personal control, including health issues. There was to be no means test for eligibility, but instead the same level of social benefit was to be afforded to everyone irrespective of income. It was the beginning of the comprehensive British welfare state, and its roots would sink deep into popular understanding of the essential functions of democratic governance.[27]

Center-left political parties across post-war Western Europe accepted comparable notions of human flourishing. For these defenders of the new welfare state, individual well-being was relational in nature and included social, intellectual, and emotional goods. In a world of contingency, accident, and frailty, care and support had to be assumed by a wider network of social order. The democratic state now became the formal instrument of this communal vision, advancing the greater good of all by removing the stigma of failure and irresponsibility from those who had been left behind in the new industrial economy. In practical terms, the state was now to assume some of the functions formally carried out by family and church. This broader mandate included regulatory control of the workplace, economic planning at the national level, and full oversight of education. The betterment of society increasingly became the measure of morality in public and private action. Human rights shed its singular identification with the solitary individual and assumed a connection with community purposes, collective ends that advanced social harmony.

The Keynesian middle way

It was a Cambridge graduate with little liking for the working man who provided the most compelling case for state intervention, especially during periods of economic uncertainty. John Maynard Keynes (1883–1946) began his career as a civil servant before being assigned to the Treasury Department during World War I. At the end of the conflict he was dispatched to Paris as an economic advisor to the Versailles Peace Conference, but left that meeting deeply disillusioned by the terms of the final peace treaty. His prescient *Economic Consequences of the Peace* (1919) criticized the harsh treatment of Germany and argued that the demand for reparations would further political instability in Europe over the long term. The book sold well, making Keynes a minor celebrity long before he became a respected economist. The message at the heart of the book would inform post–World War II reconstruction policy, with the allies committed to rebuilding Germany instead of again punishing it.[28]

Keynes published his best known work, *The General Theory of Employment, Interest and Money* (1936), in the midst of the Great Depression when the unemployment rate reached as high as 20 percent. Taking the highly unorthodox view that governments should take a leading role in promoting economic growth and full employment through public "deficit" spending, Keynes argued for the possibility of a middle ground between socialism and unregulated capitalism, between a command and a market economy. "The outstanding faults of the economic society in which we live," he wrote, "are its failure to provide for full employment and its arbitrary and inequitable distribution of wealth and income." Financial stability and economic growth were not, he argued, the natural outcomes of an unregulated, and allegedly self-adjusting, marketplace. Instead, the state must assume the task of regulating the market economy, together with the right of infusing public funds into the economy at critical junctures to preserve jobs and stimulate growth. In essence, since there was no natural law of economic equilibrium in a free market, the state had a duty to stimulate the economy during periods of high unemployment in ways that ensured growth and general prosperity. This more expansive state, Keynes argued, although it controlled interest rates and raised and lowered taxes, need not undermine liberal principles of personal freedom, private ownership of property and the means of production, or individual economic initiative.[29]

Keynes was one of the first academic economists to play a leading role in shaping public policy in the twentieth century. Although principally a theorist, he served as an advisor to the British government during World War II and played a leading role in allied post-war planning. At the 1944 Bretton Woods Conference in New Hampshire, for example, Keynes helped in the development of the post-war monetary order and the establishment of the World Bank. His arguments virtually banished the old-style liberal economists to the shadows of public and academic life, as Western democracies embraced the idea of using fiscal and monetary policy to increase consumer demand and bolster employment. The unprecedented use of public funds to strengthen private sector enterprise stood as perhaps the most forceful affirmation of the interventionist state on behalf of a newly agreed notion of public good.

Interrogating the welfare state

The Austrian-born economist Friedrich von Hayek (1899–1992), in the provocatively titled *The Road to Serfdom* (1944), took issue with the Keynesian paradigm and with the type of central planning characteristic of the welfare state, arguing that interventionism ineluctably ends with the destruction of personal freedoms. Although the book sold well in the United States (especially its abridgements), few professional economists stepped forward to support its main thesis. Indeed, as evidence mounted during the 1950s that the expansion of the welfare state did not lead to a deterministic erosion of economic, personal, and political freedoms, Hayek's defense of an older-style market solution to economic setbacks seemed quite out of touch with the new reality.[30]

But the marginalization of Hayek and other conservative economists proved to be temporary. Although most conservative thinkers accepted the main outlines of the welfare state after 1945, they remained wary of the growth of centralized power in democratic countries. Every European had been witness to the massive abuse of state power under the now vanquished dictatorship in Germany, and most were thoroughly disillusioned by a comparable abuse of power in Stalin's Soviet Union. Concern was deep over the potential of mass parties and mass media to again misuse the power of the state and avoid democratic accountability. There was also apprehension that the new welfare states would create a culture of dependency and a threat to democracy insofar as anyone in receipt of state support would be less apt to challenge those in power. Finding the proper equilibrium between state activism to advance the general welfare and constitutional restraints that preserved the freedom and autonomy of the individual raised vital questions for those employed in the work of reconstruction.

Insisting that personal liberty and the free market were inseparable—abiding tenets of nineteenth-century classical liberalism—post–World War II conservatives remained firm in their conviction that humans are malleable only in the most limited sense, and that the amelioration of social ills through directive state action overestimates the capacity of institutions to amend and redirect the irrational side of human nature. Instead of relying heavily on the state to create the good society, leading conservatives continued to emphasize the older nostrums about self-discipline and the individual cultivation of character as foundational to the betterment of society. The political philosopher Michael Oakeshott (1901–1990) described the conservative temperament as an allegiance to the familiar, "to prefer the tried to the untried, fact to mystery, the actual to the possible, the limited to the unbounded, the near to the distant, the sufficient to the superabundant, the convenient to the perfect, present laughter to utopian bliss."[31]

By the early 1970s, a series of interrelated developments led to a renewed debate over the viability, and the desirability, of the comprehensive welfare state. Europe's declining population raised concerns that an ageing population would soon place inordinate demands on the fiscal resources of the national government. Pension requirements and health care costs would inevitably outstrip the ability of a shrinking workforce to sustain. Europe's declining productivity and rising wage and benefits obligations put it at a competitive disadvantage with other economies in the emerging global marketplace. For some observers the greatly feared culture of dependency was manifest in the high incidence of strikes and union demands for better wages and benefits, including a shorter work week.

The 1973 oil crisis marked the turning point in the post-war effort to achieve through public ownership of the means of production the equality of outcomes that had been envisioned by socialists since the early nineteenth century. Prior to 1973, the industrialized West enjoyed full access to inexpensive supplies of crude oil from the Middle East, where two-thirds of the world's proven reserves were located. When war broke out between Israel and its Arab neighbors, United States' support for the Jewish state led first to an Arab oil embargo and then to a rapid escalation in the price of oil sold to Western states. This punitive move by OPEC contributed to the most serious economic downturn in the West since the Great Depression of the 1930s. The entire decade was marked by rising unemployment, high interest rates, sluggish economic growth, and rising labor unrest. As disenchantment with government-led solutions to economic problems intensified, conservative opponents of the interventionist state seized the opportunity to win the support of a public that was calling for a new direction.

The election of Margaret Thatcher in Britain in 1979 and Ronald Reagan in the United States in 1980 signaled an important turning point, as both leaders pledged to shrink the size and purview of government. They presided over a period of deregulation, privatization, and a return to the principles of market economics.[32] In Britain, powerful unions were confronted and defeated after a series of bitter strikes, a number of public services were de-nationalized, and key sectors of the economy like transportation and communications were sold to private investors, all in line with the neo-liberal economic theories of Friedrich von Hayek. Long overshadowed by the theories of his better-known rival, Hayek came "to dominate the debate on the relationship between politics and markets in the closing decades of the twentieth century, as Keynes had dominated it during the inter-war and post-war decades."[33] Hayek was joined by American economist

Milton Friedman (1912–2008) and his "Chicago School" acolytes, conservatives who skillfully married their faith in market economics with folksy appeals to rugged individualism, patriotism, and law and order.

Conservative writers of the 1980s and 1990s maintained that all citizens should enjoy equal rights, including the right to free speech and assembly, freedom of religion, and due process under law. But they also allowed that the robust exercise of these freedoms would enable some individuals to acquire a better education and more wealth, and as a result more power, than their neighbors. Freedom thus led naturally to economic and political inequalities that could not be avoided short of denying some persons the fruits of their labors. In essays and books that recalled the core convictions of early nineteenth-century liberals, late twentieth-century conservatives held that the so-called disadvantaged were no more than free and equal citizens who had failed to take full advantage of their opportunities in a competitive, individualistic society. These new conservatives declared that it was both practically unworkable and morally problematic for the state to set itself the task of reducing economic inequalities through laws and regulations. In the view of the American journalist Irving Kristol (1920–2009), conservatism must be "reformationist," reaching beyond contemporary liberalism "by a return to the original sources of liberal vision and liberal energy so as to correct the warped version of liberalism that is today's orthodoxy."[34]

By the mid-1980s, the political left found itself on the defensive throughout the West, and socialist parties struggled to present a viable alternative to de-regulation and market-based capitalism. The historic distinction between left–right politics began to blur as all parties started to accept the logic of the marketplace, the profit motive, and the inequality of outcomes resulting from free competition. This trend was confirmed, ironically, with the victory of the Democrats under Bill Clinton in 1992 and the triumph of "New Labour" under the leadership of Tony Blair in 1997. Both administrations adopted the small government rhetoric of their predecessors and presided over a dramatic expansion of the private sector economy. Now muted were the left's historic calls to remedy inequalities of status and condition through political action. Gone was the pointed interrogation of the meaning of social equality and the distrust of markets. Social democracy and equality of outcomes, the cradle-to-grave welfare system that had been at the core of the left's post-war political program, was now deemed both unsustainable and undesirable. President Clinton's ill-fated 1992 attempt to create a universal health care system, and the subsequent conservative takeover of Congress in 1994, testified to the new political realities.

Losing the center: Globalization and difference

The end of the Cold War, symbolized most memorably by the fall of the Berlin Wall in 1989, ushered in a decade of Western triumphalism and faith in the universality of democratic constitutionalism. Neo-conservative theorists like the American Francis Fukuyama (b. 1952) wrote buoyantly about the end of ideological conflict, of a new dawn where nations the world over would embrace Western-style democratic politics, market economics, and a broad social consensus based on competitive individualism.[35] With the unexpected break-up of the Soviet Union, socialism as an economic system received a body blow from which it has yet to recover. The United States assumed the role of monopoly superpower, leading a powerful 1991 military coalition of oil-consuming countries against the upstart Iraqi regime of Saddam Hussein (1937–2006) after his forces invaded neighboring Kuwait. There was much talk in Washington and in London about the dangers of appeasement, of the need to send an unequivocal message to modern dictators who threatened the growing liberal consensus. The rapid and decisive military ouster of Iraqi forces from Kuwait seemed to pave the way for the global convergence of Western values and the repositioning of local identities and cultural expression into the sphere of the private.

Nowhere was that confidence more apparent than in the burgeoning global financial markets, where regulatory protocols were difficult to agree, much less to enforce, across international boundaries. By the 1990s, the economies of the world's major states had become deeply interwoven and the wealthier inhabitants of cosmopolitan cities often had more in common with each other than with their fellow nationals. Since the largely unregulated market economy was trumpeted as the sole model for progress irrespective of place or culture, the accelerated outsourcing of both manufacturing and service jobs in pursuit of the lowest cost became a feature of developed economies in the West. Even thoughtful and highly regarded journalists were caught up in the general giddiness. One best seller of the early twenty-first century declared in its title that the world was "flat" and that those who did not embrace the new interconnected global economy would soon be left behind.[36] In reality, of course, the world's growing material inequality was the salient feature of the new economy, while within affluent Western states a greater percentage of national income was being concentrated in ever fewer hands.

By the start of the new century the general mood of confidence and optimism was compromised by an upsurge in anti-Western sentiment, fueled largely by Islamic religious fundamentalists and by a global economic crisis the scale of which had not been seen since the 1930s. The hegemony of the United States, if it existed at all, proved to be short-lived. After garnering worldwide sympathy and support in the aftermath of the 9/11 terrorist attacks, a coalition of Western countries joined with the United States to remove the loathsome Taliban regime in Afghanistan. But support for the Americans in the so-called war on terror declined precipitously after the pre-emptory invasion of Iraq in 2003. Specious claims about weapons of mass destruction and direct links between the Hussein regime and the Taliban proved to be a fiction, an "intelligence" failure where ideology drove policy and compensated for the paucity of hard evidence. The result was mounting skepticism about American intentions and rejection of the "with us or against us" posture of the single superpower. By late 2010, the "coalition of the willing" in Iraq had dwindled to the preoccupation of the one, while the conflict in Afghanistan was hampered by endemic corruption within the US-backed government in Kabul.[37]

The high cost, both human and fiscal, of the West's military involvement in Iraq and Afghanistan was compounded in the fall of 2008 by a near implosion of major financial markets and the onset of a significant global recession. Two decades of deregulation in the financial markets, together with a consumer mentality that, encouraged by irresponsible lending practices, disparaged savings and applauded debt, set the stage for disaster. The danger inherent in the internationalization of financial markets was revealed most starkly in the mortgage industry, where loans were made to unqualified buyers on the specious assumption that real estate always appreciates. Thousands of mortgages were bundled and sold to investors worldwide who knew little about the fiscal status of individual borrowers, and when the housing market began to soften, foreclosures multiplied and major financial institutions slipped toward the precipice. The US government was compelled to abandon the talisman of the marketplace, infusing billions of taxpayer dollars to prop up irresponsible banks and rapacious Wall Street firms that were deemed "too big to fail."[38] Even Alan Greenspan (b. 1926), disciple of Hayek and chairman of the US Federal Reserve from 1987–2006, testified before a Congressional committee in late 2008 that his career-long opposition to the regulation of lending institutions may have been misplaced. The entire experience raised anew important questions regarding the delicate balance between civic virtue and private interest. In a business culture where money managers were provided inordinate bonuses for short-term risk-taking with other people's money, civic virtue was demoted to an inconvenience. Once again debate over human nature and the most appropriate model for achieving a peaceful and prosperous social order moved to the foreground of public policy.

The postmodern critique

Assertions about the end of history and the definitive victory of liberal democracy could not entirely overshadow an influential trend in post-war philosophical thought that questioned the ability of reason to establish an unequivocal foundation for all moral and political values, even democratic ones. In the wake of World War II and the deaths of over 50 million people, a new generation of thinkers describing themselves as postmodernist stepped forward to disavow the integrity of all large theories of how society should be organized. They called into question the entire concept of political ideology because of its tendency to "totalize" solutions to matters of social organization, to offer a monolithic "one size fits all" formula for humans in community, and to abridge individual autonomy while paying it lip service.[39]

Postmodern writers took special aim at what they termed the West's reliance on "metanarratives," purportedly universal conceptions of truth that underlay all programs of social and political reconstruction.[40] These "metanarratives" have been a feature of Western history since the early Christian era, but they assumed directive power in Western culture beginning in the eighteenth century, when the laws of nature, rights of man, principles of reason, and progressive view of history all became part of the political vocabulary. Postmodernists like the Frenchman Jean-Francois Lyotard (1924–1998) questioned whether any homogenizing or generalist view could claim validity in a world of multiple identities and social fragmentation—an age of decolonization and increased multiculturalism. Writers and their systems, it seemed, were bounded by culture, by perspective, and by historical context. As participants in the whirl and tumble of everyday life, no theorist or political actor could formulate grand theories in a neutral, detached manner.

Another important feature of postmodern thought involved a denial that progress, social improvement, and inclusive narratives of history had any objective reality outside the minds of their creators, entrapped as humans are by their local prejudices. For the postmodernist, universalism in all its forms led not to liberation, a core aspiration of the Enlightenment project, but to greater control and domination by elites. Indeed the entire ideological mode of thinking, when coupled with the power of new communications technologies, had facilitated some of the worst horrors of the twentieth century. Too often, homogenized notions of nation, race, and class—all purportedly leading to the creation of a transformed human nature—had ended in violence, domination, and degradation. According to these writers, all modern ideologies, from liberalism to Fascism, in revisionist socialism and revolutionary Marxism, have totalizing worldviews that translate into multiple forms of domination.

The politics of difference

Postmodernism claimed a space for singularity, fragmentation, and the valorization of difference. And perhaps the most recognizable manifestation of the postmodern critique of ideology was in the emergence of a politics of subjective identity. Finding its earliest origins in the anti-colonialism of the post-war world, identity politics took myriad forms and involved a large number of minority groups. Feminists, gays, lesbians, refugees, legal immigrants, members of religious groups, peoples claiming indigenous status, and non-European populations each called for legal and constitutional recognition, greater social acceptance of lifestyle choices, and the right not to participate in the project of assimilation into the dominant culture. [41] For champions of identity politics, the legal equality of citizens at the core of traditional liberalism had failed to secure the equitable treatment of citizens. To a certain degree, identity supplanted class in the struggle against oppression, and in this respect, ironically perhaps, the politics of identity derived from a commitment to Enlightenment humanism, with calls for full equality, due process, mutual respect and tolerance, and personal self-determination that assumed a universally agreed standard.[42]

Difference was a major theme in liberal feminist thought during the final half of the century. While the political ideas that dominated the discourse since the eighteenth century were framed in terms of human nature, feminists advanced the possibility of values and interests that were principally feminine. They also pointed out that conceptions of happiness, private versus public sphere, individual autonomy, acquisitiveness, and the good life have been framed throughout Western history in societies dominated by males who assumed the natural inferiority of women. The possibility that other perspectives might be of equal or even superior value had never been considered. Even with the vote, feminists argued, the subordinate position of most women within the private sphere has negative consequences for democratic practice in the public sphere, most notably in lawmaking. The unequal division of labor in the household, and women's unequal earning power in the labor market, unfairly raised the cost of their full and equal participation in the public sphere. Feminists within the liberal democratic tradition deployed the language of difference as a means of securing an even playing field in terms of access to power, to realize genuine democracy where for centuries difference in the form of patriarchal thought had served to reinforce inequalities.

In many cases, members of identity groups had overlapping interests. A feminist, for example, might also be a member of an immigrant rights group, or a particular religious minority. Similarly, the position of one identity group might line up with the majority culture on another issue of identity, as in the case of a religious minority that does not support extending marriage rights to gays and lesbians. But one feature of identity politics applied to every group: The nature of the essential self was never static but always in formation, always affirmed by the bearer and never imposed from without.[43] In the work of scholars like Michel Foucault (1926–1984), particular humans must define their own reality, their own being, without the crutch of all-encompassing and ultimately oppressive ideological formations. There could be no comprehensive theory of the good life, only perspectives anchored in personal experience. And since self was the product of social or contingent factors, individuals had no legitimate claim to normative authority over others.[44]

Migration and identity

The postmodern perspective on identity formation had particular relevance for international migration. By the close of the twentieth century the economic model that had propelled Europe and America into the industrial age was in transition. The era of heavy industry and manufacturing was nearing its close as consumer products were now made at a lower cost in developing states. New economic trends, fueled by technology and service-related factors, put an end to the physical landscape of large urban factories and the social reality of big labor unions and extended careers with the same firm. Employment became more flexible but also more uncertain as companies reduced lifetime benefit programs and outsourced projects to third parties in the global marketplace. Dual-income families became normative, and the consumer economy expanded at the same time that birth rates dropped to near or below replacement rates.

There was still an unskilled underclass in the West, but it was increasingly the preserve of indigenous minorities and newcomers from abroad. It was the latter group that posed the greatest challenge to Western democratic theory, as the dynamism of multicultural societies existed in tension with majority cultures that prioritized the alleged virtues of assimilation. Temporary and undocumented workers, a population welcomed in Europe and America during economic good times when natives refused to accept "Three D" jobs (dull, dirty, and dangerous), were recast during periodic downturns in the economy as unwelcome aliens who unfairly strained the state's welfare apparatus.[45] This unequal pattern of embrace and rebuff began with the European guestworker programs of the 1950s and continued for the next half century. It was not the type of treatment envisioned by the United Nations in 1948 when it adopted a non-binding "Universal Declaration of Human Rights" that was intended for "all members of the human family" irrespective of nationality. The principal architect of the resolution, former First Lady Eleanor Roosevelt, anticipated a world where freedom of movement across international borders would bolster global understanding and respect for cultural differences. Most international migration flows since the 1950s have been across frontiers of adjacent poor countries, but the movement from poor to affluent countries in the West has been considerable, creating an unprecedented situation for many European receiving states. For 400 years Europeans had been the world's primary migrants; after 1945, the continent became a net immigration zone. By the 1990s, a continent-wide backlash against immigrant populations that allegedly refused to assimilate aggravated tensions and led to a greater sense of alienation amongst the descendants of non-European immigrants.

Ethno-nationalism

The core message of postmodern thought paralleled the rise of new emphases in national identity. The Enlightenment formulation of nationalism, we recall, stressed a democratic citizenry where a common education and a uniform civic spirit were actively pursued. In the post–Cold War era a more ethnically and religiously based understanding of the nation served to undermine the assimilative project which was now adjudged to be another chapter in the totalizing endeavor. More benign forms of regionalism emerged in established democratic states like Great Britain, where citizens in Scotland and Wales, for example, called for greater federalism and the creation of local parliaments. Most disturbingly, allegedly homogeneous nation-states now discovered plural voices within their midst emphasizing the primacy of religious, ethnic, linguistic, and even regional identity over common civic bonds. In some cases, religious minorities made claims for special treatment like the establishment of faith-based schools and exemptions from the established legal system on the grounds that secular liberal culture is by definition hegemonic.

Ethnic nationalism and a focus on what divides, rather than unites people, reached genocidal proportions in the former Yugoslavia during the mid-1990s and, beyond the West, in the impoverished state of Rwanda in 1995. After much indecision and delay, a coalition of Western democracies finally put a stop to the killing of innocents in Southeastern Europe and brought some of the perpetrators to justice in The Hague, but nothing comparable was done to staunch the violence in black Africa. Tragically, some who had questioned the validity of universal moral principles by privileging cultural difference and a radical pluralism ended by undercutting the very basis of international standards of accountability and human rights. The result was a level of social fragmentation so severe that the very idea of the nation became untenable. The ethno-nationalist rump that remained found its only source of unity in the exclusion and persecution of its neighbors.

John Rawls and the fate of liberal universalism

Trends in the direction of greater fragmentation were countered by efforts to re-conceptualize Enlightenment universalism. And one of the more compelling efforts to forge a synthesis between the foundational principles of classical liberalism (including social contract theory) and its Marxist and postmodern detractors was provided by the American-born philosopher John Rawls (1921–2002). Arguably the most influential political thinker of the twentieth century, Rawls began his professional career at a time when Anglo-American philosophy was largely dismissive of large metaphysical theories in the tradition of Aristotle, Hobbes, Locke, Kant, and Hegel. The focus had narrowed to investigations into matters of fact, and conceptual studies of the meanings of language and terms.[46] Rawls successfully revived substantive, "big question" political philosophy while vigorously contesting the postmodern view that morality is no more than a particular social construction.

Of equal importance was Rawls's challenge to a form of mid-century utilitarianism that equated good public policy with the maximization of social welfare at the minimum social cost. This he considered to be a threat to individual liberty, since the principle of the greatest good (or social benefit) for the greatest number could trample what Rawls called "the separateness of persons" or the dignity and humanity of other individuals. "Whenever a society sets out to maximize the sum intrinsic value or net balance of the satisfaction of interests, it is liable to find that the denial of liberty for some is justified in the name of this single end."[47] Evidence for this was everywhere in the 1950s and 1960s, from the Soviet Union, to Mao's China, to a number of developing postcolonial states. In his *Theory of Justice* (1971) Rawls set out to equip liberalism with a robust strategy for defending egalitarian and humane values against the attacks of relativism and utilitarianism. His entire academic life was devoted to exploring, refining, and articulating the notion of "justice as fairness," where a good society is measured by its ability to set up structures that afford all citizens a set of basic goods.

Beginning with a simple thought experiment, Rawls asked his readers to imagine themselves in an "original position," as part of society and familiar with human affairs, but with no knowledge of whether they are male or female, white or black, rich or poor, gifted or handicapped (characteristics of no moral significance but that in reality often place individuals at a disadvantage). Under this "veil of ignorance" as he called it, the individual is asked to adopt a set of principles that would inform the institutions of society—to enter into a social contract. Rawls assumes that rational, risk-averse, self-interested persons in such a hypothetical position of ignorance, and aware of the normal course of human affairs, would adopt principles and advocate rights that maximize a fair distribution of advantages in employment, educational opportunity, housing, health care, and other "primary goods" that allow one to live in dignity. In advancing this argument about moral decision making, Rawls deflected the criticism of Marxists who contended that classical natural rights theory was little more than an intellectual prop for the bourgeois capitalist. For under this theory of justice, individual, social, and economic liberties are arranged in such a manner as to offer the greatest advantage to the least privileged, who can then make decisions about their lives from a position of autonomy, safety, and security. Rawls believed that such a theory accorded with common intuitions that all people share and therefore provided a logical foundation for evaluating current social and economic structures. It also charted a middle way between the inequalities associated with an unregulated market society and the stultifying conformism attendant upon communist systems. Rawls' book aligned well with the move across Europe in the years after World War II, and to a lesser degree in America, to create a welfare state and a civil rights program where access to primary goods was made more equitable.[48]

A Theory of Justice reinvigorated discussion concerning the relative value of individual versus social or communitarian freedom. While he advanced the idea that individual rights were the product of a contractual process originating from "the veil of ignorance," his Harvard colleague and critic Robert Nozick (1938–2002) argued in *Anarchy, State, and Utopia* (1974) for the traditional notion that rights were inviolable and fundamentally constitutive of humanity. But both men set important limits to state power and prioritized the rights of individuals against the state and society in general. An alternative, communitarian, perspective was advanced by theorists like the Canadian Charles Taylor (b. 1931), the Briton Alasdair MacIntyre (b. 1929), and the Americans Michael Walzer (b. 1935) and Michael Sandel

(b. 1953). The communitarian read on modern liberal theory emphasized the importance of humans in overlapping relationships and communities, not individuals as isolated atoms making contracts with one another. Sandel has argued that highly individualized traditional liberal theory is empirically false, that one's location in community is the starting point of rights formation. Healthy republics require active citizens with "knowledge of public affairs and also a sense of belonging, a concern for the whole, a moral bond with the community whose fate is at stake."[49] For some liberal critics of communitarian theory, however, the idea of embedded communities was inherently conservative and relativistic; it too easily accepted existing community norms and discouraged dissent and alternative perspectives.

*   *   *

A number of critical issues stood at the foreground of late twentieth-century political thought: How could nation-states forge a renewed sense of identity and common civic purpose that was respectful of cultural difference? How could representative democracies reconcile the classical liberal defense of personal freedoms while also acknowledging that in an environment of deep economic inequality such freedoms were of little moment to the outcast? How might civic engagement be deepened and expanded in an age of media manipulation, consumerist distraction, and economic uncertainty? And how could the Western model of the autonomous nation-state, a model of civil order that has been adopted by peoples around the globe, be reconciled with the need for greater international cooperation and decision making? With memories of the tragic failures of the twentieth century still fresh, the answers to each of these questions remained elusive, even as anti-Western sentiment and totalizing religious answers to political questions gained new momentum.

Conclusion: New Trials for Old Ideas

The democratic ideal of classical antiquity was predicated on the capacity of humans to act rationally in a social setting, to establish consensus on the nature of the good life, the life worth living, and to pursue this goal in community. The individual city-state or *polis* was successful so long as citizen engagement remained strong, so long as every citizen attended, spoke, and voted on the great issues of state at formal meetings of the assembly. Men, not gods, determined the balance between freedom and order. But it was assumed also that physical labor and wealth creation were to be shouldered mainly by those who were not free (dependent women, children, and slaves), enabling a privileged minority of male citizens to engage in the project of democratic self-government. Human rationality had its limits, and for the Greek and Roman world humanity was clearly divided between the minority who were capable of rational thought and action, and the greater part that were fitted only to toil and serve.

During the medieval centuries, the pre-eminent purpose of temporal authority was to guide subjects toward salvation in the next life. In this respect the State was but an adjunct of the Church, the ruler chosen by God but subject in theory to the discipline of the papacy. Progress, happiness, and personal freedom were attributes of the next life, not this one. The earthly passage was best understood as a time of trial and preparation. Social *stasis* was divinely ordained, as were existing inequalities and social hierarchies. This theoretical structure underlays a deeply inegalitarian social order, where a privileged and parasitic few extracted agrarian surplus from a numerous and oppressed rural labor force. In medieval culture the idea of social transformation through political action was anathema, a manifestation of the sin of pride that was at the root of the first transgression. Reason, although an inherent God-given attribute of all humans, had been so compromised by the biblical fall that only a temporal kingdom wielding full coercive authority could preserve order and protect subjects from their tendency to do that which was against God's will. The coercive function of the state was deployed as an obligatory shield against the malevolence and immorality that afflicted sinful humanity.

This transcendent focus of medieval Christendom was challenged during the course of the Renaissance and then unceremoniously dislodged by the Enlightenment of the eighteenth century. In a fairly brief time frame St Augustine's undying city of God capitulated to the market-driven, transient city of man. And while in principle the language of the Enlightenment was inclusive, most of the *philosophes* shared with their medieval forebears a distinct lack of confidence in the ability of the masses to construct a rationally organized society. Most, like Kant and Voltaire, supported enlightened Monarchy and strong coercive powers. For the American and French revolutionaries of the late eighteenth century, responsible republics demanded an enlightened and informed citizenry, and the masses were neither. The revolutionary elite, it was thought, would be obliged to build the type of political and social institutions that over time would improve the capacity of the majority to engage as active participants in civil society. Republics were precarious arrangements, demanding a specific set of virtues and an educated public committed to the betterment of the whole. At the outset, however, the discovery and implementation of rational principles that were applicable to all human beings was to be the work of an enlightened minority.

During the nineteenth century, the age of industrialization and growing working-class consciousness, the democratic principles implicit in the Enlightenment began to unfold, haltingly at first, but completely by 1900. Profound social and economic changes led to the extension of political rights to the majority of males, and the beginning of serious efforts to enfranchise women, allowing the working class a direct voice in the political system for the first time. Writers from across the political spectrum acknowledged an inevitable dimension to the process of democratization. Employing the disciplined regime of modern political parties, conservatives adopted a familiar paternalistic posture and pressed their nationalist credentials in appealing to the newly enfranchised masses, while liberals stressed the primacy of individual autonomy and negative rights against the state. Only slowly did the concept of state intervention in areas of housing, education, employment, and public health ameliorate the harsh conditions of industrial society. By 1900, the threat of working-class revolution had been blunted through the extension of the vote and the enactment of legislation that addressed important issues of material well-being. So completely had the proletariat been assuaged that when a general European war erupted in 1914, those few citizens who were brave enough to stand against the fratricidal conflict earned the enmity of their fellow citizens as traitors to the sacred cause of the nation-state.

The experience of totalitarianism in the mid-twentieth century, both in its Fascist and Communist forms, severely tested the Enlightenment faith in human rationality. For intellectuals of the interwar period who had blithely criticized mass democracy and made themselves amenable to authoritarian rule, the horrors of World War II disabused them of their misplaced sympathies. The indoctrination and manipulation of the masses, even highly educated citizens, by leaders who were committed to the destruction of the liberal vision, sobered the post-war climate of ideas and provided a platform for the anti-ideological stance of postmodern thought. Although the centralization of power continued during the second half of the century with the advent of the welfare state and the onset of the Cold War, a residual suspicion of the all-powerful state remained strong, especially within conservative political circles. With conservatives, individual autonomy and economic freedom were the bulwarks of any constitutional democracy; social solidarity was a matter of voluntary association and mutual sympathies, not well-meaning bureaucratic mandates. For most of the second half of the twentieth century, Western political thought navigated between conservative small state theory, and liberal and socialist commitment to the activist state and a rough belief in the rightness of an equality of outcomes.

At the start of the new century, and despite the interrogations of postmodernism, representative, constitutional democracies continue to operate on the assumption that eternal truths exist in the realm of political theory. The language of human equality, the rule of law, inalienable rights, the market economy, and the possibility of progress continue to shape Western democratic political culture. Legitimate political authority is understood in terms of enhancing human well-being, while the nation-state continues to be advanced as the best setting for the exercise of that authority by individuals empowered to lead through free and fair elections. Civilized dissent and peaceful challenges to state policies continued to be interpreted by most observers as essential elements of a healthy political system.

The material affluence of the West since the end of World War II, together with the emergence of the welfare state, has served to blunt the impact of traditional class divisions, but new concerns that cut across class lines have emerged. For example, despite multiple warning signals, Western definitions of the "good society" continue to be framed in terms of the manipulation of nature for human purposes, of development and consumption, all under the auspices of the nation-state. But in an age of environmental stress, economic globalization, and the valorization of particular identities within states, the paradigm may not be sustainable over the long term. And addressing this issue in a meaningful way requires trans-state cooperation and coordination, not boundary-intensive nostrums.

Thankfully, Western political thought continues to take up those fundamental questions whose roots were first established in the ancient Judeo-Christian stories and which were later given explicit secular validation as moral principles during the Enlightenment. The principles demanded that the essential equality of humans is not diminished by individual material circumstances, that dignity and respect be accorded to all, that people be treated as ends, not means. How to live out these principles, how to apply them within changing social and environmental contexts, remains the ongoing focus of political debate in the West and beyond. The bedrock need for a rational politics, for a deliberative process in which plans for the amelioration of the human condition emerge through debate, compromise, and consensus, continues into the new century. It is especially required in a multipolar world where Western values have come under increasing scrutiny. When coupled with ongoing threats to free society by non-state actors who employ violence to realize their fundamentalist vision of the good, the defense of responsible, constitutional government requires unceasing alertness, the type of care and watchfulness that the Greeks thought are only within the clutch of a few men. Proving them wrong is the test of the twenty-first century.

Notes

Introduction

1 George Sabine, *A History of Political Theory* (Hinsdale, IL, 4th edn., 1973), p. 3.
2 Christopher Rowe and Malcolm Schofield, eds, *The Cambridge History of Greek and Roman Political Thought* (Cambridge, 2000), pp. 1–2.
3 Sheldon Wolin, *Politics and Vision: Continuity and Innovation in Western Political Thought* (Princeton, 2004), p. 10.
4 Ibid., p. 4.

Chapter 1: City-States and Republics c. 400 BCE–c. 400 CE

1 Paul Cartledge, "Greek Political Thought: The Historical Context", in Christopher Rowe and Malcolm Schofield, eds, *The Cambridge History of Greek and Roman Political Thought* (Cambridge, 2000), p. 11. Helpful introductions are provided by Ryan Balot, *Greek Political Thought* (Oxford, 2006) and David Stockton, *The Classical Athenian Democracy* (Oxford, 1990).
2 L. S. Stavrianos, *Lifelines from Our Past: A New World History* (Armonk, NY, 1997), argues for the communal nature of kinship societies. See also Felipe Fernandez-Armesto, *The World: A History* (Mahwah, NJ, 2007), Chapters 1 and 2, and William McNeill, *A History of the Human Community* (Mahwah, NJ, 1997), Chapter 1.
3 William H. McNeill, *A World History* (New York, 1999), p. 16.
4 H. A. Frankfort, John Wilson, and Thorkild Jacobson, *Before Philosophy: The Intellectual Adventure of Ancient Man* (New York, 1964), pp. 88–9.
5 Dean Hammer, *The Iliad as Politics: The Performance of Political Thought* (Norman, OK, 2002), pp. 80–92; Balot, *Greek Political Thought*, pp. 18–19; Robin Barrow, *Athenian Democracy* (London, 1999), pp. 7–10.
6 Jonathan M. Hall, *A History of the Archaic Greek World, ca. 1200–479 BCE* (Malden, MA, 2007), pp. 93–100; Robin Osborne, "Archaic and Classical Greece", in *The Edinburgh Companion to Ancient Greece and Rome* (Edinburgh, 2006), p. 93.
7 Susan Price, "The Organization of Knowledge", in Konrad H. Kinzl, ed., *A Companion to the Classical Greek World* (Malden, MA, 2006), pp. 432–9; Martin West, "Early Greek Philosophy", in John Boardman, Jasper Griffin, and Oswyn Murray, eds, *The Oxford History of the Classical World* (New York, 1986), pp. 112–23.
8 Simon Hornblower, "Creation and Development of Democratic Institutions in Ancient Greece", in John Dunn, ed., *Democracy: The Unfinished Journey, 508 B.C. to 1993* (Oxford, 1993), p. 3.
9 Paul Cartledge, "Greek Political Thought: The Historical Context", in *Cambridge History of Greek and Roman Political Thought* (Cambridge, 2000), p. 11.
10 Janet Coleman, *A History of Political Thought*, 2 vols (Malden, MA, 2000), 1: 23.
11 Thucydides, *History of the Peloponnesian War*, in Robert B. Strassler, ed., *The Landmark Thucydides* (New York, 1996), pp. 111–2. See also Donald Kagan, *Pericles of Athens and the Birth of Democracy* (New York, 1991).
12 Coleman, *Political Thought*, 1: 70.

13 R. M. Hare, "Plato", in R. M. Hare, Jonathan Barnes, and Henry Chadwick, eds, *Founders of Thought* (Oxford, 1991), pp. 12–13.

14 Plato, *The Republic*, trans., Paul Shorey (Cambridge, MA, 1963), p. 129.

15 Quoting Sabine, *History of Political Theory*, p. 60.

16 Jonathan Barnes, *Aristotle* (Oxford, 1982), is a good starting point. See also the same author's overview of Aristotle's life and work in Jonathan Barnes, ed., *The Cambridge Companion to Aristotle* (Cambridge, 1995), pp. 1–26.

17 Aristotle, *The Politics and the Constitution of Athens*, ed., Stephen Everson, (Cambridge, 1996), p. xi.

18 Barnes, *Aristotle*, p. 79.

19 Balot, *Greek Political Thought*, p. 232.

20 C. C. W. Taylor, "Politics", in Barnes, ed., *The Cambridge Companion to Aristotle*, p. 236; Abraham Edel, *Aristotle and His Philosophy* (Chapel Hill, NC, 1982), pp. 320–1.

21 Roger Crisp and Trevor J. Saunders, "Aristotle: Ethics and Politics", in David Furley, ed., *From Aristotle to Augustine* (London, 1999), pp. 130–5.

22 Aristotle, *Politics*, ed., Everson, p. 195.

23 Aristotle, *Nicomachean Ethics*, Book 10, Chapter 9, ed., Everson.

24 Aristotle, *Politics*, Book I, 2 (1253), ed., Everson, p. 14.

25 Wolin, *Politics and Vision*, pp. 65, 70.

26 J. M. Roberts, *A Concise History of the World* (Oxford, 1995), p. 140.

27 J. S. McClelland, *A History of Western Political Thought* (London, 1996), p. 84.

28 John Moles, "The Cynics", *Cambridge History of Greek and Roman Political Thought* (Cambridge, 2000), p. 419.

29 Norman Lillegard, *On Epicurus* (Belmont, CA, 2003) offers a short overview. See also James H. Nichols, Jr, *Epicurean Political Philosophy: The De rerum natura of Lucretius* (Ithaca, NY, 1972), pp. 13–24.

30 Wolin, *Politics and Vision*, p. 71.

31 Malcolm Schofield, "Epicurean and Stoic Political Thought", in *Cambridge History of Greek and Roman Political Thought* (Cambridge, 2000), p. 442.

32 Malcolm Schofield, "Stoic Ethics", in Brian Inwood, ed., *The Cambridge Companion to the Stoics* (Cambridge, 2003), pp. 233–56.

33 Marcus Aurelius, *Meditations*, trans., Maxwell Staniforth (Harmondsworth, 1964), pp. 88–9, 96.

34 Romans, 13.1–6.

35 Matthew Innes, *Introduction to Early Medieval Western Europe, 300–900* (London, 2007), pp. 41–2; Roger Collins, *Early Medieval Europe, 300–900* (New York, 1991), pp. 17–24.

36 Julia M. H. Smith, *Europe after Rome: A New Cultural History, 500–1000* (Oxford, 2005), p. 220; Ian Wood, "Christianisation and the Dissemination of Christian Teaching", in Paul Fouracre, ed., *New Cambridge Medieval History, c. 500–c.700*, pp. 710–711.

37 Bertrand Russell, *History of Western Philosophy* (London, 1969), p. 290.

38 St Augustine, *The City of God*, trans., Marcus Dods (New York, 1950), p. 709.

39 Peter Brown, *Augustine of Hippo: A Biography* (New York, 1967), pp. 360–1.

40 Quoting McClelland, *History of Western Political Thought*, p. 102.

41 1 Corinthians 12, 4–12.

42 Cicero, *On the Commonwealth*, ed., James E. G. Zetzel (Cambridge, 1999), p. 71 (Book 3, 33); Francis Oakley, *Natural Law, Laws of Nature, Natural Rights: Continuity and Discontinuity in the History of Ideas* (New York, 2005), pp. 39–40.

Chapter 2: Heavenly Mandates, 400–1500

1 Quoting Antony Black, *Political Thought in Europe 1250–1450* (Cambridge, 1992), p. ix. See also Marcus Bull, *Thinking Medieval: An Introduction to the Study of the Middle Ages*

(Houndmills, 2005), pp. 15–18, where the author discusses the variety of modern responses to the Middle Ages.

2 D. E. Luscombe, "The Formation of Political Thought in the West", in J. H. Burns, ed., *The Cambridge History of Medieval Political Thought, c. 350–1450* (Cambridge, 1988), pp. 158–9.

3 R. N. Berki, *The History of Political Thought: A Short Introduction* (London, 1977), p. 103.

4 C. Warren Hollister, *Medieval Europe: A Short History* (Boston, 1998), p. 59; Robert T. Howe and Helen Howe, *The Medieval World* (White Plains, NY, 1988), pp. 86–7; Edward Peters, *Europe and the Middle Ages* (Englewood Cliffs, NJ, 1989), pp. 88–9.

5 Michael Oakeshott, *Lectures in the History of Political Thought* (Charlottesville, VA, 2006), p. 255; A. Daniel Frankforter, *The Medieval Millennium* (Upper Saddle River, NJ, 1999), p. 49.

6 Hollister, *Medieval Europe*, p. 33; Jacques Le Goff, *The Birth of Europe* (Maldon, MA, 2005), pp. 200–28. See also Brian Tierney, *Western Europe in the Middle Ages, 300–1475* (Boston, 1999).

7 Joseph Canning, *A History of Medieval Political Thought, 300–1450* (London, 1996), p. 17; Eamon Duffy, *Saints and Sinners: A History of the Popes* (New Haven, 2002), p. 48. John B. Morrall, *Political Thought in Medieval Times* (New York, 1958), p. 13, discusses the "elective" principle.

8 Luscombe, "Formation of Political Thought in the West", in *The Cambridge History of Medieval Political Thought*, pp. 169–70.

9 Ibid., pp. 168–9.

10 Patrick Wormald, "Kings and Kingship", in Paul Fouracre, ed., *The New Cambridge Medieval History, c. 500–c. 700* (Cambridge, 1995), pp. 571–604, provides a good overview of early Germanic kingship.

11 Warren Treadgold, *A History of the Byzantine State and Society* (Stanford, 1997), offers a comprehensive survey. See also Mark Whittow, *The Making of Byzantium, 600–1025* (Berkeley, 1996). On the transition of the empire to the east, see Michael Grant, *From Rome to Byzantium: The Fifth Century AD* (New York, 1998).

12 Canning, *Medieval Political Thought*, p. 4.

13 R. W. Southern, *Western Society and the Church in the Middle Ages* (New York, 1970), pp. 94–6; Roger Collins, *Early Medieval Europe, 300–1000* (New York, 1991), pp. 64–70.

14 Jeffrey Burton Russell, *A History of Medieval Christianity: Prophecy and Order* (Arlington Heights, Illinois, 1968), pp. 35–41.

15 Gelasius quoted in Brain Tierney, ed., *The Crisis of Church and State, 1050–1300* (Englewood Cliffs, NJ, 1964), p. 13.

16 Oakeshott, *Lectures*, p. 266.

17 David Nicholas, *The Evolution of the Medieval World*, (London, 1992), pp. 118–20; Canning, *Medieval Political Thought*, p. 55. Later Caolingian annals portrayed the conflicts leading up to the *coup* as religious wars designed to protect the Church. See Philippe Buc, "Political Rituals and Political Imagination in the Medieval West from the Fourth Century to the Eleventh", in Peter Linehan and Janet L. Nelson, eds, *The Medieval World* (London, 2001), p. 191.

18 Matthew Innes, *Introduction to Early Medieval Western Europe, 300–900* (New York, 2007), pp. 400–7; John A. F. Thomson, *The Western Church in the Middle Ages* (London, 1998), pp. 42–4; Joseph H. Lynch, *The Medieval Church: A Brief History* (New York, 1992), pp. 59–64.

19 Quoted in Janet Nelson, "Kingship and Empire", in *Cambridge History of Medieval Political Thought*, p. 221.

20 Hollister, *Medieval Europe*, pp. 95–6.

21 Le Goff, *The Birth of Europe*, pp. 32–5; Thomas F. X. Noble, "The Papacy in the Eighth and Ninth Centuries", in Rosamond McKitterick, ed., *The New Cambridge Medieval History, c. 700–900* (Cambridge, 1995), pp. 568–9.

22 R. W. Southern, *Western Society and the Church*, p. 92.

23 Ibid., p. 99.

24 Janet L. Nelson, "Kingship and Royal Governance", in *The New Cambridge Medieval History, c. 700–900*, p. 393.
25 R. H. C. Davis, *A History of Medieval Europe: From Constantine to Saint Louis* (London, 2nd edn., 1988), pp. 156–64.
26 Nelson, "Kingship and Empire", in *Cambridge History of Medieval Political Thought*, pp. 226–7.
27 Brian Tierney, *Western Europe in the Middle Ages*, p. 205; Le Goff, *Birth of Europe*, pp. 40–1.
28 Tierney, *Western Europe in the Middle Ages*, p. 208.
29 Ibid., p. 214.
30 Hollister, *Medieval Europe*, pp. 228–9.
31 Ibid., p. 230.
32 "Dictates of the Pope", in C. Warren Hollister, ed., *Medieval Europe: A Short Sourcebook* (New York, 1997), pp. 260–1.
33 John B. Morrall, *Political Thought in Medieval Times* (New York, 1958), pp. 34–6.
34 Tierney, *Western Europe in the Middle Ages*, pp. 220–3.
35 Tierney, ed., *Crisis of Church and State*, pp. 76, 78, 83. See also selections from Mangold of Lautenbach and Hugh of Fleury, in Ewart Lewis, *Medieval Political Ideas* (London, 1954), pp. 164–8.
36 Frank Barlow, *The Feudal Kingdom of England, 1042–1216* (New York, 1988), pp. 122–33.
37 Tierney, *Western Europe in the Middle Ages*, p. 225.
38 Sabine, *History of Political Theory*, p. 216.
39 Le Goff, *Birth of Europe*, pp. 100–9.
40 John of Salisbury quoted in Canning, *Medieval Political Thought*, p. 112.
41 John of Salisbury, *Policraticus*, trans. and ed., Gary J. Nederman (Cambridge, 1990), pp. 28, 30.
42 Tierney, *Western Europe in the Middle Ages*, p. 313.
43 Hollister, *Medieval Europe*, pp. 298–9.
44 Fernand Van Steenberghen, *Aristotle in the West*, trans., Leonard Johnston (Louvain, 1970), pp. 8–22.
45 Eleanor Stump, *Aquinas* (London, 2003), 314–6, discusses the role of the state in forwarding justice. Alexander Passerin D'Entreves, *The Medieval Contribution to Political Thought: Thomas Aquinas, Marsilius of Padua, Richard Hooker* (New York, 1959), pp. 22–3; Berki, *History of Political Thought*, p. 106.
46 Berki, *History of Political Thought*, p. 107. Arthur Lovejoy, *The Great Chain of Being* (Cambridge, MA, 1936) is the classic survey.
47 From Aquinas, *Summa Theologica*, in Ralph McInery, ed. and trans., *Thomas Aquinas: Selected Writings* (London, 1998), p. 613. See also Sabine, *History of Political Theory*, pp. 241–3.
48 David Nicholas, *The Transformation of Europe, 1300–1600* (London, 1999), pp. 53–84, reviews the secularizing tendencies in government.
49 *Unam Sanctum* in Tierney, ed., *The Crisis of Church and State, 1050–1300*, p. 189.
50 Black, *Political Thought in Europe, 1250–1450*, pp. 48–9.
51 Barbara Tuchman, *A Distant Mirror: The Calamitous Fourteenth Century* (New York, 1972); Robin Winks and Lee Palmer Wandel, *Europe in a Wider World* (New York, 2003), pp. 32–40.
52 Nicholas, *Transformation of Europe*, pp. 128–9.
53 Dante, *On World Government*, trans., Herbert W. Schneider (Indianapolis, 1957), pp. 52–80; John A. Scott, *Understanding Dante* (Notre Dame, IN, 2004), pp. 144–5; Sabine, *History of Political Theory*, p. 246.
54 Marsilius of Padua, *Defensor Pacis*, trans., Alan Gewirth (Toronto, 1980), p. 23. See also Leo Strauss, "Marsilius of Padua", in Leo Strauss and Jospeh Cropsey, eds, *History of Political Philosophy* (Chicago, 1987), pp. 276–95.
55 Canning, *Medieval Political Thought*, pp. 155–6.
56 Marsilius, *Defensor Pacis*, p. 45.

57 Francis Oakley, *The Medieval Experience: Foundations of Western Cultural Singularity* (New York, 1974), pp. 106–7.
58 David Nicholas, *The Evolution of the Medieval World: Society, Government and Thought in Europe, 312–1500* (London, 1992), pp. 461–4; Albert Rigaudiere, "The Theory and Practice of Government in Western Europe", in Michael Jones, ed., *The New Cambridge Medieval History, c. 1300–1415* (Cambridge, 2000), pp. 31–2.
59 Nicholas, *Evolution of Medieval World*, pp. 465–6.
60 Quentin Skinner, *Machiavelli* (Oxford, 1996), provides a short overview of Machiavelli's life and work.
61 Quoting Wolin, *Politics and Vision*, p. 188. See also Elena Fasano Guarini, "Machiavelli and the Crisis of the Italian Republics", in Gisela Bock, Quentin Skinner, and Maurizio Viroli, eds, *Machiavelli and Republicanism* (Cambridge, 1993), pp. 17–40.
62 Machiavelli, *The Discourses*, ed., Bernard Crick (Harmondsworth, 1986), p. 132.
63 E. A. Rees, *Political Thought from Machiavelli to Stalin* (Houndmills, 2004), p. 7. On Machiavelli and natural law, see J. N. Figgis, *Political Thought from Gerson to Grotius, 1414–1625* (New York, 1960), pp. 97–9.
64 Wolin, *Politics and Vision*, pp. 180–1.
65 Sabine, *History of Political Theory*, p. 323.
66 Machiavelli, *The Discourses*, p. 515.
67 Machiavelli, *The Prince*, trans., George Bull (Harmondsworth, 1981), p. 96.
68 Machiavelli, *The Discourses*, p. 268.
69 Quentin Skinner, *Machiavelli*, p. 59.
70 Machiavelli, *The Prince*, p. 91.

Chapter 3: The Emergence of the Sovereign State, 1500–1700

1 Theodore Rabb, *Origins of the Modern West* (New York, 1993), p. 21. See also Rabb, *The Struggle for Stability in Early Modern Europe* (New York, 1975) for an overview of the period 1500–1700; and Thomas Munck, *Seventeenth-Century Europe, 1598–1700* (Houndmills, 1991).
2 Fernand Braudel, *Capitalism and Material Life, 1400–1800* (New York, 1973) provides a comprehensive overview.
3 Herschel Baker, *The Image of Man* (New York, 1947), part III, and the same author's *The Wars of Truth* (Cambridge, MA, 1952), focus on the Renaissance view of human nature. See also De Lamar Jensen, *Renaissance Europe: Age of Recovery and Reconciliation* (Lexington, MA, 1992).
4 Richard Mackenny, *Sixteenth Century Europe* (New York, 1993), p. 58.
5 Roland Bainton, *The Age of the Reformation* (New York, 1956), p. 12. See also Alister McGrath, *The Intellectual Origins of the European Reformation* (Malden, MA, 2004).
6 Berki, *History of Political Thought*, p. 126.
7 Franklin Le Van Baumer, ed., *Main Currents of Western Thought* (New Haven, 1978), p. 169.
8 Garrett Mattingly, introduction to the Harper Torchbook edition of J. N. Figgis, *Political Thought from Gerson to Grotius, 1414–1625* (New York, 1960), p. xiv.
9 Mackenny, *Sixteenth-Century Europe*, pp. 60–1. See also Paul Kennedy, *The Rise and Fall of the Great Powers* (New York, 1988), chapter 1.
10 Lewis W. Spitz, *The Renaissance and Reformation Movements*, 2 vols (St Louis, 1987), 2: 359; De Lamar Jensen, *Reformation Europe* (Lexington, MA, 1992), p. 34.
11 Euan Cameron, *The European Reformation* (Oxford, 1991), pp. 99–103, 106–8. Martin Marty, *Martin Luther* (New York, 2004), is the most recent scholarly biography.
12 Wolin, *Politics and Vision*, p. 148.
13 Luther, "An Appeal to the Ruling Class", in Lewis W. Spitz, ed., *The Protestant Reformation* (Englewood Cliffs, NJ, 1966), p. 54.

14 Ibid., p. 55.
15 Hans J. Hillerbrand, *Men and Ideas in the Sixteenth Century* (Prospect Heights, IL, 1969), pp. 28–9.
16 Quentin Skinner, *The Foundations of Modern Political Thought*, 2 vols (Cambridge, 1978), 2: 15.
17 Jensen, *Reformation Europe*, p. 88.
18 Cameron, *European Reformation*, p. 153.
19 Quoting Skinner, *Foundations*, 2: 71. The point is reaffirmed on p. 113. See also Francis Oakley, "Christian Obedience and Authority, 1520–1550", in J. H. Burns, ed., *The Cambridge History of Political Thought, 1450–1700* (Cambridge, 1991), pp. 170–1.
20 Skinner, *Foundations*, 2: 113.
21 Dennis Sherman and Joyce Salisbury, *The West in the World* (New York, 2001), p. 377.
22 Robin Briggs, *Early Modern France, 1560–1715* (Oxford, 1977), pp. 14–24. See also Richard S. Dunn, *The Age of Religious Wars, 1559–1689* (New York, 1970), pp. 20–31.
23 W. M. Spellman, *European Political Thought, 1600–1700* (Houndmills, 1998), p. 53.
24 Skinner, *Foundations*, 2: 87. John Guy, *Tudor England* (Oxford, 1988), provides the best overview of the period.
25 G. R. Elton, *The Tudor Revolution in Government* (Cambridge, 1966), makes the case for the revolutionary nature of the English Reformation under Cromwell's guidance.
26 A. G. Dickens, *The English Reformation* (New York, 1964), p. 71; Skinner, *Foundations*, 2: 33.
27 On Elizabeth's reign, a good starting point is Carole Levin, *Elizabeth I* (Houndmills, 2000). See also John Neale, *Elizabeth I and Her Parliaments*, 2 vols; A. G. R. Smith, *The Government of Elizabethan England* (New York, 1967).
28 Charles H. MacIlwain, ed., *The Political Works of James I* (New York, 1965), p. 62; *Trew Law of Free Monarchy*, in Johann P. Sommerville, ed., *King James VI and I: Political Writings* (Cambridge, 1994), p. 69.
29 Spellman, *European Political Thought, 1600–1700*, p. 59.
30 The best recent treatment is Johann P. Somerville, *Thomas Hobbes: Political Ideas in Historical Context* (Houndmills, 1992).
31 Thomas Hobbes, *Leviathan*, ed., Richard Tuck (Cambridge, 1991), p. 89.
32 Roland Stromberg, *An Intellectual History of Modern Europe* (Englewood Cliff, NJ, 1975), p. 88.
33 Quoting Noel Malcolm, "Hobbes and Spinoza", in *Cambridge History of Political Thought, 1450–1700*, p. 535.
34 Hobbes, *Leviathan*, p. 124.
35 Henry Bertram Hill, ed., *The Political Testament of Cardinal Richelieu* (Madison, WI, 1961).
36 Bossuet, *Politics* quoted in J. P. Sommerville, "Absolutism and Royalism", in *Cambridge History of Political Thought, 1450–1700*, p. 350.
37 Jensen, *Reformation Europe*, pp. 109–11.
38 Calvin, "The Geneva Confession of Faith" (1526) in Spitz, ed., *Protestant Reformation*, p. 115.
39 Sabine, *History of Political Theory*, p. 340.
40 Knox's attack on female monarchs in general, and Elizabeth I in particular, began in 1558 with *The First Blast of the Trumpet Against the Monstrous Regiment of Women*. See Marvin Breslow, ed., *The Political Writings of John Knox* (Washington, 1985).
41 Allen, *Political Thought*, pp. 346–52; Kingdom, "Calvinism and Resistance Theory", in *Cambridge History of Political Thought, 1450–1700*, pp. 216–8.
42 Christopher Goodman, *How Superior Powers Ought to be Obeyed of Their Subjects*, in Edmund Morgan, ed., *Puritan Political Thought* (Indianapolis, 1965), pp. 2, 9.
43 Ponet quoted in Peter Holmes, *Resistance and Compromise: The Political Thought of the Elizabethan Catholics* (Cambridge, 1982), p. 4.
44 Francis Hotman, *Francogallia*, in Julian H. Franklin, ed., *Constitutionalism and Resistance in the Sixteenth-Century: Three Treatises by Hotman, Beza and Mornay* (New York, 1960), p. 55.

Donald Kelley, *Francis Hotman: A Revolutionary's Ordeal* (Princeton, 1973), offers a good analysis.

45 Beza, *Right of Magistrates*, in Franklin, ed., *Constitutionalism*, p. 108. On the book's publishing history, see Robert M. Kingdom, "Calvinism and Resistant Theory, 1550–80", in *Cambridge History of Political Thought, 1450–1700*, p. 211.

46 Quoting J. W. Allen, *A History of Political Thought in the Sixteenth Century* (London, 1967; originally published 1928), p. 315.

47 Spellman, *European Political Thought, 1600–1700*, pp. 82–3.

48 Mariana, "The King and the Education of the King" (1599) quoted in Richard Bonney, *The European Dynastic States, 1494–1660* (Oxford, 1991), p. 311. For a treatment of Catholic resistance theory see Frederic Baumgartner, *Radical Reactionaries: The Political Thought of the Seventeenth-Century Catholic League* (Geneva, 1976).

49 Robert Filmer, *Patriarcha* in J. P. Somerville, ed., *Patriarcha and Other Writings* (Cambridge, 1991), p. 2.

50 John Locke, *Two Treatises of Government*, ed., Peter Laslett (Cambridge, 1963), Book 1: 52; Book 2: 56.

51 Ibid., 2: 124, 125, 126.

52 Ibid., 2: 4, 6, 23.

53 John Milton, *A Defense of the People of England*, in Martin Dzelzainis, ed., *John Milton: Political Writings*, trans., Claire Gruzelier (Cambridge, 1991), p. 108.

54 Andrew Sharp, ed., *The English Levellers* (New York, 1998) provides a selection of important Leveller tracts.

55 Gerrard Winstanley, *The New Law of Righteousness*, in George H. Sabine, ed., *The Works of Gerrard Winstanley* (New York, 1965), p. 159.

56 Sabine, *History of Political Theory*, pp. 447, 451.

57 Grotius, *The Law of War and Peace*, trans., Francis W. Kelsey (Indianapolis, IN, 1925), p. 38.

58 Hobbes, *Leviathan*, ed., Richard Tuck (Cambridge, 1991), p. 91.

59 Grotius quoted in Michael Zuckert, *Natural Rights and the New Republicanism* (Princeton, 1994), p. 122.

60 Stromberg, *Intellectual History of Western Europe*, p. 74.

Chapter 4: From Subject to Citizen, 1700–1815

1 A useful starting point is Roy Porter, *The Enlightenment* (Atlantic Heights, NJ, 1990). Peter Gay, *The Enlightenment: An Interpretation*, 2 vols (New York, 1969), treats the relationship between the Enlightenment and classical antiquity, while Carl Becker, *The Heavenly City of the Eighteenth-Century Philosophers* (New Haven, 1932), explores the century's faith in reason.

2 Philipp Blom, *Enlightening the World: Encyclopédie, The Book That Changed the Course of History* (New York, 2005), traces the history of the project.

3 David J. Sturdy, *Louis XIV* (New York, 1998), provides a solid introduction to the reign. See also, Anthony Levi, *Louis XIV* (New York, 2004).

4 Bettina L. Knapp, *Voltaire Revisited* (New York, 2000), pp. 6–8, and Roger Pearson, *Voltaire Almighty: A Life in Pursuit of Freedom* (New York, 2005), pp. 69–84, examine his exile in England. Voltaire, *Letters on England*, trans., Leonard Tancock (New York, 1980).

5 Constance Rowe, *Voltaire and the State* (New York, 1968), pp. 132–3. Peter Gay, *Voltaire's Politics: The Poet as Realist* (Princeton, 1959), offers the best analysis of Voltaire's monarchism.

6 Maurice Cranston, *Philosophers and Pamphleteers: Political Theorists of the Enlightenment* (Oxford, 1986), p. 46. See also Gay, *The Enlightenment*, 2: 471–2.

7 Voltaire, *Philosophical Dictionary*, 2 vols, trans., Peter Gay (New York, 1962), 2: 413.

8 Judith N. Shklar, *Montesquieu* (Oxford, 1987), pp. 1–28, provides an overview of his life and work.

9   Montesquieu, *The Spirit of the Laws*, trans., Thomas Nugent (New York, 1949), p. 1.
10 Ibid., p. 6.
11 J. Robert Loy, *Montesquieu* (New York, 1968), p. 85.
12 Peter V. Conroy, *Montesquieu Revisited* (New York, 1992), pp. 74–6.
13 John Plamenatz, *Man and Society*, 2 vols (London, 1963), 1: 253. Berki, *History of Political Thought*, p. 152.
14 Maurice Cranston, *Jean-Jacques: The Early Life and Work* (Chicago, 1991), treats the period to 1754.
15 Rousseau, *Discourse on the Origin of Inequality*, in Roger Masters and Christopher Kelly, eds, *The Collected Writings of Rousseau*, 4 vols (Hanover, NH, 1992), 3: 37.
16 Ibid., 3: 43.
17 Ibid., 3: 54.
18 Stromberg, *Intellectual History of Western Europe*, p. 147.
19 Patrick Riley, "Social Contract Theory and Its Critics", in Mark Goldie and Robert Wolker, eds, *The Cambridge History of Eighteenth-Century Political Thought* (Cambridge, 2006), p. 362.
20 Jean-Jacques Rousseau, *The Social Contract*, trans., Maurice Cranston (London, 1968), p. 96.
21 Rousseau, *Social Contract*, p. 65. See the discussion in Jonathan Wolfe, *An Introduction to Political Philosophy* (Oxford, 1996), pp. 95–7 and Dupre, *The Enlightenment and the Intellectual Foundations of Modern Culture*, pp. 167–8.
22 Paul Rahe, *Republics Ancient and Modern* (Chapel Hill, 1992), explores the links between the ancient republics and the American Revolution.
23 Gordon Wood, "The American Revolution", in *The Cambridge History of Eighteenth Century Political Thought*, eds, Mark Goldie and Robert Wokler (Cambridge, 2006), p. 601. See also the same author's *The Creation of the American Republic, 1777–1787*, (Chapel Hill, 1969).
24 Wood, "The American Revolution", pp. 601–2.
25 The classic exposition of this thesis is Bernard Bailyn, *The Ideological Origins of the American Revolution* (Cambridge, MA, 1967). Jeremy Black, *George III: America's Last King* (New Haven, 2006), pp. 209–19, examines the king's role in the lead-up to war. See also Charles R. Ritcheson, *British Politics and the American Revolution* (Norman, OK, 1954), pp. 3–5.
26 Edmund Burke, "Speech on Moving Resolutions for Conciliation with the Colonies" (March 1775) in Ross J. S. Hoffman and Paul Levack, eds, *Burke's Politics: Selected Writings and Speeches* (New York, 1967), p. 69.
27 Thomas Paine quoted in Wood, "The American Revolution", p. 611.
28 James Madison, Federalist # 51 in Terence Ball, ed., *The Federalist* (Cambridge, 2003), p. 255.
29 For an introduction to the Anti-Federalists, see Ralph Ketcham, ed., *The Anti-Federalist Papers and the Constitutional Convention Debates* (New York, 1986) and W. B. Allen and Gordon Lloyd, eds, *The Essential Anti-Federalist* (New York, 1985).
30 Hamilton, Federalist #1 in Ball, ed., *The Federalist*, p. 1.
31 The financial and political crises facing the French government prior to 1789 are described by William Doyle, *Origins of the French Revolution* (Oxford, 2nd edn., 1988), pp. 43–65.
32 Alan Forrest, *The French Revolution* (Oxford, 1995), pp. 24–39.
33 Bruce Haddock, *History of Political Thought, 1789 to the Present* (Cambridge, 2005), p. 11.
34 See, for example, Brian Tierney, *The Idea of Natural Rights* (Atlanta, 1977) and the review of recent interpretations in Francis Oakley, *Natural Law, Laws of Nature, Natural Rights* (New York, 2005), pp. 87–109.
35 Louis Dupre, *The Enlightenment and the Intellectual Foundations of Modern Culture* (New Haven, 2004), pp. 159–60.
36 Ibid., pp. 154–9.
37 Oakley, *Natural Law*, pp. 108–9; Locke, *Second Treatise of Government*, ed., C. B. Macpherson (Indianapolis, IN, 1980), p. 66.
38 Edmund Burke, *Reflections on the Revolution in France*, in L. G. Mitchell, ed., *The Writings and Speeches of Edmund Burke*, 8 vols (Oxford, 1989), 7: 92.

39 Ibid., 7: 72.

40 Berki, *Short History of Political Theory*, pp. 170–1.

41 A. J. Ayer, *Thomas Paine* (New York, 1988), pp. 1–10.

42 Mark Philp, *Paine* (Oxford, 1989), pp. 10–11; Bruce Kuklick, ed., *Paine: Political Writings* (Cambridge, 1989), p viii.

43 George Spater, "American Revolutionary, 1774–89", in Ian Dyck, ed., *Citizen of the World: Essays on Thomas Paine* (New York, 1988), pp. 28–30.

44 Philp, *Thomas Paine*, pp. 12–13.

45 Paine, *Common Sense*, in Kuklick, ed., *Political Writings*, p. 3.

46 Paine, *Rights of Man, Part II*, in *Political Writings*, p. 155.

47 Ibid., p. 155.

48 Ibid., p. 157.

49 Ibid., pp. 161, 172.

50 William Godwin, *Enquiry Concerning Political Justice*, ed., F. E. L. Priestley, 3 vols (Toronto, 1946), 2: 119.

51 Patrick Riley, "Social Contract Theory and Its Critics", in *Cambridge History of Eighteenth-Century Political Thought*, p. 356. David Miller, *Philosophy and Ideology in Hume's Political Thought* (Oxford, 1981), p. 187 concludes that for Hume "moral judgement necessarily involved an element of feeling".

52 Hume quoted in Melvin Richter, "The Comparative Study of Regimes and Societies", in *Cambridge History of Eighteenth-Century Political Thought*, p. 163.

53 Jack Fruchtman, *The Apocalyptic Politics of Richard Price and Joseph Priestly* (Philadelphia, 1983); Helvetius, *De L'Esprit or Essays on the Mind* (New York, 1970), pp. 62–3; Beccaria, *Of Crimes and Punishments* (Oxford, 1964), p. 11.

54 Jeremy Bentham, *An Introduction to the Principles of Morals and Legislation* (Oxford, 1967), p. 125; John Dinwiddy, *Bentham* (Oxford, 1989), pp. 7–8.

55 Gianni Vaggi, *The Economics of Francois Quesnay* (Durhan, NC, 1987), p. 18, writes that for Quesnay, "economic events are the result of the working of objective laws, which describe the systematic order of society".

56 Iain McLean, *Adam Smith, Radical and Egalitarian: An Interpretation for the Twenty-First Century* (New York, 2007), pp. 88–95, discusses Smith's view of markets and government intervention.

57 Adam Smith, *The Wealth of Nations*, ed., Edwin Cannan (New York, 1937), p. 423. See also John H. Hallowell, *Main Currents in Modern Political Thought* (New York, 1960), p. 139 and Emma Rothschild and Amartya Sen, "Adam Smith's Economics", in Knud Haakonssen, ed., *The Cambridge Companion to Adam Smith* (Cambridge, 2006), p. 347 on the essential duties of the sovereign.

58 Mary Astell, *Political Writings*, ed., P. Springborg (Cambridge, 1996), p. 18.

59 Karen Offen, *European Feminisms, 1700–1950: A Political History* (Stanford, CA, 2000), p. 31.

60 Paine quoted in Micheline R. Ishay, *The History of Human Rights: From Ancient Times to the Globalization Era* (Berkeley, 2004), p. 110.

61 Rachel G. Fuchs and Victoria E. Thompson, *Women in Nineteenth-Century Europe* (Houndmills, 2005), pp. 5–7.

62 Quoted in Offen, *European Feminisms*, pp. 51–2.

63 Ibid., p. 54.

64 Condorcet quoted in Offen, *European Feminisms*, p. 57.

65 Olympe de Gouge, "Declaration of the Rights of Women and Citizen", in Hilda L. Smith and Bernice A. Carroll, eds, *Women's Political and Social Thought: An Anthology* (Bloomington, IN, 2000), p. 150.

66 Williams, *Letters Written in France*, in Adriana Craciun, ed., *British Women Writers and the French Revolution* (Houndmills, 2005), p. 1.

67 John Davidson, trans., *Persian and Chinese Letters* (New York, 1901); Immanuel Kant, *Toward Perpetual Peace and Other Writings on Politics, Peace, and History*, Pauline Kleingeld, trans., David L. Colclasure (New Haven, 2006), pp. 74–5.
68 Quoting Barbara Taylor, "Mary Wolstonecraft and the Wild Wish of Early Feminism", in Fiona Montgomery and Christine Collette, eds, *The European Women's History Reader* (New York, 2002), p. 53.
69 Mary Wolstonecraft, *A Vindication of the Rights of Women* (New York, 2004), p. 19, where she begins her attack on Rousseau.
70 Olwen Hufton, *The Prospect Before Her: A History of Women in Western Europe, 1500–1800* (New York, 1996), p. 454.
71 Quoting Sylvana Tomaselli, in Mary Wolstonecraft, *A Vindication of the Rights of Man and A Vindication of the Rights of Women*, ed., Sylvana Tomaselli (Cambridge, 1995), p. xxvi.
72 Adams quoted in Paul Schumaker, *From Ideologies to Public Philosophies: An Introduction to Political Theory* (Oxford, 2008), pp. 31–2.

Chapter 5: Ideology and Equality, 1815–1914

1 Robert Tombs, "Politics", in T. C. W. Blanning, ed., *The Nineteenth Century: Europe 1789–1914* (Oxford, 2000), pp. 10–11. Historian Harry Hearder has written that "Much of the thought of the period 1830–1880 was to have a greater influence on the post-1880 period than on its own". *Europe in the Nineteenth Century, 1830–1880* (New York, 2nd edn., 1988), p. 41.
2 Tom Kemp, *Industrialization in Nineteenth-Century Europe* (New York, 2nd edn., 1985), provides a useful overview of industrial change and its impact on society.
3 T. C. W. Blanning, ed., *The Nineteenth Century: Europe, 1789–1914* (Oxford, 2000), p. 2.
4 Franklin L. Ford, *Europe, 1780–1830* (New York, 2nd edn., 1989), chapters 8 and 9 treat the career of the emperor. See also Robert Gildea, *Barricades and Borders: Europe 1800–1914* (Oxford, 1987), pp. 35–56.
5 Charles S. Maier, "Democracy Since the French Revolution", in John Dunn, ed., *Democracy: The Unfinished Journey* (Oxford, 1992), p. 126. See also Jacques Droz, *Europe Between Revolutions, 1815–1848*, trans., Robert Baldick (New York, 1967), pp. 9–17 and Arthur J. May, *The Age of Metternich, 1814–1848* (New York, 1963), chapters 1 and 2.
6 Thomas Carlyle, *Past and Present*, ed., Richard D. Altick (Boston, 1965), p. 148.
7 Thomas Carlyle, *On Heroes, Hero-Worship, & the Heroic in History* (Berkeley, CA, 1993), p. 3. Walter Waring, *Thomas Carlyle* (Boston, 1978), pp. 91–4.
8 Hugh Brogan, *Alexis de Tocqueville: A Life* (New Haven, 2006), pp. 253–82, describes the writing and publication of *Democracy in America*.
9 Alexis de Tocqueville, *Democracy in America*, ed., Richard D. Heffner (New York, 1956), p. 114.
10 Ibid., p. 118.
11 Jack Lively, trans., *The Works of Joseph de Maistre* (New York, 1965), p. 126; Coleridge, "Second Lay Sermon (1817)", in R. J. White, ed., *The Conservative Tradition* (New York, 1957), p. 82. See also Peter Viereck, *Conservative Thinkers* (London, 2006), pp. 33–7.
12 Harry Hearder, *Europe in the Nineteenth Century, 1830–1880* (New York, 1988), p. 227.
13 Benjamin Disraeli, *Sybil*, ed., Tom Braun (London, 1985); E. J. Feuchtwanger, *Disraeli, Democracy and the Tory Party* (Oxford, 1968), pp. 80–102, describes the Tory effort to broaden the Party's electoral appeal.
14 Jill Harsin, *Barricades: The War of the Streets in Revolutionary Paris, 1830–1848* (Houndmills, 2002), pp. 251–318.
15 Tocqueville quoted in Roger Price, ed., *Documents of the French Revolution of 1848* (New York, 1996), p. 117.
16 J. M. Thompson, *Louis Napoleon and the Second Empire* (New York, 1955), pp. 232–7.

17 August Comte, *Course of Positive Philosophy*, in Gertrud Lenzer, ed., *August Comte and Positivism: The Essential Writings* (Chicago, 1975), p. 219; Arline Reilein Standley, *August Comte* (Boston, 1981), p. 25.

18 Alain Plessis, *The Rise and Fall of the Second Empire, 1852–1871* (Cambridge, 1985), provides a brief overview.

19 Lynn Abrams, *Bismarck and the German Empire, 1871–1918* (New York, 2nd edn., 2006), pp. 40–1; Edgar Feuchtwanger, *Bismarck* (New York, 2002), pp. 219–22.

20 Giuseppe Mazzini, "On the Superiority of Representative Government" (1832), in Stephano Recchia and Nadia Urbinati, eds, *A Cosmopolitanism of Nations: Giuseppe Mazzini's Writings on Democracy, Nation Building, and International Relations* (Princeton, 2009), p. 49.

21 Thomas Malthus, *An Essay on the Principle of Population (1798)*, ed., Philip Appleman (New York, 2004), p. 36; David Ricardo, *The Principles of Political Economy and Taxation (1817)*, ed., Ernest Rhys (London, 1933), pp. 52–3.

22 See the discussion in Bruce Haddock, *History of Political Thought: 1789 to the Present* (Cambridge, 2005), p. 91.

23 John Stuart Mill, *On Liberty*, in *Collected Works of John Stuart Mill*, eds, J. M. Robson and Alexander Brady (Toronto, 1977), XVIII, p. 220.

24 Ibid., p. 223.

25 John Stuart Mill, *Considerations on Representative Government* (London, 1963), p. 168.

26 Wendy Donner, *The Liberal Self: John Stuart Mill's Moral and Political Philosophy* (Ithaca, NY, 1991), pp. 126–7.

27 Gail Tulloch, *Mill and Sexual Equality* (Worcester, 1989) and William Thomas, *Mill* (Oxford, 1985), pp. 120–1.

28 J. S. McClelland, *A History of Western Political Thought* (New York, 1996), p. 514. See also David O. Brink, *Perfectionism and the Common Good* (Oxford, 2003), pp. 4–5. A Useful study of Green is M. Ricter, *The Politics of Conscience: T. H. Green and His Age (1964)*.

29 Alon Kadish, *Apostle Arnold: The Life and Death of Arnold Toynbee, 1852–1883* (Durham, NC, 1986).

30 Morley quoted in Walter L. Arnstein, *Britain Yesterday and Today* (Lexington, MA, 6th edn., 1992), p. 196. Lloyd George quoted in Arnstein, ed., *The Past Speaks: Sources and Problems in British History* (Lexington, MA, 2nd edn., 1993), p. 304.

31 Sophia A. van Wingerden, *The Women's Suffrage Movement in Britain, 1866–1928* (Houndmills, 1998), pp. 55–69; David Morgan, *Suffragists and Liberals: The Politics of Woman Suffrage in England* (Totawa, NJ, 1975), pp. 14–19.

32 Krishan Kumar, *Utopia and Anti-Utopia in Modern Times* (Oxford, 1987), pp. 49–65.

33 John F. C. Harrison, *Quest for the New Moral Order: Robert Owen and the Owenites in Britain and America* (New York, 1969), p. 163, writes that 7 British and 16 American cooperative communities were undertaken.

34 Ruth Levitas, *The Concept of Utopia* (Syracuse, NY, 1990), pp. 36–9; Spencer M. DiScala and Salvo Mastellone, *European Political Thought, 1815–1989* (Boulder, CO, 1998), p. 28.

35 Peter Singer, *Hegel* (Oxford, 1983), pp. 9–23 treats Hegel's understanding of history.

36 Terrell Carver, *Engels* (Oxford, 1981), pp. 10–11.

37 A solid survey of the 1848 revolutions is Peter Stearns, *1848: The Revolutionary Tide in Europe* (New York, 1974).

38 Karl Marx and Friedrich Engels, *Manifesto of the Communist Party*, in Robert C. Tucker, ed., *The Marx-Engels Reader* (New York, 1972), p. 336. See also Marx's *Wage Labor and Capital* in the same volume, pp. 167–90. Marx published the first volume of *Capital* in 1867. The final two volumes were edited and published posthumously by Engels in 1885 and 1891.

39 Robert Tombs, "Politics", p. 25.

40 Hallowell, *Main Currents in Modern Political Thought*, p. 449.

41 Peter Gay, *The Dilemma of Democratic Socialism: Eduard Bernstein's Challenge to Marx* (New York, 1952), is a good starting point.

42 Carlton J. H. Hayes, *A Generation of Materialism, 1871–1900* (New York, 1941), p. 190; Jack J. Roth, *The Cult of Violence: Sorel and the Sorelians* (Berkeley, CA, 1980), pp. 45–53.

43 Quoted in Hallowell, *Main Currents in Modern Political Thought*, p. 464. On the origins of the Fabians, see Margaret Cole, *The Story of Fabian Socialism* (New York, 1964), pp. 338.

44 Blatchford, *Merrie England* quoted in Arnstein, ed., *The Past Speaks*, p. 292.

45 Peter Marsh, *Joseph Chamberlain: Entrepreneur in Politics* (New Haven, 1994), pp. 83–9.

46 *Rerum Novarum* in Charles J. Dollen, James K. McGowan and James J. Megivern, eds, *The Catholic Tradition*, 14 vols (Wilmington, NC, 1979), I: 357–8, 375. Eric O. Hanson, *The Catholic Church in World Politics* (Princeton, NJ, 1987), pp. 40–1, 49–50.

47 See Laurence Lafore, *The Long Fuse: An Interpretation of the Origins of World War I* (New York, 2nd edn., 1971), offers a thorough analysis of the European state system in the years before the war. Jeremy Black, "European Warfare, 1864–1913", in Black, ed., *European Warfare, 1815–2000* (Houndmills, 2002), pp. 51–78.

48 Felix Gilbert, *The End of the European Era, 1890 to the Present* (New York, 1970), pp. 22–7.

49 Heinrich von Treitschke, *Politics*, ed., Hans Kohn (New York, 1963), pp. 3, 35, 39.

50 J. M. Roberts, *Europe, 1880–1945* (New York, 2nd edn., 1989), p. 229.

51 M. S. Anderson, *The Ascendancy of Europe, 1815–1914* (New York, 2nd edn., 1985), pp. 364–9; Robert Gildea, *Barricades and Borders: Europe 1800–1914* (Oxford, 1987), pp. 388–9.

52 Peter Fritzsche, ed., *Nietzsche and the Death of God: Selected Writings* (Boston, 2007), pp. 1–36, is an accessible introduction.

53 Di Scala and Mastellone, *European Political Thought*, pp. 127–31.

54 Lenin, *What is to be Done?* in Franklin Lee Van Baumer, ed., *Main Currents of Western Thought* (New Haven, 4th edn., 1978), p. 726.

Chapter 6: Breakdown and Uncertainty, 1914–2010

1 Niall Ferguson, *The War of the World: Twentieth-Century Conflict and the Descent of the West* (New York, 2006), provides a comprehensive overview. See also Daniel Brower, *The World in the Twentieth Century* (Upper Saddle River, NJ, 6th edn., 2006).

2 Grey quoted in Walter Arnstein, *Britain Yesterday and Today*, p. 245. On the lead-up to war in 1914, see Spencer C. Tucker, *The Great War, 1914–1918* (Bloomington, IN, 1998), pp. 1–16.

3 Roland Stromberg, *Democracy: A Short, Analytical History* (London, 1996), pp. 49–54.

4 Michael Howard, "Europe in the Age of the Two World Wars", in Howard and Wm. Roger Louis, eds, *The Oxford History of the Twentieth Century* (Oxford, 1998), pp. 108–9. See also Alan Sharp, *The Versailles Settlement: Peacemaking in Paris, 1919* (New York, 1991), pp. 19–41.

5 Adolf Hitler, *Mein Kampf*, trans., Ralph Manheim (Boston, 1971), p. 180. John Toland, *Adolf Hitler* (New York, 1976), Chapters 4–6 covers the rise to power in the 1920s.

6 Alexander De Grand, *Italian Fascism: Its Origins and Development* (London, 2000), pp. 22–37.

7 Mussolini, "Fascism's Myth: The Nation", in Roger Griffin, ed., *Fascism* (Oxford, 1995), p. 42.

8 Philip Morgan, *Italian Fascism, 1919–1945* (New York, 1995), pp. 64–97; Martin Clark, *Mussolini* (Edinburgh, 2005), pp. 38–61.

9 Patricia Clavin, *The Great Depression in Europe, 1929–1939* (Houndmills, 2000), especially pp. 110–46, 179–183 on conditions in Eastern Europe.

10 Sigmund Freud, *Civilization and Its Discontents*, trans., James Strachey (New York, 1961), especially pp. 68–9, 81–2. Roland Stromberg, *European Intellectual History Since 1789* (Englewood Cliff, NJ, 6th edn., 1994), pp. 200–2. See also Alastair Hamilton, *The Appeal of Fascism: A Study of Intellectuals and Fascism, 1919–1945* (New York, 1971).

11 Carl Becker, "Liberalism – A Way Station", in *Everyman His Own Historian and Other Essays* (Chicago, 1966), pp. 91–100; Keith Robbins, *Appeasement* (Oxford, 1988), pp. 78–82.

12 J. M. Roberts, *Europe, 1880–1945* (New York, 2nd edn., 1989), p. 422.

13 Lenin, *"What is to be Done?" in Collected Works*, 45 vols (Moscow, 1977), 5: 354. See also Beryl Williams, *Lenin* (Harlow, Essex, 2000), pp. 35–8.

14 Richard Stites, "The Russian Empire and the Soviet Union, 1900–1945", in Michael Howard and Wm. Roger Louis, eds, *The Oxford History of the Twentieth Century* (Oxford, 1998), pp. 121–3.

15 Stites, "Russian Empire and Soviet Union", p. 124; Robert Conquest, *The Harvest of Sorrow: Soviet Collectivization and the Terror Famine* (New York, 1986) covers the late 1920s and 1930s.

16 W. M. Spellman, *A Concise History of the World Since 1945* (Houndmills, 2006), pp. 11–17.

17 Herbert Butterfield, *Christianity and History* (London, 1949), pp. 46–7.

18 Karl Popper, *The Open Society and Its Enemies*, 2 vols (Princeton, 1963), traces totalitarian tendencies in thinkers as varied as Plato and Marx.

19 Noel O'Sullivan, *European Political Thought Since 1945* (Houndmills, 2004).

20 Michael Bess, *Choices Under Fire: Moral Dimensions of World War II* (New York, 2006), pp. 263–7; Johannes Morsink, *The Universal Declaration of Human Rights: Origins, Drafting, Intent* (Philadelphia, 1999), pp. 1–12.

21 Karl Dietrich Bracher, *The Age of Ideologies: A History of Political Thought in the Twentieth Century*, trans., Ewald Osers (New York, 1984), pp. 191–2. See also Roland N. Stromberg, *After Everything: Western Intellectual History Since 1945* (New York, 1975), pp. 26–30.

22 David Reynolds, *One World Divisible* (New York, 2000); David Brower, *The World Since 1945: A Brief History* (Upper Saddle River, NJ, 2000), pp. 27–49.

23 William R Keylor, *A World of Nations: The International Order Since 1945* (New York, 2003), pp. 64–9.

24 Michael Freeden, "The Coming of the Welfare State", in Terence Ball and Richard Bellamy, eds, *The Cambridge History of Twentieth-Century Political Thought* (Cambridge, 2003), p. 9.

25 L. T. Hobhouse, *Liberalism* (New York, 1911), pp. 158–9. D. J. Manning, *Liberalism* (New York, 1976), p. 102.

26 R. H. Tawney, *Equality* (New York, 1931), especially Chapter 1, "The Religion of Inequality". Ross Terrill, *Richard Tawney and His Times: Socialism as Fellowship* (Cambridge, MA, 1973).

27 Donald Sassoon, "Politics", in Mary Fulbrook, ed., *Europe Since 1945* (Oxford, 2001), p. 21.

28 Paul Davidson, *John Maynard Keynes* (Houndmills, 2007), pp. 1–12.

29 John Maynard Keynes, *The General Theory of Employment, Interest, and Money* (New York, 1936), p. 372.

30 Robert Skidelsky, "Hayek versus Keynes: The road to reconciliation", in Edward Feser, ed., *The Cambridge Companion to Hayek* (Cambridge, 2006), pp. 82–108.

31 Michael Oakeshott, "On Being Conservative", in Russell Kirk, ed., *The Portable Conservative Reader* (New York, 1982), p. 569.

32 Spellman, *World Since 1945* (Houndmills, 2006), p. 179; Jules Tygiel, *Ronald Reagan and the Triumph of American Conservatism* (New York, 2005), pp. 125, 128, 133–5; Peter Clarke, *Hope and Glory: Britain 1900–1990* (New York, 1996), pp. 367–72.

33 Wayne Parsons, "Politics and Markets: Keynes and His Critics", in *Cambridge History of Twentieth-Century Political Thought*, p. 60.

34 Irving Kristol, *Reflections of a Neoconservative* (New York, 1983), p. 75; Sheldon Wolin, *Politics and Vision*, pp. 525–6.

35 Francis Fukuyama, *The End of History and the Last Man* (New York, 1992).

36 Thomas Friedman, *The World is Flat: A Short History of the 21st Century* (New York, 2005).

37 David S. Mason, *The End of the American Century* (Lanham, Maryland, 2009), pp. 133–52.

38 Richard A. Posner, *A Failure of Capitalism: The Crisis of '08 and the Descent into Depression* (Cambridge, MA, 2009), especially pp. 148–219.

39 John Schwarzmantel, *The Age of Ideology: Political Ideologies from the American Revolution to Postmodern Times* (New York, 1998), p. 175.

40 John Morrow, *History of Political Thought*, pp. 371–2.

41 Brian Barry, *Culture and Equality: An Egalitarian Critique of Multiculturalism* (Cambridge, 2001), p. 12; Michael Kenny, *The Politics of Identity* (Cambridge, 2004), pp. 1–11.
42 John Gray, *Endgames: Questions in Late Modern Political Thought* (Cambridge, 1997), p. x.
43 James Tully, "Identity Politics", in *Cambridge History of Twentieth Century Political Thought*, pp. 517–9.
44 Clare O'Farrell, *Michel Foucault* (London, 2005), offers an accessible overview of Foucault's life and work.
45 W. M. Spellman, *Uncertain Identity: International Migration Since 1945* (London, 2008), pp. 22–60.
46 See Martha Nussbaum's essay on the significance of Rawls' work in *Chronicle of Higher Education* (20 July 2001).
47 John Rawls, *A Theory of Justice*, revised ed. (Cambridge, MA, 1999), p. 185.
48 Louis I. Katzner, "The Original Position and the Veil of Ignorance", in H. Gene Blocker and Elizabeth H. Smith, eds, *John Rawls' Theory of Social Justice* (Athens, OH, 1980), pp. 42–58.
49 Michael Sandel, *Democracy's Discontent: America in Search of a Public Philosophy* (Cambridge, MA, 1996), p. 5. See also Michael Walzer, *Politics and Passion: Toward a More Egalitarian Liberalism* (New Haven, 2004).

Further Reading

Recent general surveys include Sheldon Wolin, *Politics and Vision: Continuity and Innovation in Western Political Thought* (Princeton, 2004); John Morrow, *The History of Western Political Thought: A Thematic Introduction* (New York, 2005); John Dunn, ed., *Democracy: The Unfinished Journey, 508 B.C. to 1993* (Oxford, 1993); J. S. McClelland, *A History of Western Political Thought* (London, 1996); N. Berki, *The History of Political Thought: A Short Introduction* (London, 1977); Jonathan Wolfe, *An Introduction to Political Philosophy* (Oxford, 1996); Roland Stromberg, *Democracy: A Short, Analytical History* (London, 1996).

For the ancient world, see Christopher Rowe and Malcolm Schofield, eds, *The Cambridge History of Greek and Roman Political Thought* (Cambridge, 2000); Helpful introductions are provided by Ryan Balot, *Greek Political Thought* (Oxford, 2006) and David Stockton, *The Classical Athenian Democracy* (Oxford, 1990); Robin Barrow, *Athenian Democracy* (London, 1999); Janet Coleman, *A History of Political Thought*, 2 vols (Malden, MA, 2000); Jonathan Barnes, ed., *The Cambridge Companion to Aristotle* (Cambridge, 1995); Robin Barrow, *Athenian Democracy* (London, 1999); Donald Kagan, *Pericles of Athens and the Birth of Democracy* (New York, 1991); R. M. Hare, Jonathan Barnes, and Henry Chadwick, eds, *Founders of Thought* (Oxford, 1991).

Studies of the medieval period include J. H. Burns, ed., *The Cambridge History of Medieval Political Thought, c. 350–1450* (Cambridge, 1988); Marcus Bull, *Thinking Medieval: An Introduction to the Study of the Middle Ages* (Houndmills, 2005); Antony Black, *Political Thought in Europe 1250–1450* (Cambridge, 1992); Joseph Canning, *A History of Medieval Political Thought, 300–1450* (London, 1996); John B. Morrall, *Political Thought in Medieval Times* (New York, 1958); David Nicholas, *The Evolution of the Medieval World* (London, 1992); Matthew Innes, *Introduction to Early Medieval Western Europe, 300–900* (New York, 2007); R. W. Southern, *Western Society and the Church in the Middle Ages* (New York, 1970); John A. F. Thomson, *The Western Church in the Middle Ages* (London, 1998); David Nicholas, *The Evolution of the Medieval World: Society, Government and Thought in Europe, 312–1500* (London, 1992).

On the early modern period see J. H. Burns, ed., *The Cambridge History of Political Thought, 1450–1700* (Cambridge, 1991); Theodore Rabb, *The Struggle for Stability in Early Modern Europe* (New York, 1975); Alister McGrath, *The Intellectual Origins of the European Reformation* (Malden, MA, 2004); J. N. Figgis, *Political Thought from Gerson to Grotius, 1414–1625* (New York, 1960); Quentin Skinner, *The Foundations of Modern Political Thought*, 2 vols (Cambridge, 1978); W. M. Spellman, *European Political Thought, 1600–1700* (Houndmills, 1998); J. W. Allen, *A History of Political Thought in the Sixteenth Century* (London, 1967); Richard Bonney, *The European Dynastic States, 1494–1660* (Oxford, 1991).

Good introductions to the eighteenth century include Mark Goldie and Robert Wolker, eds, *The Cambridge History of Eighteenth-Century Political Thought* (Cambridge, 2006); Roy Porter, *The Enlightenment* (Atlantic Heights, NJ, 1990); Peter Gay, *The Enlightenment: An Interpretation*, 2 vols (New York, 1969); Maurice Cranston, *Philosophers and Pamphleteers: Political Theorists of the Enlightenment* (Oxford, 1986); Paul Rahe, *Republics Ancient and Modern* (Chapel Hill, 1992); Bernard Bailyn, *The Ideological Origins of the American Revolution* (Cambridge, MA, 1967); Louis Dupre, *The Enlightenment and the Intellectual Foundations of Modern Culture* (New Haven, 2004); John H. Hallowell, *Main Currents in Modern Political Thought* (New York, 1960); Karen Offen, *European Feminisms, 1700–1950: A Political History* (Stanford, CA, 2000); Olwen Hufton, *The Prospect Before Her: A History of Women in Western Europe, 1500–1800* (New York, 1996).

On the nineteenth century see Bruce Haddock, *History of Political Thought, 1789 to the Present* (Cambridge, 2005); Spencer M. DiScala and Salvo Mastellone, *European Political Thought, 1815–1989* (Boulder, CO, 1998); M. S. Anderson, *The Ascendancy of Europe, 1815–1914* (New York, 2nd edn., 1985); Robert Gildea, *Barricades and Borders: Europe 1800–1914* (Oxford, 1987); Hearder, *Europe in the Nineteenth Century, 1830–1880* (New York, 1988); David O. Brink, *Perfectionism and the Common Good* (Oxford, 2003); Sophia A. van Wingerden, *The Women's Suffrage Movement in Britain, 1866–1928* (Houndmills, 1998).

Overviews of recent political thought include Terence Ball and Richard Bellamy, eds, *The Cambridge History of Twentieth-Century Political Thought* (Cambridge, 2003); Noel O'Sullivan, *European Political Thought Since 1945* (Houndmills, 2004); Karl Dietrich Bracher, *The Age of Ideologies: A History of Political Thought in the Twentieth Century*, trans., Ewald Osers (New York, 1984); Roland N. Stromberg, *After Everything: Western Intellectual History Since 1945* (New York, 1975); David Reynolds, *One World Divisible* (New York, 2000); William R. Keylor, *A World of Nations: The International Order Since 1945* (New York, 2003); Michael Kenny, *The Politics of Identity* (Cambridge, 2004); Alastair Hamilton, *The Appeal of Fascism: A Study of Intellectuals and Fascism, 1919–1945* (New York, 1971); John Gray, *Endgames: Questions in Late Modern Political Thought* (Cambridge, 1997).

Index